The Korean Developmental State

Kyung Mi Kim

The Korean Developmental State

palgrave
macmillan

Kyung Mi Kim
Seoul National University
Seoul, Korea (Republic of)

ISBN 978-981-15-3464-5 ISBN 978-981-15-3465-2 (eBook)
https://doi.org/10.1007/978-981-15-3465-2

This Palgrave Macmillan imprint is published by the registered company Springer Nature Singapore Pte Ltd.
The registered company address is: 152 Beach Road, #21-01/04 Gateway East, Singapore 189721, Singapore

PREFACE

The Asian developmental states have attracted the attention of scholars and policymakers for decades. Until the 1990s, the developmental state school gained ascendancy based on its rich empirical studies in how to understand rapid economic development in East Asian economies, including Japan, South Korea (hereafter Korea), and Taiwan. Many developing countries were recommended to, and actually tried to, replicate aspects of the East Asian developmental state model.

However, since the Asian financial crisis of 1997, the relevancy of the developmental state for economic development has been seriously discredited. It is a widely held belief that in an era of globalization, such an interventionist state's role is anachronistic at best and inimical to further development at worst. In actuality, Korea, as an ideal type of East Asian developmental state, suffered from a deep recession and experienced serious structural and strategic adjustments. In such circumstances, neoliberalism and the thesis of developmental state demise gained ascendancy. It is widely believed that the developmental state could not continue in Korea and it would emulate the Anglo-Saxon free-market model.

This book focuses on the following questions: How should we understand the continuing growth of the Korean economy even after the crisis of 1997? Is the recession because of the classical developmental state system or the neoliberal free market? To what extent has the Korean development model changed since 1997? Does it converge toward an Anglo-Saxon-style free-market economy, or can it be still classified as a variant of developmentalism? What explains the cause and mechanism of change?

Based on in-depth field research and historically tracing its changes, this book suggests that in contrast to the neoliberal arguments and the developmental state demise literature, the state has played an important role in the Korean economic system since 1997 despite significant changes in the postcrisis period; the ongoing growth of the Korean economy in the 2000s can be understood by a new version of state-led capitalism, rather than by a neoliberal free-market system. More importantly, this book holds that unlike the institutionalist argument, the continuity of the state's active role in the Korean economy is not because of path dependency, institutional "stickiness," or historical legacies but because of the changes in developmental strategies and methods, that is, from classical authoritarian and exclusive to democratic and inclusive developmentalism, as well as from input-driven to innovation-driven strategy.

Seoul, Republic of Korea　　　　Kyung Mi Kim

Acknowledgements

Since I launched this project in 2009, I have benefited from many people. It is a great pleasure to acknowledge numerous debts I owe to my committee, friends, and family. Without their support and encouragement, I could not have finished this project.

First and foremost, I would like to express my deepest appreciation to Professor Su-Ik Hwang, Myung Chey, Jung Bock Lee, Honglim Ryu, and Kyung Hoon Leem. They are all my mentors who guided me through the murky and turbulent process of undergraduate and graduate studies as well as after graduation. I also appreciate my doctoral committee members, Professors Chang Jae Baik, Hae Ran Lim, Toh-Kyeong Ahn, Suk-Jin Lew, Joo-myung Song, and Hyeong-ki Kwon, who provided me with tremendous encouragement, tough and insightful criticism, and soul-caring advice.

I will never forget the indispensable help offered by many people during my field research from 2010 to 2016: managers of supplier companies and original equipment manufacturers (OEMs), associations, and research institutes in the Korean government. In particular, I would like to give special thanks to former and current officials and policymakers in Korean government.

I also would like to thank many friends in the department of political science at Seoul National University, particularly Hyun Lee, Hee-Jung Sohn, Mi-hyun Yun, and In-Kyung Chung, who virtually broadened my intellectual horizon and made graduate life greatly joyful.

Finally, but most greatly, I would like to thank my family for their endless sacrifice, love, and encouragement. My sister Soo-hong, brother-in-law Joon-oh, my brother Tae-hwan, sister-in-law Bong-jung, my lovely nephew Ji-ahn, and nieces Do-yun, Na-ri, and Su-yun deserve my deepest appreciation. Finally, I dedicate this book to my parents, Yong Kim and Soon Ja Park, who taught me how to live a meaningful life by their own example.

About the Book

Chapter 1 introduces the puzzles and main arguments of this book and the methods and objects of study.

Chapter 2 with a critical examination of existing studies on the changes and continuity of Korean state-led capitalism, and presents theoretical alternatives and analytic frameworks.

Chapter 3 presents an overview of the history of Korean economic growth and what caused such rapid growth over 50 years, mainly based on economic statistical data. In this chapter, I offer reference points for discussions in the next chapters by showing that the driving forces behind Korea's economic growth have significantly changed.

In Chaps. 4, 5, and 6, this study argues that the qualitative transition of the Korean economy is not through the private firms' voluntary actions in the free market but by the state's strategic attempts and their interactions with corporations.

Specifically, Chap. 4 analyzes the classical model of state-led capitalism in Korea. The traditional Korean developmental state established in the 1960s and 1970s was an authoritarian state dirigisme system, a variant of state-led capitalism.

Chapter 5 focuses on the extent to which Korean state-led capitalism has changed, and why we can understand Korea's current political and economic system as another variant of state-led capitalism despite significant changes in its industrial policies and institutions.

Chapter 6 explores why and how Korean state-led capitalism has evolved. Specifically, we examine why Korean capitalism gave up its traditional model of state-led capitalism but did not converge toward Anglo-Saxon-style free market system or change toward a European corporatist coordination system.

Finally, Chap. 7 summarizes the key questions and concludes with key arguments.

Contents

About the Author

Kyung Mi Kim holds a PhD from Seoul National University in 2017 and works as a research professor of the Philosophy, Politics, and Economics program at Seoul National University. Her dissertation discusses changes and continuity in the Korean developmental state. Her main works are "The State's Role in Globalization: Korea's Experience from a Comparative Perspective" published in *Politics & Society* (2017) and "Varieties of globalisation and national economy: Korea's experience from a comparative perspective" published in the *Journal of International Relations and Development* (2018, available online).

List of Figures

List of Tables

CHAPTER 1

Introduction

This book analyzes, from a historical comparative perspective, the Korean economic development model, the extent to which it has changed from its classical model, and what constitutes its changes and continuity.

The Korean economy has been studied by policymakers as well as political economists around the world. Interest in the Korean economic model started in the 1980s when the success of the Japanese economy was receiving global attention, followed by the emerging economies of East Asia, with their unique method of state-led development. The reason for continued interest in the Korean economy is that in contrast to Japan, which experienced a long-term economic decline known as the "lost decade" or "the lost 20 years," the Korean economy has recovered quickly from the severe economic crisis in 1997 and shown steady economic growth in the process of globalization. In fact, since the start of industrialization in the 1960s, Korea has experienced continued rapid growth compared to both developed and emerging economies. The Korean economic model has also maintained its characteristics of state-led capitalism despite significant changes in its global integration, revealing a diverse pattern of capitalism, unlike neoliberal patterns of convergence in the era of globalization. In practical terms, the Korean economic model has been of great interest to policymakers in developing countries such as China and other late developing countries in Asia and Africa (Kim 2006; Bobo and Sintim-Aboagye 2012; Interview with former President Roh Moo-hyun's economic advisor, April 19, 2013). As recent Korean governments have tried to export

K. M. Kim, *The Korean Developmental State*,
https://doi.org/10.1007/978-981-15-3465-2_1

the Korean development model in order to cooperate with developing countries, defining the model has become an important issue within and beyond Korea.

Nonetheless, what the genuine Korean development model is, how it could transform a devastatingly poor country to a developed country, and how it could continuously grow from initial industrialization in the 1960s until the 2010s all remain controversial issues. The neoliberal perspective attributes Korean economic success to market-adaptive policies, while the developmental state theory argues that Korea's notable economic growth was due to state-led capitalism (World Bank 1993; Krueger 1980; Amsden 1989; Woo 1991; Haggard 1990). Until the mid-1990s, the developmental state theory had been more persuasive, because Korea's market-adaptive, export-oriented policies and temporary interest rate liberalization measures—key evidence of market liberalism—had been coordinated by the Korean government's highly selective strategies.

However, the debate on the Korean development model significantly changed following the 1997 Asian financial crisis, when the neoliberal view gained ascendancy. The dominant view is that in overcoming the 1997 crisis, the Korean political economic model shifted to neoliberal market capitalism. The traditional developmental state now became an obstacle to, rather than the cause for, rapid growth (Kang 2002; Kirk 2000; Jayasuriya 2000; Noland and Pack 2003; Pirie 2005; Yoon 2009; Ji 2009; Hall 2003; Kim 1999; Minns 2001). Even developmental theorists tend to believe that since 1997, Korea has shifted to a neoliberal regulatory state (Lee et al. 2002; Shin and Chang 2003).

If this is so, should the continuing growth of the Korean economy be understood as based on state-led capitalism before 1997 and on the free-market system after 1997? How should the Korean capitalism model be defined? To what extent has the Korean development model changed since 1997? What constitutes the changes? Does it converge toward an Anglo-Saxon free-market economy, or can it be still classified as a variant of developmentalism? What explains the cause and mechanism of change?

Based on in-depth field research and historically tracing its changes, this study suggests that since 1997 the state has played an important role in the Korean economic system; the ongoing growth of the Korean economy in the 2000s can be understood by state-led capitalism rather than by a neoliberal free-market system. Existing studies on the causes for Korea's economic success reveal many limitations. First, neoliberal approaches have difficulty in understanding the characteristics of the Korean development model from a comparative perspective. Neoliberals hold that Korea's economic success resulted from an open and free-market system, disregarding the state's role in upgrading its national industrial system (World Bank 1993; Krueger 1980). However, the shift in the 1960s from an import substitution to an export-oriented strategy, and the transition from labor-intensive light industries to capital-intensive heavy chemical industries in the 1970s, cannot be explained except by the strategic intervention of the Korean state. Even after 1997, the Korean state played a pivotal role in transforming its industrial system to a more knowledge-intensive and high value-added system in the 2000s. These were not voluntary changes by private large corporations in the free market. Furthermore, Korea's strategic intervention and coordination policies reveal an intentional and ongoing pattern of developmentalism with mid- and long-term prospects for economic and industrial competitiveness.

On the other hand, many studies based on the developmental state theory have limitations in understanding the changes in Korea's economic and industrial systems in the 2000s by conflating certain elements of the classical authoritarian developmental state as an ideal type of developmental state in general. They argue for the demise of the Korean developmental state in the 2000s by exclusively drawing on elements of the 1970s, such as direct state control of banks and credit distribution and the existence of a pilot agency like the Economic Planning Board (EPB). For instance, although Lee et al. (2002), Shin and Chang (2003), and Kim (2014) categorized the pre-1997 Korean economic system as a developmental state, they held that the system has dissolved or converged toward a neoliberal regulatory state since 1997. Yet from a comparative perspective, it is difficult to identify the Korean capitalist model as an Anglo-Saxon-style neoliberal system in which the state is a neutral regulator rather than a strategic actor in upgrading industrial competitiveness. As we will examine in Chap. 5, the Korean state still plays an important role in upgrading the national industrial structure with changed strategies and methods of industrial policy.

This study explores three main questions concerning the Korean economic development model. First, what are its typical characteristics? Second, to what extent has the model changed in the 2000s? Finally, why and how has this model evolved?

This study argues that despite significant changes in policies and instruments, the Korean political economy is still a variant of state-led capitalism if we consider it from a comparative perspective of structural state-business and interfirm relations, rather than focusing on elements of context-specific policies and instruments, particularly in the 1970s authoritarian developmental era. Typical elements of the traditional developmental state in the era of Park Chung-hee, such as state control over banks and direct control of credit distribution—deemed symbolic of the developmental state by institutional theorists—were appropriate to build national industrial champions that could compete internationally through economies of scale and cheap prices. However, mobilizing and funneling massive capital to a few large corporations in strategic industries proved ineffective as the Korean state aimed to build a knowledge-intense and innovation-oriented economic system. Traditional methods of excluding small- and medium-sized enterprises (SMEs) while favoring chaebols, or large industrial conglomerates controlled by an owner or family, became obstacles to developing innovative industrial ecosystems that allow competent SMEs to collaborate with large assemblers.

Policies and instruments for Korean developmentalism have significantly changed due to the success of existing developmental policies. As the domestic economy grew and international competition changed, Korea had to change its developmental strategies from traditional input-driven growth centered on large corporations' economies of scale to innovation-driven growth centered on components and materials companies. Since 1997, Korea's industrial policies have fostered technology-intensive and high value-added industries through synergistic cooperation among SMEs, large firms, and public research institutes. Consequently, key policy instruments have also shifted, from massive capital inputs to research and development (R&D) support and building innovative industrial ecosystems. This is the Korean state's initiative, not the free market or private firms' voluntary action. Now the state coordinates a consortium of private companies and government-funded research centers.

Changes in growth strategy triggered changes in governance systems, from closed and exclusive relations between the state and a few chaebols to relations inclusive of small- and medium-sized companies. More importantly, changes in growth strategy have brought a qualitative change to interfirm relations. While somewhat closed and confrontational subcontracting relations remain, relationships between large assemblers and key component suppliers in main industries have grown more collaborative.

This study, however, emphasizes that giving up traditional methods of mobilizing massive capital and rationing it to a few chaebols does not mean the demise of the developmental state. Rather, Korea recognized the need for new strategies and methods to continue to achieve its original developmental goal of improving national industrial competitiveness in an international environment.

The role of the Korean state—proposing and creating specific programs for continuous industrial advancement—continues with each new government: for instance, the Kim Dae-jung government's policies to promote venture companies and to develop components and materials, the Roh Moo-hyun government's Chasedaisungjangdongrykjungchaik, the Lee Myung-bak government's Sinsungjangdongrykjungchaik to promote new industries, and the Park Geun-hye government's Creative Economy Policy. In most cases, these policies are consistent with mid- to long-term goals to improve main industries' competitiveness. In fact, continuity of these state-led industrial policies has been fundamentally supported by Korea's persistent export-led growth strategy in changing global contexts.

To underscore the continuity of state-led capitalism during changes in policies and instruments, we emphasize both developmentalism's basic goals and institutional arrangements for its execution from a comparative perspective, rather than focusing on context-specific institutions and policies, as the demise theorists emphasize (Thurbon 2016, pp. 1–10). For example, developmental states such as Korea and Taiwan are similar in the developmental goal of upgrading national techno-industrial competitiveness, but they differ in their use of policies and instruments with Korea using more state-directed credit rationing, unlike Taiwan. State-led financial lending is not a decisive criterion for the developmental state. Rather than focusing on policy elements of time-specific developmental states, this study emphasizes the ideal types of state-led capitalism in general from a comparative perspective: What are the state's roles in the economy? Does it serve as a neutral regulator for the free market, or does it actively intervene to promote national industrial competitiveness? Does the state initiate transformation of industrial structure, or negotiate collectively with labor as European corporatism does, or does it let private firms voluntarily act in the free market?

This study holds that the Korean state maintains its characteristics of state-led capitalism despite significant changes in policies and instruments, rather than converging toward an Anglo-Saxon-style free-market system. Korea's R&D policy differs from that of the United States. Korea focuses more on applied research in strategic industries, while the United States focuses on basic and general science. Korean state R&D supports a consortium of companies and government-affiliated research centers to improve national industrial competitiveness. Unlike European corporatism, such as in Germany, where civil actors negotiate industrial governance independent of the federal government, the Korean state strategically initiates programs to transform the industrial structure.

How can we best understand the continuity and changes in Korean capitalism? Why has Korean capitalism neither converged toward a neoliberal free market nor transformed toward European-style social democratic corporatism? To account for the evolution of Korean capitalism, first we differentiate the state elites' goal of developmentalism in the contexts of international competition. Here, we contrast the existing literature on the debate in which change and continuity are mutually exclusive: some arguing for convergence toward neoliberal free market while others argue for path-dependent continuity.[1] We emphasize that the continuity of state-led capitalism is compatible with institutional change. In other words, Korean capitalism could sustain its state developmentalism by changes in policies and instruments to improve national industrial competitiveness in the changed context of international competition. The politics of readjustment combine principles of national developmentalism or liberalism with suitable policies and measures.

Second, to understand the direction and actual mechanisms of changes, this study emphasizes endogenous changes rather than exogenous shocks including globalization and global economic crises. Most of the existing literature emphasizes the external shocks, such as the 1997 Asian financial crisis. Many studies argue that the Korean developmental state underwent its demise due to external shock and pressure for liberalization (Lee et al. 2004; Shin and Chang 2003; Kirk 2000; Kong 2000; Kim 1997, 1999; Lee and Han 2006; Lim and Jang 2006). Surely these external shocks ignite

[1]A notable exception is Thurbon (2016). We agree with Thurbon (2016) in that the definition of developmental state lies not in the context-specific elements, but in the ideal type of developmental state in general. While Thurbon (2016) emphasized the state elites' consensus and mindset for developmentalism, this study underlines more detailed principles from a comparative perspective as criteria to differentiate the developmental state from other types of capitalism. For example, after the Second World War, West German elites had consensus for national recovery and development. However, they did not adopt the principle of statism in which the state could better intervene in coordinating industrial actors. In the postwar era, West German elites placed significant constraints on the government's ability to undertake industrial structure reform while they had economic nationalism similar to Korea's. For national economic development, German elites developed decentralized but coordinated institutions in civil society (Fioretos 2011, pp. 138–144). By contrast, Korean elites adopted the principle of state intervention to undertake industrial structure reform.

important changes. However, external shocks alone cannot account for the direction of national adjustments. Similar external shocks have evoked other national responses. In response to globalization, Ireland established a model of social concertation, while the United Kingdom shifted its economic system radically toward a free-market system, giving up postwar collective coordination (Kwon 2012). In the 1997 financial crisis, the Korean government did not simply follow the International Monetary Fund (IMF) agreement. Rather, the Korean government developed a reform package exceeding the IMF's demands in order to discipline large corporations and to advance its own domestic reform agenda. The direction of the Kim Dae-jung government's reform to discourage large corporations from pursuing debt-based overexpansion and to encourage specialization for high value-added production resulted solely from industrial bureaucrats' deliberation for developmentalism in the changed context of international competition (Mathews 1998; Kim 2003; Hundt 2009; Thurbon 2016, p. 185, endnote 6). This study holds that in order to understand the evolutionary path of Korean capitalism, we must follow the endogenous politics as Korean key actors contested over interpreting challenges and looking for solutions in domestic and international political economic contexts.

This study explores different arrangements of key political actors across national economies.[2] Key political actors include public and private entities regarded as having a stake in the social and economic institutions that govern their interactions and who also have a public voice or parapublic decision-making status. While the Korean working people rapidly organized in the democratization process in the late 1980s, they have not achieved parapublic status as in European corporatist economies. This inability to organize stems historically from Korean industrialization in which labor was politically excluded and public status was not allowed. Therefore, Korea has difficulty in shifting to a European-style corporatist system. On the other hand, the Korean state's active role has been justified since its early industrialization, which explains why workers wanted the state to actively solve economic problems in the late 1990s, although those problems resulted mainly from state-led development in the 1970s.

This study draws from the literature of historical institutionalism, particularly the recently developed version of historical institutionalism

[2] For key political actors, see Fredrick (1985, pp. 127–152). For social actors' parapublic status, see Katzenstein (1978), Schmitter (1979), and Kwon (2014, pp. 252–254).

concerning endogenous changes (Mahoney and Thelen 2010; Thelen 2004; Streeck and Thelen 2005; Kwon 2013, 2014; Schmidt 2008; Blyth 2002; Herrigel 2010). Accordingly, we emphasize the politics of discursive interactions of key institutional actors, in contrast to unilateral institutional constraint proposed by institutionalist path dependency (Kwon 2013; Schmidt 2008; Blyth 2002; Herrigel 2010). Traditional institutionalists underscore path dependency to account for the continuity of state-led capitalism. However, proponents of path dependency clearly emphasize institutions' unilateral constraints over actors and thus explain changes only by external shocks to shake the existing institutional equilibrium. However, many evolutionary adjustments happen without severe external shocks, such as wars and global economic crises (Streeck and Thelen 2005, pp. 4–9; Mahoney and Thelen 2010, pp. 1–14). This study examines discursive politics among key actors who reflect upon challenges and reinterpret the meaning of institutions rather than focus on institutional constraints (Mahoney and Thelen 2010; Thelen 2004; Streeck and Thelen 2005). Key actors constantly seek new grounds for justification by redefining their roles, which engenders endogenous institutional changes.

Continuity and change within economic systems result from key actors' political interactions, which are continuously reinterpreted in light of their partners' choices. For example, in the Korean development model, the state sought legitimacy for state intervention whenever the effectiveness of state-led developmentalism was questioned, and state elites therefore continually attempted to change their methods and means to justify their developmental policies. But the process of justifying the role of the state itself was a process of political interactions in which policies sometimes were accepted and sometimes failed. Political interactions for Korean developmentalism are mainly located between state and large corporations, as well as between bureaucratic departments. Labor, for the most part, is excluded. Although labor in Korea has gained more of a public voice since democratization, it has failed to propose a new strategy of national economic development.

Korea has continued its state-led capitalism mainly because state bureaucrats have successfully initiated a new growth strategy and implemented the state's new developmentalism in political interactions with large corporations. For instance, large corporations in Korea were not interested in transforming existing strategies of market share and volume expansion to innovation-driven growth. If the Korean state had not intervened, the transformation to a knowledge-intensive and innovation-driven system might not have happened. Criticizing large corporations' immoral and unfair actions that violated market norms, including land speculation and volume expansion strategies based on their market power, Korean state elites justified their developmental policies by changing various measures. These state attempts to redirect economic growth strategies did not achieve immediate success. Only since the 1997 financial crisis has the state institutionalized its innovation-driven system, with changes in large corporations' growth strategies.

Research Methods and Data

With its focus on the historical evolution of Korean state-led capitalism, this study examines the relationships between the state and business as well as interfirm relationships. By analyzing Korean state-business relations from a comparative perspective, this study identifies Korean capitalism as a variant of state-led capitalism, despite its significant changes from traditional dirigisme, or state control of economic and social matters, that is distinct from Anglo-Saxon-style free-market and European corporatist systems. This study explores the changes in state developmentalism at both the macro and micro levels. At the macro level, this study focuses on the policy goals and means of the Korean state. At the micro level, it analyzes how the government and firms interact with each other in the process of policy decision and implementation, and interfirm relationships of lead companies and components suppliers in Korean flagship industries, including the automobile and electronics industries.

I focus on the automotive and electronics industries since they share a major portion of the Korean economy. In 2014, these two industries accounted for 34% of manufacturing production, 40% of added value, and 39% of exports. These industries also have wide-ranging effects on related industries through backward and forward industrial linkages. More importantly, these Korean flagship industries show the characteristics and mechanisms of Korean state-led capitalism because they have grown through the state's strategic policies since the 1960s. In the 1960s and the 1970s, the automobile and electronics industries were built by the state's strategic supports, including industry promotion policies. In the 2000s, these two industries became the most globalized, thus serving as test cases for the effectiveness of state-led capitalism in globalization. This study shows how state developmentalism has changed in the process of key corporations' globalization. I maintain that the Korean state continues its developmentalism by changing from its traditional methods of exclusively nurturing large corporations to developing a more inclusive industrial ecosystem. Here, the state actively develops collaboration among large original equipment manufacturers (OEMs), components suppliers, and research institutes. This study explores interfirm collaboration and industrial ecosystems at the micro level.

I use quantitative as well as qualitative data. In order to profile the basic characteristics of Korean state-led capitalism and its growth strategies, this study draws from official statistical data collected by Korean and international organizations, including statistical data collected by the National Statistical Office, the Bank of Korea, the Organisation for Economic Co-operation and Development (OECD), and the United Nations Conference on Trade and Development (UNCTAD). It also references reports published by national research institutes, including the Korea Institute for Industrial Economics and Trade (KIET) and the Science and Technology Policy Institute. To capture the historical evolution of Korean state-led capitalism, this study relies on qualitative data, including memoirs of bureaucrats and businessmen who were involved in policy-making processes, drawing from the existing literature, newspapers, and industry journals. But the primary data for qualitative exploration were collected through extensive and intensive personal interviews with former and current bureaucrats and corporate executives, officials of major government agencies and government-funded institutes, and trade association and trade union officials. Personal interviews enable us to trace changes in actors' understanding: how and why major actors responded, with particular considerations, when they faced challenges; how they perceived their counter components' responses; and how they reconsidered their strategies.

Interviews were conducted from May 2010 to June 2016 over eight periods, totaling 66 interviews with 72 people. For interviews with officials in government, government affiliates, and government institutes, 28 people were interviewed on 26 occasions. A total of 27 company officials were interviewed on 25 occasions, while 17 people from industry associations, trade unions, and private experts were interviewed on 15 occasions. The first survey spanned from May to August 2010, the second from March to July 2011, the third in February 2012, the fourth from April to June 2013, the fifth from September to November 2014, the sixth from February to August 2015, the seventh from October 2015 to February 2016, and the eighth in June 2016. Specific dates and times of interviews as well as the list of interviewees are attached as appendices.

Table 1.1 Overview of survey respondents

	Sector	*Employees*	*Sales*
Survey results	Electric/electronic: 28 companies Automobile: 71 companies	Average of 403 people	Average of KRW 229 billion
Number of respondents (response rate)	99 companies (41%)		

Note: The total number of survey respondents is 242 companies; 65 electric/electronic companies; 177 automobile companies

To track actual changes in interfirm relations and innovation networks at the micro level, I conducted a questionnaire survey of private companies in the Korean automobile and electronics industries from June to December 2011. This survey supplements the reliability of the interview data from these industries by tracking the overall tendency of changes at the micro level. For the automobile industry, I contacted 177 components suppliers listed in the *2009 Automotive Industry Directory* with 50 or more employees. For the electronics industry, I contacted 65 companies from *The KEA 2007 Membership List* with 50 or more employees. To map interfirm relations in the two Korean flagship industries, the survey included mainly the first-tier suppliers. The survey questionnaire was sent to those best positioned to understand the company's overall situation—intermediate managers of planning departments or executives. As shown in Table 1.1, the collected responses consisted of 28 electrical and electronic companies and 71 automobile companies. The overall response rate was 41% on average: 43% for electrical and electronics and 40% for automobile.

References

Amsden, A. H. (1989). *Asia's next giant: South Korea and late industrialization*. New York: Oxford University Press.

Blyth, M. (2002). *Great transformation: Economic ideas and institutional change in the twentieth century*. New York: Cambridge University Press.

Bobo, B. F., & Sintim-Aboagye, H. (2012). *Neo-liberalism, interventionism and the developmental state: Implementing new partnership for Africa's development*. Trenton: Africa World Press.

Fioretos, O. (2011). *Creative Reconstructions: Multilateralism and European Varieties of Capitalism after 1950*. Ithaca: Cornell University Press.

Fredrick, W. F. (1985). The Problem of Actor Designation in Political Analysis. *Comparative Politics, 17*(2), 127–152.

Haggard, S. (1990). *Pathways from the periphery: The politics of growth in the newly industrializing countries*. Ithaca, NY: Cornell University Press.
Hall, R. B. (2003). The discursive demolition of the Asian development model. *International Studies Quarterly, 47*(1), 71–99.
Herrigel, G. (2010). *Manufacturing possibilities: Creative action and industries recomposition in the United States, Germany, and Japan*. Oxford and New York: Oxford University Press.
Hundt, D. (2009). *Korea's development alliance: State, capital and the politics of rapid development*. London: Routledge.
Jayasuriya, K. M. (2000). Authoritarian liberalism, governance and the emergence of the regulatory state in post-crisis East Asia. In R. Robison, M. Beeson, K. Jayasuriya, & H. Kim (Eds.), *Politics and markets in the wake of the Asian crisis, Asian capitalisms* (pp. 315–330). London and New York: Routledge.
Ji, J.-H. (2009). The shift in the state form and mode of power exercise in South Korea: From the authoritarian developmental state to neoliberal state power. *Korean Political Science Review, 43*(4), 175–203.
Kang, C. W. (2002). Bad Loans to Good Friends: Money Politics and the Developmental State in South Korea." *International Organization, 56*(1), 177–207.
Katzenstein, P. J. (1978). *Between Power and Plenty: Foreign Economic Policies of Advanced Industrial States*. Madison: University of Wisconsin Press.
Kim, E. M. (1997). *Big business and strong state: Collusion and conflict in South Korean developments, 1960–1990*. Albany: State University of New York Press.
Kim, Y.-T. (1999). Neoliberalism and the decline of the developmental state. *Journal of Contemporary Asia, 29*(4), 441–461.
Kim, K.-H. (2003). Kim Chae-ik soosukgwa kookjehwa. In D.-W. Nam et al. (Eds.), *80nyundae kyungjegyehyukgwa Kim Chae-ik soosuk* (pp. 143–170). Seoul: Samsung Economic Research Institute.
Kim, C.-Y. (2006). *Choibingookesu sunjingook moontukggaji: Hangook kyungjejungchek 30nyunsa*. Seoul: Randomhouse Korea.
Kim, E. M. (2014). The South Korean developmental alliance between business, labor and government. In I.-C. Yi & T. Mkandawire (Eds.), *Learning from the South Korean developmental success: Effective developmental cooperation and synergistic institutions and policies* (pp. 235–258). New York: Palgrave Macmillan.
Kirk, D. (2000). *The unravelling of the Korean miracle in the IMF era*. New York: St Martin's Press.
Kong, T.-Y. (2000). *The politics of economic reform in South Korea: A fragile miracle*. London and New York: Routledge.
Krueger, A. O. (1980). Trade policy as an input to development. *American Economic Review, 70*(2), 288–292.
Kwon, H.-K. (2012). Politics of globalization and national economy: The German experience compared with the U.S. *Politics & Society, 40*(4), 581–607.
Kwon, H.-K. (2013). Politics of institutional change: Evolution of the Irish social concertation model. *Comparative European Politics, 11*(4), 481–510.

Kwon, H.-K. (2014). *Politics of social pacts in the era of globalization: Evolution of the Irish social concertation model.* Seoul: Humanitas.
Lee, S.-J., & Han, T.-J. (2006). The demise of 'Korea, Inc.': Paradigm shift in Korea's developmental state. *Journal of Contemporary Asia, 36*(3), 305–324.
Lee, Y. H., Lim, Y.-J., & Chung, S.-K. (2002). The rise of the regulatory state and government-business relations in South Korea. *Korean Political Science Review, 36*(3), 199–222.
Lee, Y.-H., Chung, S.-K., & Lim, Y.-J. (2004). A comparative study of 'industrial rationalization' and 'corporate reform'—The Chun Doohwan and the Kim DaeJung government cases. *21st Century Political Science Review, 14*(1), 25–54.
Lim, H.-C., & Jang, J.-H. (2006). Between neo-liberalism and democracy: The transformation of the developmental state in South Korea. *Development and Society, 35*(1), 1–28.
Mahoney, J., & Thelen, K. (2010). *Explaining institutional change: Ambiguity, agency, and power.* Cambridge: Cambridge University Press.
Mathews, J. (1998). Fashioning a New Korean Model Out of the Crisis: The Rebuilding of Institutional Capabilities." *Cambridge Journal of Economics, 22*(6), 747–759.
Minns, J. (2001). Of miracles and models: The rise of and decline of the developmental state in South Korea. *Third World Quarterly, 22*(6), 1025–1043.
Noland, M., & Pack, H. (2003). *Industrial policy in an era of globalization: Lessons from Asia.* Washington, DC: International Economic Institute.
Pirie, I. (2005). The new Korean state. *New Political Economy, 10*(1), 25–42.
Schmitter, P. C. (1979). Still the Century of Corporatism? In P. C. Schmitter & G. Lehmbruch (Eds.), *Trends Toward Corporatist Intermediation.* London: Sage.
Schmidt, V. A. (2008). Discursive institutionalism: The explanatory power of ideas and discourse. *Annual Review of Political Science, 11*, 303–326.
Shin, J.-S., & Chang, H.-J. (2003). *Joosikhwoisa hangookui goojojojung: Moousi moonjeinga* (Restructuring Korea Inc.). Paju: Changbi Publishers.
Streeck, W., & Thelen, K. (2005). *Beyond continuity: Institutional change in advanced political economies.* Oxford and New York: Oxford University Press.
Thelen, K. (2004). *How institutions evolve: The political economy of skills in Germany, Britain, the United States, and Japan.* Cambridge and New York: Cambridge University Press.
Thurbon, E. (2016). *Developmental mindset: The revival of financial activism in South Korea.* Ithaca, NY: Cornell University Press.
Woo, J.-E. (1991). *Race to the swift: State and finance in Korean industrialization.* New York: Columbia University Press.
World Bank. (1993). *The East Asian miracle: Economic growth and public policy.* New York: Oxford University Press.
Yoon, S.-W. (2009). Woihwanwigi ihoo Hangookui baljunjoouijuk sinjayoojooui-hwa [Internalizing neoliberal globalization in Korea—A case for 'developmental neoliberalization']. *Economy and Society, 83*, 40–68.

CHAPTER 2

Current Debates and Theoretical Arguments

With the Korean economy's accelerated growth between the 1960s and the 1980s, early debates regarding Korea's economic development model focused on "what is the Korean economic development model" that made this impressive success possible. Neoliberal economists represented by the World Bank (1993) claimed that the success of the Korean economy was possible through market-adaptive strategies like export-led policies, rather than state intervention (World Bank 1993; Yoo 2004; Frank 1975; Krueger 1978, 1980, pp. 288–292; Bhagwati 1978, pp. 1–38; Little et al. 1970; Balassa 1978, pp. 37–45; Hong 1975). In contrast, Amsden (1989) and other developmental theorists argued that the Korean economy's rapid catch-up is a product of state-led developmentalism based on unique institutions established in the 1960s and 1970s (Amsden 1989; Wade 1990; Haggard 1990; Woo 1991; Mason et al. 1980; Jones and Sakong 1980; Johnson 1982, 1985; Cole and Lyman 1971).

However, prevalent theories that analyzed the reasons for the Korean economy's success focused on one dimension of the Korean economic model and overlooked the dynamic process that the model has undergone, given the changes in the domestic and international political economic environment. Despite the static limitations shared by these two dominant perspectives, the Korean economic development model received more attention as a type of state-led capitalism until the mid-1990s.

With East Asia facing economic crisis in the late 1990s, the focus of the debates rapidly changed. In particular, most of the former developmental

K. M. Kim, *The Korean Developmental State*,
https://doi.org/10.1007/978-981-15-3465-2_2

states that faced the crisis, including Korea, have adopted neoliberal reform measures, moving the core of the debate to "Have the developmental states shifted to a free-market system or have they continued with developmentalism?" or "Is the development model still valid in the era of globalization?" And in the changed debate, leadership was passed on to the neoliberalists. As a matter of fact, the effectiveness of free-market competition had dominated the global market in the aftermath of the 1980s, so the Asian economic crisis in the late 1990s was a prime opportunity to attack the inefficiency of state intervention (Krugman 1998). In fact, the Asian states in crisis at the time implemented neoliberal reforms not only because of external pressures but also as a result of the endogenous political processes, which combined reflective thinking about the appropriateness and effectiveness of state intervention and expectations for neoliberal alternatives.

Nevertheless, the question of how to define the changes in the Korean economic development model that have occurred after the 1997 crisis remains controversial. The dominant viewpoint focuses on neoliberal liberalization measures of the Korean economy before and after the crisis and interprets changes in the Korean economic development model as the dissolution of the existing model of state-led developmentalism (Shin and Chang 2003; Chang and Evans 2005; Lee et al. 2002, 2004; Kirk 2000; Kong 2000; Kim 1999; Kim 2014; Moon and Kim 1996; Moon 1994; Kang 2000, 2003; Lee and Han 2006; Lim and Jang 2006; Jayasuriya 2000; Noland and Pack 2003; Yoon 2009; Ji 2009, 2011; Stubbs 2011; Pirie 2005).

In contrast, approaches that explain changes in the Korean economic model from the perspective of continuity focus on the persistence of growth-oriented economic policies and institutions and a sustained economic structure centered on the state and large conglomerates. Within this perspective, recent changes such as liberalization in the financial system are still interpreted as changes within the framework of developmentalism (Witt 2015; Cherry 2005; Yoon 2012; Koo 2010; Amsden and Chu 2003; Wong 2004; Lim and Lee 2009; Chu 2009; Hundt 2005; Thurbon and Weiss 2006; Kim et al. 2008; Kim 2012a).

Unlike the demise theory of developmentalism, the continuity theory has an advantage in understanding the Korean model from a comparative perspective. However, both approaches face the same limitations. First, they presuppose the unique characteristics of the classical Korean developmental system as the only ideal type of developmentalism. Second, they fail to capture the direction of the evolution of the Korean political economic model, which was not a transition to "a European corporatist capitalism" or "an Anglo-Saxon free market system," nor a simple continuity of the past system, but a transition to "a new version of developmentalism."

How then should we understand the evolution of Korean capitalism, which is a complex reconstruction of change and continuity? How can we characterize the current Korean political economic system? What might be a better theoretical alternative to understand the continuity and change of the Korean development model?

From the comparative perspective, this study shares the continuity perspective in that it argues that the Korean development model should be classified as a variant of state-led capitalism, not Anglo-Saxon market liberalism or European corporatism (Schmidt 2002, pp. 1–9). However, this study notes that the goals and means of state-led industrial policy in the Korean developmental system have changed drastically and that the governance system of industrial policy has also changed to something more comprehensive and democratic. Further, this study argues for the importance of the political process of endogenous interactions of major actors, not just exogenous shocks or isolated events, in the Korean political economy adapting to changes in domestic and international political economic environments.

This chapter critically reviews the prevalent literature on the Korean economic development model and how changes in this model should be viewed and presents a theoretical alternative.

Section 1: Explaining Growth: Liberalism vs. Institutionalism

Liberalism and the Korean Political Economy

Classical economists argue that latecomers in East Asia have achieved rapid economic growth through export-oriented industrialization, unlike developing countries in South America and Africa. In the same vein, mainstream economists who are interested in the cause of Korean economic growth generally claim that Korea's successful catch-up depended on market-adaptive and export-oriented economic policies after the mid-1960s, such as the adoption of the uniform exchange rate system, the easing of import controls, and the introduction of export incentives (Krueger 1978, pp. 277–300, 1980, pp. 288–292; Bhagwati 1978, pp. 1–38; Little et al. 1970; Balassa 1978, pp. 37–45; Hong 1975; World Bank 1993; Yoo 2004; Frank 1975). They essentially equate a domestic market opening and export-oriented strategy with a liberal market economy, the opposite of a protectionism and import substitution strategy. From this perspective, Korea, which has adopted an export-oriented strategy, is understood as one variant of a liberal market economy.

This argument of classical economists gained influence in the 2000s following the Asian crisis of 1997. As many late developing economies, including the emerging Asian economies, showed continued economic growth after the 1997 crisis, they argued that the economic success of Brazil, Russia, India, China, Singapore, and Taiwan in the 2000s was a result of neoliberal reforms and nonintervention, rather than of successful industrial policies, and that developmentalism is no longer a growth model of late industrializing economies (Pack and Saggi 2006). Likewise, neoliberals hold that the rapid recovery and sustained growth of the Korean economy since the crisis have resulted from various restructuring measures introduced to improve the productivity of the Korean economy (CCKE 2011, p. 107).

However, classical market economists ignore the fact that the export-led industrialization strategy of the East Asian countries was possible through the state's active economic intervention, including legal and institutional reforms. For example, the transition from an import substitution to an export-oriented industrial strategy in Korea in the mid-1960s was not the result of market actors' autonomous choices but the result of the state's active intervention. In fact, private businessmen had no incentive to switch to an export-oriented strategy because they could gain much more profit in the protected domestic market under the import substitution strategy. Thus, without strong state intervention, switching to an export-oriented strategy would have been impossible (Kim 2006). Similarly, the transition from light industry to heavy chemical industry in the 1970s was driven solely through the state's intentional intervention. The state attracted and encouraged private corporations by concentrating capital for the industrialization of heavy chemical industries.

Market economists tend to identify openness with market liberalism and protection with state intervention, a simple dichotomy. Market economists mistakenly think that an open strategy itself defines the nature of the domestic economic system. However, state intervention, open economy, and market-friendly policies have coexisted in Korea ever since the introduction of export-led growth strategies in the mid-1960s. The heavy chemical industrialization policy of the 1970s, typical of Korea's developmentalism, was an industrial policy to maintain an export-led economy. In other words, the open market economy strategy can coexist with an Anglo-Saxon liberalist system in the United States, a corporatist system in the Nordic countries, or even a developmental system in the Asian countries (Katzenstein 1985, pp. 17–38). Hence a comparative perspective is needed to understand the nature of a state's political economy.

Finally, neoliberal market economists cannot account for changes in the Korean economic development model. The Korean economy has maintained an export-oriented growth strategy since the 1960s, but the domestic system supporting it has changed significantly to maintain export-oriented growth. However, market economists fail to capture these changes and have a limited understanding of the implications of these changes.

Institutionalism and the Korean Political Economy

By focusing on the political, social, and institutional elements of East Asian economic systems, developmental state theory has gained more persuasiveness in explaining the East Asian development model since the late 1990s Asian economic crisis. This theory argues that East Asian countries gained rapid economic growth through state-led industrial policies promoting the competence, rationality, and relative autonomy of bureaucrats (Amsden 1989; Wade 1990; Haggard 1990; Woo 1991; Mason et al. 1980; Jones and Sakong 1980; Johnson 1982, 1985; Cole and Lyman 1971). Developmental state theory is fundamentally based on institutionalism, emphasizing the rationality and relative autonomy of bureaucrats and the state's ability to take advantage of international political and economic environments and historical legacies (Evans 1995; Acemoglu 2005, pp. 1199–1226; Davidheiser 1992, pp. 463–475; Woo 1991; Shin and Chang 2003).

According to developmental state theory, the success of the Korean economy—one of the most representative East Asian economies showing impressive economic growth—was due to state, not market, intervention. According to Shin and Chang (2003), Korea pursued an imbalanced growth strategy that concentrated resources on specific strategic industries, as Japan, first noted as the exemplar of the East Asian development model, did. Despite being a global latecomer, Japan gained rapid economic growth through its focus on the heavy chemicals and electronics industries. Korea, an even later developing country, focused on more limited fields in similar industries and showed a faster growth rate than Japan, thanks to state intervention (Shin and Chang 2003, p. 35).

These studies emphasized that state intervention reduces the possibility of market failure. Amsden (1989) pointed out that private firms are reluctant to enter new industries because of uncertainties and worries about short-term low profits (pp. 84–85). According to Amsden (1989), Korea could not switch to the heavy chemical industry, which required large investments, if it relied on the interests of private corporations. In fact, during Korea's industrial move from light industry to heavy chemicals in the 1970s, light industry profits were much higher than those of heavy industry, a disincentive for private companies. Here, the state changed the direction of investment while considering the long-term interests of the entire national economy (Amsden 1989, p. 88).

Developmental state theory pays attention to the institutional bases for the effectiveness of state intervention. The first basis is the bureaucracy's professionalism and relative autonomy. Evans (1995) argued that Korea's successful industrialization could be achieved through a Weberian competent bureaucracy and its relative autonomy, which restricted rent-seeking between the state and businesses. Evans and Rauch (1999) showed that bureaucrats' relative autonomy is positively correlated with the state's economic performance. Woo (1991) also claimed that the Korean state was able to enter full-fledged industrialization by shifting from external reliance on the United States and internal capital in the 1950s to becoming a state of relative autonomy in the 1960s (Woo 1991, pp. 7–14).

Another institutional basis for effective state intervention is the state's ability to attract and control business. Many studies analyzing the Korean economic development model from the 1960s to the 1980s, including Amsden (1989), noted that Korea was able to pursue strong industrial policies, such as heavy chemicals, in the 1970s due to the Korean government's control of finance (Amsden 1989; Woo 1991; Shin and Chang 2003).

Although effective in explaining the Korean development model of the 1960s and 1970s, developmental state theory takes an overly static approach, similar to classical economic theory, in its focus on fixed institutional foundations. While static implies resistance to change, the institutional foundations on which developmental state theory depends are transformed and restructured in response to the pressures of continuous change. Developmental state theory lacks an internal logic to interpret these transformations and reconstructions. Many studies that have attempted to explain the characteristics of the Korean economic development model struggle to explain the evolutionary process of its developmental system, which has been adapting to changes in political economic environments, such as globalization and democratization, since the 1990s.

Moreover, developmental state theory tends to rely too heavily on the rationality of bureaucracy, positing that state intervention works because bureaucrats correctly determine market failure and provide a correct solution. While competent bureaucrats are important for the effectiveness of state intervention, competency itself does not determine rationality. Such rationality is not a given but is constantly reconstructed in response to changing circumstances. The state presents a vision, and subsequent processes are readjusted through continuous interaction of state and market actors. In Korea, policies for heavy chemicals and components industries were ineffective at first due to the resistance of businesses and wrong policy programs. These policies began to work once they were revised and adjusted through continuous interactions between the state and businesses.

In sum, developmental state theory, which explains Korea's economic development model based on the state's competency and capability, is limited in explaining change by failing to see the political processes in which the developmental system works. For this reason, internal differentiation in the theory to analyze change came after the 1997 economic crisis.

Section 2: Explaining Change: Differentiation Within Developmental State Theory

With the economic crisis of 1997, the core of the debate on the Korean political economic model shifted to whether the Korean developmental state has been dismantled and how to explain institutional changes after the crisis. As a result, developmental state theory has differentiated into two positions: one that claims the dissolution of the developmental state and the other that claims its continuity.

Dissolution of Developmentalism

Most studies claiming dissolution largely see the transition of the Korean developmental state to a neoliberal regulatory state, although some consider the possibility of a transition to a corporatist model due to the growth of social forces including business and labor since democratization in the 1980s. They point to the following: the dismantling of policy means such as financial control and strengthening of liberal measures against chaebol conglomerates, the dissolution of past developmental coalitions between state and large conglomerates, and the weakening of bureaucratic coherence (Lee et al. 2002, 2004; Pirie 2008; Shin and Chang 2003; Jayasuriya 2000; Pirie 2005, 2008; Chang and Evans 2005; Kirk 2000; Kong 2000; Kim 1999, Kim 2014; Moon and Kim 1996; Moon 1994; Kang 2000, 2003; Lee and Han 2006; Lim and Jang 2006; Noland and Pack 2003; Yoon 2009; Ji 2009, 2011; Stubbs 2011; Lew and Wang 2007).

Shin and Chang (2003) argued for the breakdown of Korea's developmental state based on financial liberalization measures since the mid-1990s. According to Shin and Chang (2003), the inevitable result of Korea's traditional catch-up strategy is the relatively late development of the financial sector. Since the early 1980s, financial liberalization measures have been partially implemented to improve the efficiency of the financial sector. The liberalization process greatly accelerated during the Kim Young-sam government. The five-year financial liberalization plan promulgated by the Kim government in 1993 included deregulation of interest rates, abolition of policy fund loans, strengthening of banks' management autonomy, reduction of entry barriers to financial business, and capital account liberalization (Shin and Chang 2003, pp. 114–116, 121–123).[1] In addition, Pirie (2005) and Jayasuriya (2000) argued that after the financial crisis, Korea has rapidly transformed into a neoliberal state through the strengthening of the Bank of Korea's independence and the establishment of financial supervisory bodies (Pirie 2005, p. 38).

By analyzing changes in the roles of government and financial institutions in the process of industrial restructuring, Lee et al. (2004) argued that the traditional methods of the Korean developmental state, which regulated the market through the intermediary of banks, have been dismantled. According to their study, the traditional characteristics of Korea's

[1] However, Shin and Chang (2003) pointed out that this program was incorrectly designed and not properly managed, becoming a major cause of the 1997 financial crisis (pp. 123–129).

developmental state have changed considerably when comparing the industrial rationalization measures of the Chun Doo-hwan government and the restructuring process of the Kim Dae-jung government. While the industrial restructuring measures of the 1980s were government-led corporate restructuring, the corporate restructuring of the 1990s, such as the workout program, were led by main creditor banks rather than direct state intervention. Funding for restructuring also changed from an increased issuance of currency from the Bank of Korea to a far more market-oriented approach of purchasing weak credits through public fundraising and selling after normalization of management. Although controversy exists over government intervention in the case of the "Big Deal," the business exchange between chaebol groups initiated by the Kim Dae-jung government, Lee et al. (2004) pointed out that the Big Deal was different from past practices, in that the government tried to induce autonomous restructuring among big businesses.

Some studies focused on the strengthening of regulations against large conglomerates, claiming that the Korean developmental state has declined and converged toward a regulatory state (Lee et al. 2002; Shin and Chang 2003; Noland and Pack 2003). According to Lee et al. (2002), the transition to a liberal regulatory state in Korea began under the Chun Doo-hwan government, during which time Korea tried to curb the chaebols' concentration of economic power through the introduction of the Fair Trade Act. Moreover, during the Kim Young-sam government, the Fair Trade Commission was made independent to strengthen fair competition in the market, and market entry regulation was removed in 1996. In order to meet IMF requirements, the Kim Dae-jung government strengthened the fair trade system under the framework of economic liberalization and economic democratization, reducing cross-shareholding among affiliates, preventing unfair internal transactions, reintroducing the equity investment limit (25% of net assets), and introducing a debt guarantee restriction system among affiliates of conglomerates (Lee et al. 2002, pp. 205–211).

Shin and Chang (2003) pointed out that the restructuring during the crisis at the end of the 1990s was concentrated in the corporate sector, following IMF programs. At that time, restructuring of the chaebols was "in-depth" enough to break up the chaebols' corporate governance structures. Key measures for restructuring the chaebols included prohibition of intragroup transactions, restriction of debt-capital ratio, strengthening of minority shareholders' rights, improvement of accounting transparency, and introduction of an outside director system. They saw that financial reform was also part of corporate sector reform (Shin and Chang 2003, pp. 16–20). Noland and Pack (2003) argued that after the 1997 financial crisis, the principle of free market gained strength due to its emphasis on corporate governance restructuring and sound monitoring by the Korean market. They claimed that the state's industrial policies could no longer be normatively or realistically justified (Noland and Pack 2003).

Studies that claim the demise of Korean developmentalism hold that financial liberalization and reforms against chaebols disorganized the traditional developmental coalition and weakened the autonomy and capacity of Korean bureaucracy. According to this view, the Korean government's measures for financial liberalization and regulation of large corporations in the 1980s and 1990s broke down the political coalition of developmentalism (Moon and Kim 1996; Moon 1994; Kim 1997, 2014). Moreover, some studies pointed out that the state's internal coherence had been weakened and that policy coordination and authority within the bureaucracy had not been properly arranged, weakening both bureaucratic coherence and state capacity (Ji 2009; Lew and Wang 2007).

On the other hand, some studies paid attention to the decline of authoritarianism and the strengthening of interest group politics after democratization in the late 1980s, considering the possibility that the Korean political economic system could develop into a corporatist model (Moon and Kim 1996; Moon 1994; Kim 1997, 2014). With the relative weakening of state power in state-conglomerate relations, and the increased voice of organized labor after the 1980s, the corporatist system has actually emerged as an alternative model of the Korean political economy.

For example, although taking a somewhat vague position, Kim's (2014) research focused on the dissolution of Korea's traditional developmental coalition and the expansion of labor participation in social and economic decision-making processes (Kim 2014, p. 246). According to Kim (2014), the Korean government had to abolish trade policies to protect domestic industries due to the pressure of globalization since the 1980s (Kim 2014, pp. 246–247). In addition, with their economic growth, chaebols lost interest in maintaining the close relationship with the state, which formed the axis for the traditional Korean economic model. Labor, which had been oppressed until the 1980s, began to emerge, along with democratization, as an active social actor. Kim (2014) argued that the pressure of capital to reduce the state's economic intervention and the pressure of labor to expand welfare benefits and regulate the increasing power of chaebols resulted in a considerable change in the characteristics of the Korean political economic system (Kim 2014, pp. 247–248).

However, studies that claimed the decline of the Korean developmental state and its transition to neoliberalism or corporatism are limited in their understanding of the direction of change. The demise theory of Korean developmentalism lacks a comparative perspective. Although the Korean political economic model has been moving away from its traditional system, it still cannot be understood as Anglo-Saxon free-market capitalism or European corporatist capitalism. Studies claiming the demise of Korean developmentalism tend to regard a close alliance of state and large corporations mediated by banks, which is a unique characteristic of the past Korean developmental system, as an archetype of developmentalism. Although financial control through nationalization of the bank was an important policy instrument for the traditional Korean developmental system, we cannot say that it is the only policy instrument for developmentalism.

As we will further explore in Chap. 5, the Korean developmental state changed its growth strategy from input-driven, centered on assembly industries, to innovation-driven, centered on components and materials industries, and likewise altered its method of using policy means. Rather than supplying capital for large-scale facility investments to support the input-driven growth strategy, the focus is now on providing R&D incentives to upgrade the main industries and foster new high-technology industries. For these purposes, the Korean state takes advantage of government subsidies, policy financing, and tax benefits even more broadly than comparable countries.

While current Korean developmentalism is different from the traditional Korean development model, it has become more like the traditional Japanese developmental system that was in place at least until the 1980s. In Japanese industrialization, the state took a role as enabler or benefactor, rather than as leader or organizer, for industrial catch-up and predominantly focused on organizing government-supported consortia based on comprehensive private sector participation and cooperation, rather than directly funding individual corporations (Shin and Chang 2003, pp. 35–36).

In regard to strengthening the corporatist tendency in Korea, the voices of capital and labor have grown relatively stronger. However, the nature of a system depends not on the balance of power itself, but on the way in which power is exercised. Labor in Korea remains weak in terms of how organizational power is exercised. Conglomerates also seek to benefit from individual deals rather than from organized ones with the state. A corporatist experiment such as Nosajungwiwonhwoi, the Korea Tripartite Commission (of labor, business, and government), which was established in the Kim Dae-jung government, still lacks real binding power (Kim 2010, pp. 254–255; Lee 2009; Yang 2007).

The demise theory lacks a single internal logic to explain the coexistence of change and continuity in the evolutionary process of the Korean political economic model. Hence, most studies in demise theory tend to interpret the remaining developmental attributes as remnants of past practices that will soon disappear (Lee et al. 2002). But why have some aspects changed, and why do others continue? Is the change due to exogenous shock and the persistence due to institutional path dependency?

What the demise theory misses is that exogenous factors such as globalization, or domestic events such as democratization and hence the dissolution of past institutional foundations, do not explain the direction of change. Exogenous pressures to heed the international norms of the World Trade Organization (WTO) and the OECD memberships and to follow IMF requests have not moved the Korean model specifically toward an Anglo-Saxon free-market system. Likewise, the power of private actors such as chaebols and labor has not moved the Korean political economic system toward a European corporatism. To understand the exact direction of change in the Korean political economic model, we must figure out its institutional characteristics and how the main actors actually interact with each other, from a comparative perspective.

Continuity of Developmentalism

From a comparative perspective, the Korean political economic model can be best described in terms of continuity. Continuity emphasizes the persistence of the Korean developmental system, based on extension of growth-oriented economic policies, interventionist institutions, and an economic structure centered on large conglomerates. Of course, even continuity proponents point out that the Korean developmental state has undergone a series of transformations in its financial and developmental governance systems. Yet for them, these changes are still interpreted as changes within the framework of developmentalism (Witt 2015; Yoon 2012; Lim and Lee 2009; Cherry 2005; Kim et al. 2008; Koo 2010; Amsden and Chu 2003;

Wong 2004; Chu 2009; Hundt 2005; Thurbon and Weiss 2006; Kim 2012a).

Witt (2015) noted that Korea maintains the basic framework of a developmental state, categorizing Korea as "a reconfigured developmental state" for the following reasons. First, economic growth resurfaced as a policy priority after the Lee Myung-bak government. Second, the functions of finance and budget planning, earlier separated into the Ministry of Finance and Economy and the Ministry of Planning and Budget, were reintegrated into the Ministry of Strategy and Finance in 2008, which exercises powerful authority. Third, chaebols are still allowed long-term financing as in the past. Chaebols can receive preferential long-term loans through nonbank financial institutions under their ownership. The Korean government does not intervene directly to provide preferential treatment to chaebols but tolerates their preferential status in the domestic market. Fourth, even after democratization, the power of final decision-making still lies with the president. Chaebols participate as main actors in establishing economic policies, but consultation from other social forces such as labor or small and medium corporations is limited. The Korean government's ability to enforce policy is generally superior to other countries (World Bank 2012; Witt 2015, pp. 216–219, 231).

Unlike studies that present the liberalization of the financial system as evidence of Korean developmentalism's dismantlement, Lim and Lee (2009) highlighted that despite formal changes in the financial system, the way it actually works does not differ greatly from the past. They insisted that the independence of the Bank of Korea and the creation of the Financial Supervisory Commission are not sufficient and that the state's influence on the financial sector continues through the Financial Supervisory Commission (Lim and Lee 2009).

Through research on the institutional system of Korean industrial policies, Yoon (2012) argued that Korea has continued state intervention in the market to recover from economic crises and pursue export-led growth, despite changes brought through democratization and globalization. Faced with domestic and international crises, the Korean government institutionalized industrial policies for the continuous growth of the export sectors, especially for industrial development (Yoon 2012, pp. 13, 58–60, 252).

Although liberal reforms followed the late 1990s Korean financial crisis, Koo (2010) and Thurbon and Weiss (2006) held that these policies were still developmental strategies. Koo (2010) interpreted Korea's strengthening of the open market by promoting an active free trade agreement (FTA) policy in the 2000s as the transition from developmental mercantilism to developmental liberalism. Thurbon and Weiss (2006) likewise stated that although the size of foreign direct investment (FDI) has increased since the financial crisis, the Korean government has taken a strategic approach to FDI (Koo 2010; Thurbon and Weiss 2006).

In addition, Cherry (2005) indicated that the Korean state maintains a relative advantage over chaebols by analyzing the political process of the "Big Deal," the business exchange between the five conglomerates led by the Kim Dae-jung government. Kim et al. (2008) also claimed that the Korean state has not lost its autonomy over labor or capital, even after the 1990s. Wong (2004) and Kim (2012a) noted that the establishment and coordination of industrial policies has continued despite the dismantling of the top policymaking agency—the EPB. In a study of the role of the Korean state in the development of biotechnology, Wong (2004) stated that policy overlap and coordination among ministries has been resolved through a division of labor between ministries despite the absence of the top policy coordination agency. Kim (2012a) showed that the Ministry of Information and Communication played a role of "quasi-pilot agency" in the process of developing new wireless communication technology in Korea (Cherry 2005; Kim et al. 2008; Wong 2004; Kim 2012a).

However, studies advocating the continuity of Korean developmentalism also point to changes in the state's role and method of intervention. Witt (2015) viewed liberal reforms such as privatizing banks, strengthening the Bank for International Settlements (BIS) capital adequacy ratio, authorizing chaebols' nonbank financial institutions, and restricting firms' debt ratios as changes that weaken the policy means of the traditional Korean developmental state. Nonetheless, Witt (2015) pointed out that Korean firms still depend more on indirect financing than firms in Anglo-American liberal states, which would allow long-term financing of Korean firms, including chaebols (p. 219).

Some studies emphasized the changes in the state's traditional policy means and roles. Yoon (2012) showed that the Korean industrial policy governance system has shifted from dirigiste decision-making based on the discretionary command of the president and his core group until the 1970s to an institutionalized way based on legislative and policy institutions since the 1980s (pp. 13, 58–60, 252). Cherry (2005) pointed out that the state's role in policy implementation has changed from commander-in-chief to senior partner. Kim et al. (2008) claimed that the

Korean government now seeks legitimacy in policymaking and implementation through a "coalition" with diverse social actors rather than through oppression and coercion (Cherry 2005; Kim et al. 2008; Park 2012, pp. 70–72).

Recent continuity arguments for the evolution of the Korean political economic model illustrate the present Korean economic model situated in a comparative context, distinct from the dissolution approaches of Korean developmentalism. Yet the emphasis on continuity exposes limitations in explaining change by focusing exclusively on fixed institutional foundations.

The continuity arguments notably fail to capture the implications of the Korean economic development model's recent qualitative changes because they identify the institutional foundations of the past developmental system, such as a top policymaking agency's means of financial control, as typical of developmentalism. For example, Witt (2015) emphasized that the functions of budget planning and financial affairs separated during the Kim Dae-jung government were reintegrated in the Lee Myung-bak government. However, the existence of a powerful agency controlling both budget planning and financial affairs is no longer an important part of the Korean developmental state. Currently, the decentralized Korean developmental system includes more institutional foundations—several economic ministries and their affiliates, government-funded research centers, industrial associations, and so forth—than it did in the past. This change suggests that different versions of developmentalism may work on different institutional foundations.

Continuity studies cannot explain the direction of change, much like studies on the dissolution of developmentalism. Although they recognize changes in the formal institutions of Korean developmentalism, they do not clarify how change and continuity can coexist in the Korean political economic model. They tend to exaggerate continuity at the risk of ignoring change. These studies of Korean developmentalism show continuity not as a result of adjustment to the pressure to change but as a result of resistance to it, based on the path dependency of institutions. Thus, they do not capture the direction of the evolution of Korean capitalism, which is not simply a persistence of the past model nor a transition to a free-market or corporatist model.

Like the dissolution perspective, the continuity perspective has limitations in understanding the direction of evolution of the Korean political economic model, where change and continuity coexist. How shall we describe the direction of evolution of the Korean political economic model?

Section 3: Theoretical Alternative and Analytical Framework

Based on an analysis of the Korean capitalist model, how and to what extent this model has changed, and why it has changed into a system with certain unique characteristics, this study raises three key hypotheses. First, the Korean capitalist model remains a type of state-led capitalism when viewed from a comparative institutional perspective. This claim differs from the claims of developmental, leftist, and neoliberal theorists that Korea has transformed to a neoliberal model.

The second key hypothesis is that the current Korean political economic model is not a repetition or persistence of the past model but a new version of developmentalism. This means that various versions of developmentalism exist, contrary to the prevalent developmentalists' assumption that the traditional Korean developmental system is an archetype.

The third key hypothesis is that the unique direction of the evolution of the Korean capitalist model has been determined neither by exogenous pressures nor by the path dependency of institutions but by the endogenous process of discursive politics of Korea's major political economic actors. This view is distinct from the path dependency perspective of the Korean political economic model as a "legacy" of the past developmental state, as well as from the perspective that views changes in the Korean development model as a result of exogenous pressure.

This study presents the following analytical framework to address our three hypotheses. First, this study relies on the classification based on traditional comparative political economic literature to categorize the Korean economic development model. Specifically, this study uses the classification of three types of political economic models including Anglo-Saxon liberalism, German or Nordic corporatist collectivism, and state-led capitalism, all of which are suggested as ideal types of capitalism (Shonfield 1965; Cohen 1977; Estrin and Holmes 1983; Zysman 1983; Cox 1986; Schmidt 2002; Hall 1986).

Second, this study divides the types of state-led capitalism into an authoritarian dirigisme system and an enabled developmental system, based on a comprehensive network, in order to capture the changes in the Korean developmental system (Johnson 1982; Levy 2015; Weiss 2003; Williams 2014; Stiglitz et al. 2013; Evans 2008, 2010; Evans and Heller 2015).

Third, to analyze the unique direction of the evolution of the Korean capitalist model, which cannot be explained by path dependency or exogenous pressure such as globalization, this study follows the endogenous institutional change theory developed in recent historical institutionalism and explains institutional change through active reinterpretation and recomposition of the main actors on institutions in their interactions (Mahoney and Thelen 2010; Streeck and Thelen 2005; Kwon 2013, 2014; Schmidt 2008; Blyth 2002; Herrigel 2010).

Classification of the Types of Capitalism

The Korean political economic system has undergone many changes through democratization in 1987 and the financial crisis of 1997. The debate lies in how far the system has changed and how to interpret the change. Marxist theorists, as well as neoliberalists, argue that Korea changed from a developmental state to a neoliberal state around the financial crisis (Ji 2011). However, they narrowly interpret the authoritative developmental state of the 1970s as equal to state-led capitalism in general or tend to overstate the weakening of the state and the supremacy of transnational capital, ignoring national differences in the capitalist reproduction system. This study aims to understand the capitalist reproduction model at the national level in a comparative perspective by analyzing Korea's state-business and interfirm relations.

Based on a general classification method of comparative forms of capitalism, this study identifies three categories: Anglo-Saxon free-market capitalism, European corporatist capitalism, and state-led capitalism. We follow these three classifications of capitalism for the following reasons. First, we focus on the supply side of the economy, taking note of major actors' roles in economic investment and input. Thus, this study excludes classifications that consider the demand side of the economy, such as redistribution and welfare systems (Ebbinghaus 1999; Boyer 1997; Amable 2003).

Second, this study considers state intervention in the economy as an important factor in comparative business systems. Other prevalent classifications focusing on the supply side categorize varieties of capitalism as market liberalism and coordinated capitalism (Albert 1993; Hall and Soskice 2001). By ignoring the role of the state as an actor, however, these classifications have difficulty in explaining countries in which state intervention plays an important role in the economy, including France, Taiwan, and Korea. Furthermore, this dichotomy overlooks another form of efficient "institutional complementarity" that goes beyond the two types of institutional complementarity identified by Hall and Soskice (2001).

Finally, these three types of capitalism—market liberalism, corporatism, and state-led capitalism—are among the traditional classifications in the literature on modernization and industrialization (Schmidt 1996, 2002; Hall 1986; Shonfield 1965; Cohen 1977; Estrin and Holmes 1983; Zysman 1983; Cox 1986; Johnson 1982). Shonfield (1965) distinguished the British model, in which the economy works based on market competition, from the French and German models, in which the role of public authorities is stronger than in the British model. Shonfield (1965) differentiated the French model, in which state institutions are strong, from the German model, where the role of the bank in industrial development is more important. Shonfield (1965) emphasized the effectiveness of the state intervention model, different from the traditional British free-market model, by focusing on the state's institutional structure that supports market actors with industrial strategies.

The ways in which various capitalism models work depend on who the major actors are in the national economy, the roles they play in the economy, and the relations they form with each other. Here, we will examine the characteristics of each model to understand the direction of evolution of Korean capitalism by focusing on the characteristics, roles, and relationships of the main actors in each model.

Liberal Capitalism

A main characteristic of the free-market economic model represented by the United States and the United Kingdom is that the major actors (labor and capital) are fragmented, and main decisions and coordination in the supply side of the economy are left to market competition. In this model, the state keeps an arm's length away from the market and minimizes economic intervention. The role of the state in the economy is limited to regulator and mediator.

For example, UK firms are more reliant on capital markets for financing than German and French ones; therefore, CEOs in UK firms try to maximize shareholder value by focusing on the company's short-term profit. On the other hand, UK corporations are relatively free in their relations with other corporations. UK firms develop corporate governance rules that promote transparency and accountability because they tend to rely on open official information and contracts. In short, the United Kingdom's capital market practice is a shareholder model rather than a stakeholder model (Schmidt 2002, pp. 121–122).

In the market liberalism model, labor, like capital, is often fragmented, and most negotiations occur at the local level. British labor has a single trade union at the national level, the Trades Union Congress (TUC), but it is relatively loose due to limited bureaucratic resources and lack of sanctions. Instead, substantive negotiations are centered on craft unions that are fragmented into more than 100 entities (Hall 1986, p. 250).

The state in the liberal market economy keeps the principle of arm's length economic management and limits its role to macroeconomic policies that regulate demand only through interest rate and budget balancing (Hansen 1968; Hall 1989). The state has no will to intervene directly in the economy to achieve specific economic goals and limits itself to the role of regulator to maintain macroeconomic stability (Hall 2015, pp. 426–427).

Corporatist Capitalism

The coordinated capitalist model, represented by Germany and the Nordic countries, distinguishes itself from the Anglo-Saxon free-market system in that major economic coordination is made through nonmarket mechanisms rather than market competition. For coordination, major actors in the economy, such as labor and business, are organized at the industrial, regional, or national level. Major macroeconomic decisions are made through consultations and negotiations between business and labor or tripartite concertation including the state. Important decisions even at the firm level do not depend on short-term equity values, as in the Anglo-Saxon liberal regime, but rather on the concertation of various stakeholders, such as corporate executives, work councils, unions, financial institutions, and major subcontractors in long-term business relations. Although the state formally participates as a major actor in important decisions, the state's role is limited to coordinator, unlike the role of the developmental state in state-led capitalism. Especially, its role in the supply side is limited to universal policies such as infrastructure construction and education, rather than strategic industrial policies (Hall 1986; Schmidt 2002).

In Germany, traditionally regarded as the most distinct from the UK free-market system, financial capital exercises considerable control over the operation of industrial capital. As a result, German banks have a direct interest in the long-term performance of a firm and actually influence the firm's strategy (Hall 1986, pp. 235–236). Despite recent emphasis on shareholder value in Germany, these network-based relationships contribute to strengthening the value of stakeholders rather than shareholders (Schmidt 2002, pp. 122–123).

The main partner of capital in a coordinated capitalist model is labor, based on a centralized organizational structure and a formalized collective bargaining system. For example, German laborers are members of trade unions organized at the industrial level, and almost all unions belong to the unified German Trade Union Confederation (DGB). The collective bargaining system is guaranteed by law (Hall 1986, p. 236). In addition, even at the individual firm level, important decisions are articulated in workers' terms because they formally participate on corporate supervisory boards (Schmidt 2002, p. 123).

However, a centralized organizational structure itself is dispensable for social concertation, which is characteristic of the coordinated capitalist model. Various reforms in coordinated capitalist countries since the 1980s have shown that despite the dismantlement and transformation of existing organizational structures, negotiating practices can continue. In the 1980s, for example, Denmark successfully overcame the economic crisis by reforming existing corporatist institutions and creating a so-called "flexicurity" system, a more flexible and inclusive system of deliberation (Kjær and Pedersen 2001, p. 235; Pedersen 2006, p. 255; Martin 2006, pp. 279–280).

Finally, the state's role in the coordinated capitalist model is limited to coordinator to maintain macroeconomic stability and to support the collective coordination of private actors. In Germany, for example, fiscal policy and monetary policy are strictly separated, and Germany's monetary policy is completely free from parliamentary influence and legally protected, especially since the independence of the Deutsche Bank (Hall 1986, p. 235). In addition, in the coordinated capitalist system, capital and labor expect that the state will protect nonmarket institutions and practices by establishing and periodically adjusting the legal framework that gives regulatory authority to private groups (employer groups or trade unions) rather than directly intervening in the economy (Schmidt 2002, pp. 125–126).

State-Led Capitalism

Characteristics of state-led capitalism represented by postwar France and Japan are, above all, the intentional intervention of the state in the supply side of the economy and its institutional capabilities to realize its will.

State-led capitalism distinguishes itself from the Anglo-Saxon liberal market model in that the operation of the economy is not left to the market but to nonmarket mechanisms. This model also distinguishes itself from corporatist coordinated economies since the state serves as a key actor of coordination, but the public status and role of labor are weak. While in the corporatist model, the state intervenes mainly in the demand side of the economy, in the state capitalist model, the state is mainly involved in the supply side of the economy.

In this model, the state intervenes strategically and selectively in cultivating industries, considering the ripple effects of specific industries and the priority of national industrial development. Economic planning in postwar France, as well as active and selective industrial policies in East Asian countries such as Japan and Korea, is a typical example of state intervention not found in Anglo-Saxon liberal economies and corporatist coordinated economies (Zysman 1983; Johnson 1982; Evans 1995; Shonfield 1965). These selective industrial policies distinguish state-led capitalism from the neutral regulatory policies of the Anglo-Saxon free-market model, or from universal and general policies in the corporatist model, such as highway construction or advancement of universal educational systems.

The state's economic intervention is supported by the institutional capabilities to realize it. For example, in the postwar period, state capitalist economies shared a few institutional features. First, formal and informal networks developed between the state and business through meritocratic elite schools to foster competent bureaucrats and a system in which bureaucrats transfer to firms after their retirement. France's strong state organization is based on a unique human resource system backed by the Ecole Nationale d'Administration (ENA) and the Commissariat Général du Plan (Levy 2015, p. 396; Zysman 1983; Schmidt 2002, pp. 123–125; Hall 1986, p. 243).

Second, policy instruments used in postwar state capitalist countries include protectionist tariff and trade policies, price setting modes, and selective credit allocation by the state (Levy 2015, pp. 396–397; Zysman 1983; Johnson 1982; Evans 1995). With globalization, earlier policy instruments have lost their effectiveness, but countries that maintain a framework of state-led capitalism continue industrial policies through various incentives such as policy grants, taxes, and financial benefits (Amsden 2013; Weiss 2003).

Finally, one characteristic of the state-led capitalism model is closer relations between state and business, and exclusion or suppression of labor interests. Business expects the state to play a role on their behalf, by establishing wage bargaining mechanisms, maintaining peace with labor through welfare and labor market programs, and concentrating investments through planning and industrial policies (Schmidt 2002, pp. 125–127).

Shared interests between state and business create a conservative political hegemony. According to Levy (2015), France and Japan kept workers' wages low and prioritized investment over consumption. They used policies to socialize the cost of investment for corporate competitiveness through decreased wages and distorted prices by keeping prices higher at home and selling cheaper abroad. Meanwhile, France and Japan minimized social spending (Levy 2015, p. 397).

This traditional exclusionary nature of the state-led capitalism model intensifies the underdevelopment of organized labor and restricts its role in the supply side, thereby inciting labor's political unrest and militant tendencies, which in turn reinforce or consolidate businesses' exclusion of labor. For example, French labor's organizational strength is low; unions are not unified; collective bargaining is not regulated by law; and a union has very limited status in the workplace. And while the nature of trade unions is radical and militant, their success in industrial disputes is usually very low (Hall 1986, p. 244).

Despite these generally shared features of state-led capitalism, differentiation does exist. In the next section, we analyze these differences to understand the direction of the evolution of the Korean political economic model.

Differentiation Within State-Led Capitalism

Previous studies that explain the changes in the Korean political economic model as the dissolution of developmentalism or the transition to neoliberalism understand the traditional institutional form of Korea's developmentalism as an archetype of the developmental state. Thus, they mistakenly equate the disorganization of previous institutions as the demise of the developmental state itself or a transition to neoliberalism. However, within state-led capitalism, diverse variations exist by governance method and developmental strategy.

Governance Method: Dirigisme vs. Enabling State

First, governance forms in state-led capitalism can be divided into a dirigiste state and an enabling state. An enabling state employs strategic selective industrial policy. While an enabling state relies on private-led or relatively horizontal interfirm networks based on indirect support by the state, with dirigisme, the state develops a more direct and hierarchical relationship with firms, forming detailed plans for national industrial development, fostering selective corporations, and even setting production goals. While postwar France is close to dirigisme, postwar Japan is relatively closer to an enabling state.

Dirigisme in postwar France occurred through direct production planning by the state and industrial development by state-owned firms, which occupy a large percentage of the economy. Developmental planning by industry focused on fostering one or two national champions, bringing technologies developed by national research institutes directly to selected companies to foster world leaders through a "technology leaps" strategy (Cohen 1992). With this state-led dirigisme system, France's policymaking and enforcement mechanisms took on a top-down, state-centric nature. Moreover, to foster national industry champions, France pursued Fordist mass production strategies, which led to the marginalization of small- and medium-sized firms (Levy 2015, p. 397).

On the other hand, developmentalism in postwar Japan relied on formal and informal linkages and partnerships between the state and corporations while further ensuring the autonomy of the private sector (Johnson 1982). While France depended on state-owned companies to implement planned economic industrial policies, Japan held a smaller share of state-owned companies in the economy (Samuels 1987). Unlike France, Japan's Ministry of International Trade and Industry (MITI) operated industrial policies based on the participation and cooperation of private companies. In Japan's capital structure, a conglomerate called *keiretsu* owns its affiliates in almost every industry. Thus, the government deals with five or six business groups and takes steps to support and discipline them, depending on whether they are complying with government policies (Anchordoguy 1989; Levy and Samuels 1991; Levy 2015, pp. 397–399).

Developmental Strategies

Another major aspect of state-led capitalism lies in its developmental strategies. Postwar developmental countries have in common their pursuit of strategies to nurture national champions. For instance, France selected a strategy of nurturing national champions by industry, while Japan opted to manage and cultivate selective companies across several business groups (Schmidt 2002; Johnson 1982). In the case of Japan, fostering national champions resulted in supporting the entire industrial ecosystem, due to its unique big business group structure based on widespread systemization of companies (Shin and Chang 2003).

In the postwar period, international competition based on production and export within a country required fostering national champions with economy of scale and high technology. Relying on national champions for international competition was standard in both the liberal and corporatist models. Until the 1980s, the US economy was also represented by large corporations such as General Motors (GM), Ford, and General Electric (GE), and their successes meant the success of the US economy. In Germany, companies such as Volkswagen, Mercedes-Benz, and Bosch were the leading companies. However, unlike state-led capitalist economies, national champions in liberal economies were formed by radical innovation through market competition and mergers and acquisitions, and national champions in corporatist economies by gradual innovation based on bank-led, long-term investment practices and interfirm cooperation. In short, the way of competition was the same, but the way in which competing players were cultivated varied from country to country.

However, with the globalization of finance and production, and the acceleration of technological innovation, international competition no longer depends on national champions but on national innovative ecosystems including many components and materials suppliers, public and private research institutions, financial institutions, and training and education institutes, as well as national lead firms. As globalization of production by national champions intensifies, it becomes difficult to equate the interest of an individual corporation with that of the national economy. For example, as of 2008, Japanese companies such as Toyota gained huge profits thanks to overseas production, but the entire Japanese economy lost about $420 billion in production and about 1 million jobs (*The Economist*, November 20, 2010). US automobile companies have also increased their overseas production since the 1990s, but employment in the US domestic automotive industry declined between 1998 and 2008 by 66.7% (US Bureau of Labor Statistics; *The Guardian*, February 17, 2012). Thus, the focus of international competition among nations shifted to continuing high value-added production and building an innovative ecosystem in the national economy to maintain linkages between domestic and foreign production.

This change in the way of competition has brought about a change in the growth strategy of state-led capitalism. The development strategy for fostering national champions was based on inputs, including supply of low-wage labor through labor oppression policies and supply of capital through subsidies and financial and tax benefits (Zysman 1983; Johnson 1982; Amsden 1989). The most important in competition among national champions was economic efficiency based on economies of scale. However, a new developmental strategy focused on establishing an innovative ecosystem requires productivity-driven policies to generate high added value per unit input of capital and labor (Weiss 2003, pp. 296–297).

Building an innovation ecosystem goes beyond fostering one or a few outstanding engineers or scientists who design and develop a mass production system. It requires a new production process in which various professional technical personnel and economic players work together. In the past, input-driven mass production systems in less developed countries like Korea borrowed or bought an idea or technology from advanced countries to develop industries, rather than developing them for themselves. Instead, they focused on increasing profits through scale. Here, mobilizing cheap labor and capital is more important than collecting a variety of innovative ideas. By contrast, in the innovation-driven economic system, the source of ideas is more diverse and decentralized.

Thus, while excluding various small- and medium-sized enterprises (SMEs) was dominant for the concentration of capital in input-driven economies, innovation-driven economies require inducing the participation of increasing numbers of small and medium components companies, skilled workers, and private research institutes. For example, if the state exclusively concentrates capital on a few conglomerates through the state's artificial mobilization of capital for the input-driven strategies, innovation-driven systems require joint consultation and cooperation with previously excluded small and medium components companies, public and private research institutes, labor, and lead firms. Innovation is developed not simply by superior individual actors but by industrial ecosystems designed for innovation, which organize and coordinate "industrial commons" including well-organized training programs, components companies with expertise and technology, and various research institutes in which new experiments can be conducted (Kim and Kwon 2017).

Politics of Evolution

Korea's long-term successful development is based not on a single growth principle but on its ability to adapt to changes in the international political economy and shift to a new growth principle. Korea shifted from an input-driven growth strategy that realizes economies of scale through low wages and enormous capital investment based on foreign technologies to an innovation-driven growth strategy based on productivity improvement through innovation of product and production processes. How did it achieve this shift from an input-driven strategy to an innovation-driven one?

There are multiple ways to form an industrial ecosystem to cultivate the industrial commons for an innovation-driven economy. As shown in Fig. 2.1, one method is the accumulation of innovative capabilities through "creative destruction" based on the free market, coordination through active participation by labor and civic organizations based on corporatism, and state-supported development of "industrial commons" and formation of innovative industrial ecosystems.

For instance, in corporatist countries, such as Germany, Sweden, and Denmark, labor and business associations continue to foster "industrial public goods" by renewing technology training programs and strengthening cooperation between small- and medium-sized components companies. German companies develop the national economy by upgrading their

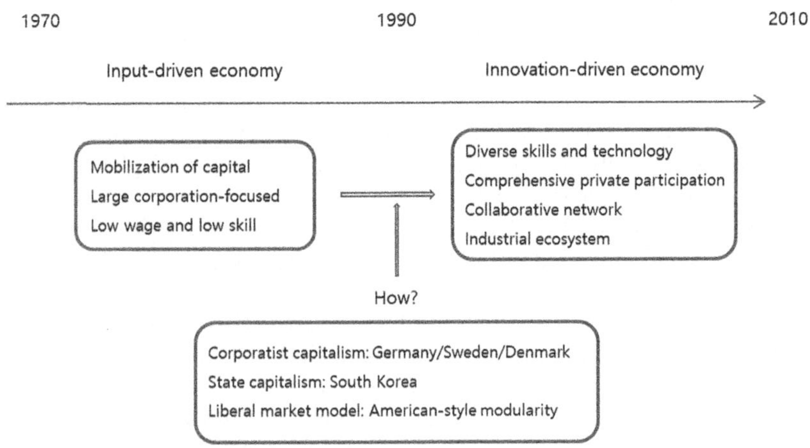

Fig. 2.1 Different ways of transition

innovation capabilities in well-developed domestic "industrial ecosystems" in the process of expanding overseas production (Kwon 2012). On the other hand, the United States has a free-market-based business relationship, which establishes a global module system that easily combines global innovation resources. This global module production system, however, has in fact produced a lot of innovation holes in the industrial ecosystem in the United States, resulting in a significant loss of industrial innovation capability (Pisano and Shih 2012; Berger 2013).

How then could Korea transform from an "input-driven" to an "innovation-driven" economy? Why did it not adopt a coordinated capitalist style like Germany, Denmark, and Sweden or pursue the free market like the United States? Why has the Korean developmental state continued while making organizational changes from its old model?

In order to analyze the direction of the evolution of the Korean capitalism model, we rely on the endogenous change theory of historical institutionalism, which focuses on the politics of strategic choices of actors, as distinguished from existing institutionalist approaches based on path dependency or exogenous change theory.

The rationale is as follows. First, actors who actively engage in industrial upgrade vary by country, resulting in variations in political economic models. In northern European countries and Germany, labor and business associations traditionally have been major actors for important industrial coordination, whereas in the United States and Korea, neither labor nor business organizations have traditionally existed as major actors with public status.

The capabilities of main actors who make their voices heard determine the choices they can make and play an important role in creating directions for change. For example, even if conditions for state autonomy are established internationally and domestically, state policy cannot be effectively carried out if the state lacks capability to implement it. Even a state with authoritarian characteristics, such as Korea in the past, still has difficulty in effectively implementing a policy unless it has the ability to make other actors actively participate in it.

Unlike institutionalists, however, we do not focus on the fixed institutional capabilities of key actors. Rather, we stress that the regeneration or continuation of institutions cannot come from institutional stasis within the existing system but only from change. Key actors ensure the continuity of the institution when they themselves can change by creating new capabilities through new strategies.

The final reason we adopt the institutional change theory of historical institutionalism is that the direction of evolution of the Korean economic development model can be explained only by the endogenous political process of key actors. The hypotheses we propose to analyze the changes and continuity of the Korean political economic model are as follows.

First, the unique direction of the Korean political economy's evolution is the result of reinterpreting new interests and strategies through interaction among main actors. The interpretation of feasible options by key actors and the politics of their interactions during a crucial phase of transition shed light on the evolutionary direction of the Korean political economic model that has adapted to changes in exogenous political economic environments.

Existing studies explaining changes in the Korean economic model tend to focus on exogenous factors. Shin and Chang (2003), Lee et al. (2004), Kim (2014), and Ji (2011) all considered exogenous factors such as globalization, financialization, economic crisis, and democratization as major factors of change. However, while these exogenous factors can serve as background for change, they themselves do not explain the direction of change. In spite of the pressures of globalization and democratization that have persisted since the late 1970s, Korea has continued its developmental system and strengthened its vertical business model rather than converging into a free-market model or transitioning to a corporatist cooperative economy. The endogenous process of changing their strategies through interaction among major actors has allowed Korea to adapt to the external shocks of the liberalization, financialization, and globalization of the international political economic order.

Second, Korea's state-led capitalism could continue because the state still dominated the discourse of change by considering the entire national economy, and state intervention could be justified by other major actors in the Korean political economy in spite of exogenous pressures. Unlike existing developmental state studies focusing on fixed institutional capacity, this study accepts that the state's ability has been weakened in terms of existing institutional capacity. Nevertheless, the state's continued economic intervention could be justified because the state could create new strategies and means in the interaction among the state and other actors. The state did not present a successful master plan from the start. State-led discourse was sometimes retracted and sometimes discarded in the interaction with other major actors, but the state continued its efforts to revise its discourse and create new discourse by observing the responses of other actors.

Third, Korea could transition from an input-driven growth strategy based on the alliance between state and big business to the innovation-driven growth strategy based on a comprehensive innovation network because it could reach a new social consensus among actors. We agree with the view of the traditional class coalition theory that the stability of a particular system should be based on a particular class coalition. However, system changes or shifts may not necessarily result from the dissolution of a traditional class coalition. If the content of consensus changes even under the same or similar class coalition, a change of system is possible. In contrast, even with the dismantling or weakening of the traditional class coalition, the existing system can continue through a new class coalition. In Korea, the narrow state-chaebol developmental coalition based on an input-driven system has weakened, but the state and large corporations remain major partners even in the new innovation-driven system. Noteworthy, however, is that the content of social consensus among the major actors has changed.

Finally, the content of social consensus among the major actors in the transition of the Korean political economic model was not presented from the start as a complete blueprint but has been reconstructed as a new discourse in the continuous interaction between actors, by reinterpreting and rearranging their interests and strategies. An effective counterstrategy to other actors' strategies is never clear from the outset. Rather, it evolves by adjusting to each other's counterstrategies. To understand the changes in the Korean economic model, we must examine historically how the actors' discourse has been restructured, rather than focus on their fixed interests or balance of power.

References

Acemoglu, D. (2005). Politics and economics in weak and strong states. *Journal of Monetary Economics, 52*(7), 1199–1226.

Albert, M. (1993). *Capitalism Against Capitalism*. London: Whurr.

Amable, B. (2003). *The diversity of modern capitalism*. Oxford and New York: Oxford University Press.

Amsden, A. H. (1989). *Asia's next giant: South Korea and late industrialization*. New York: Oxford University Press.

Amsden, A. H. (2013). *Securing the home market: A new approach to Korean development*. Research paper 2013-1. United Nations Research Institute for Social Development (UNRISD). Retrieved April 15, 2015, from http://www.unrisd.org/__80256b3c005bccf9.nsf/0/3c3c2e5f091a961dc1257b7c00470256?OpenDocument&panel=seriespapers&Click=.

Amsden, A. H., & Chu, W.-W. (2003). *Beyond late development: Taiwan's upgrading policies*. Cambridge, MA: MIT Press.

Anchordoguy, M. (1989). *Computers Inc.: Japan's challenge to IBM*. Cambridge, MA: Harvard University Press.

Balassa, B. (1978). The 'New Protectionism' and the International Economy. *The Journal of World Trade Law, 12*(5), 408–436.

Berger, S. (2013). *Making in American: From innovation to market*. Cambridge, MA: MIT Press.

Bhagwati, J. N. (1978). *Foreign trade regimes and economic development: Anatomy and consequences of exchange control regimes*. Cambridge: Ballinger Co. National Bureau of Economic Research.

Blyth, M. (2002). *Great transformation: Economic ideas and institutional change in the twentieth century*. New York: Cambridge University Press.

Boyer, R. (1997). French statism at the crossroads. In C. Crouch & W. Streeck (Eds.), *Political economy of modern capitalism: Mapping convergence and diversity* (pp. 71–101). London: SAGE Publications Ltd.

CCKE (The Compilation Committee for the Korean Economy for 60 Years). (2011). *The Korean economy: Six decades of growth and development: Summary*. Seoul: Korea Development Institute.

Chang, H.-J., & Evans, P. (2005). The role of institutions in economic change. In S. Paula & G. Dymski (Eds.), *Reimagining growth: Towards a renewal of development theory* (pp. 99–140). London and New York: Zed Books.

Cherry, J. (2005). 'Big deal' or big disappointment? The continuing evolution of the South Korean developmental state. *The Pacific Review, 18*(3), 327–354.

Chu, Y.-W. (2009). Eclipse or reconfigured? South Korea's developmental state and challenges of the global knowledge economy. *Economy and Society, 38*(2), 278–303.

Cohen, S. (1977). *Modern capitalist planning*. Berkeley: University of California Press.

Cohen, É. (1992). *Le colbertisme 'High Tech': économie des telecom et du grand projet* [High-Tech colbertism: The economics of telecoms and the grand project]. Paris: Hachette.

Cole, D. C., & Lyman, P. N. (1971). *Korean development: The interplay of politics and economics*. Cambridge, MA: Harvard University Press.

Cox, A. (1986). *State, finance and industry*. Prentice Hall: Harvester Wheatsheaf.

Davidheiser, E. B. (1992). Strong states, weak states: The role of the state in revolution. *Comparative Politics, 24*(4), 463–475.

Ebbinghaus, B. (1999). Does a European social model exist and can it survive? In G. Huemer, M. Mesch, & F. Traxler (Eds.), *The role of employer associations and labour unions in the EMU: Institutional requirements for European economic policies*. Aldershot: Ashgate.

Estrin, S., & Holmes, P. (1983). *French planning in theory and practice*. London: Allen & Unwin.

Evans, P. B. (1995). *Embedded autonomy: States and industrial transformation*. Princeton: Princeton University Press.

Evans, P. B. (2008). *In search of the 21st century developmental state*. Centre for global political economy working paper 4. Brighton: University of Sussex.

Evans, P. B. (2010). Constructing the 21st century developmental state: Potentials and pitfalls. In O. Edigheji (Ed.), *Constructing a democratic developmental state in South Africa* (pp. 37–58). Cape Town: HSRC Press.

Evans, P. B., & Heller, P. (2015). Human development, state transformation, and the politics of the development state. In S. Leibfried et al. (Eds.), *The Oxford handbook of transformations of the state* (pp. 691–713). Oxford: Oxford University Press.

Evans, P. B., & Rauch, J. (1999). Bureaucracy and growth: A cross-national analysis of the effects of 'Weberian' states structures on economic growth. *American Sociological Review, 64*(5), 748–765.

Frank, C. R. (1975). *Foreign trade regimes and economic development: South Korea*. New York: National Bureau of Economic Research.

Haggard, S. (1990). *Pathways from the periphery: The politics of growth in the newly industrializing countries*. Ithaca, NY: Cornell University Press.

Hall, P. (1986). *Governing the economy: The politics of state intervention in Britain and France*. New York: Oxford University Press.

Hall, P. (Ed.). (1989). *The political power of economic ideas*. Princeton: Princeton University Press.

Hall, P. (Ed.). (2015). The changing role of the state in liberal market economies. In S. Leibfried, E. Huber, M. Lange, J. D. Levy, F. Nullmeier, & J. D. Stephens (Eds.), *The Oxford handbook of transformation of the state* (pp. 426-444). Oxford: Oxford University Press.

Hall, P., & Soskice, D. (2001). *Varieties of capitalism: The institutional foundations of comparative advantage*. Oxford: Oxford University Press.

Hansen, B. (1968). *Fiscal policy in seven countries, 1955–1965*. Paris: OECD.

Herrigel, G. (2010). *Manufacturing possibilities: Creative action and industries recomposition in the United States, Germany, and Japan*. Oxford and New York: Oxford University Press.

Hong, W. (1975). *Trade and development in Korea*. Honolulu: University of Hawaii Press.

Hundt, D. (2005). A legitimate paradox: Neo-liberal reform and the return of the state in Korea. *Journal of Development Studies, 41*(2), 242–260.

Jayasuriya, K. M. (2000). Authoritarian liberalism, governance and the emergence of the regulatory state in post-crisis East Asia. In R. Robison, M. Beeson, K. Jayasuriya, & H. Kim (Eds.), *Politics and markets in the wake of the Asian crisis, Asian capitalisms* (pp. 315–330). London and New York: Routledge.

Ji, J.-H. (2009). The shift in the state form and mode of power exercise in South Korea: From the authoritarian developmental state to neoliberal state power. *Korean Political Science Review, 43*(4), 175–203.

Ji, J.-H. (2011). *Hangook sinjayoojoouiui giwongwa hyungsung*. Seoul: Chaegsesang.

Johnson, C. (1982). *MITI and the Japanese miracle: The growth of industrial policy, 1925–1975*. Stanford: Stanford University Press.

Johnson, C. (1985). Political institutions and economic performance: The government-business relationship in Japan, South Korea, and Taiwan. In R. A. Scalapino, S. Sato, & J. Wanandi (Eds.), *Asian economic development: Present and future* (pp. 63–89). Berkeley: University of California Press.

Jones, L. P. & Sakong, I. (1980). *Government, Business, and Entrepreneurship in Economic Development: The Korean Case*. Cambridge, Mass: Harvard University Press.

Kang, E. C. S. (2000). Segyehwa reform of the South Korean developmental state. In S. Kim (Ed.), *Korea's globalization* (pp. 76–101). New York: Cambridge University Press.

Kang, E. C. S. (2003). The developmental state and democratic consolidation in South Korea. In S. Kim (Ed.), *Korea's democratization* (pp. 220–244). New York: Cambridge University Press.

Katzenstein, P. J. (1985). *Small states in world markets: Industrial policy in Europe*. Ithaca, NY: Cornell University Press.

Kim, E. M. (1997). *Big business and strong state: Collusion and conflict in South Korean developments, 1960–1990*. Albany: State University of New York Press.

Kim, Y.-T. (1999). Neoliberalism and the decline of the developmental state. *Journal of Contemporary Asia, 29*(4), 441–461.

Kim, C.-Y. (2006). *Choibingookesu sunjingook moontukggaji: Hangook kyungjejungchek 30nyunsa*. Seoul: Randomhouse Korea.

Kim, K.-M. (2010). Changes in Korean labor market regimes. *Seoul Journal of Korean Studies, 23*(2), 247–269.

Kim, S.-Y. (2012a). Transitioning from fast-follower to innovator: The institutional foundations of the Korean telecommunications sector. *Review of International Political Economy, 19*(1), 140–168.

Kim, E. M. (2014). The South Korean developmental alliance between business, labor and government. In I.-C. Yi & T. Mkandawire (Eds.), *Learning from the South Korean developmental success: Effective developmental cooperation and synergistic institutions and policies* (pp. 235–258). New York: Palgrave Macmillan.

Kim, K.-M., & Kwon, H.-K. (2017). The state's role in globalization: Korea's experience from a comparative perspective. *Politics & Society, 45*(4), 505–531.

Kim, S.-H., Han, C.-H., & Jang, J.-H. (2008). State-society relations in South Korea after democratization: Is the strong state defunct? *Pacific Focus, 23*(2), 252–270.

Kirk, D. (2000). *The unravelling of the Korean miracle in the IMF era*. New York: St Martin's Press.

Kjær, P. & Padersen, O. K. (2001). Translating Liberalization: Neoliberalism in the Danish Negotiated Economy. In J. L. Campbell, O. K. Pedersen (Eds.), *The Rise of Neoliberalism and Institutional Analysis* (pp. 219–248). Princeton: Princeton University Press.

Kong, T.-Y. (2000). *The politics of economic reform in South Korea: A fragile miracle*. London and New York: Routledge.

Koo, M.-K. (2010). Embracing free trade agreements, Korean style: From developmental mercantilism to developmental liberalism. *The Korean Journal of Policy Studies, 25*(3), 101–123.

Krueger, A. O. (1978). *Foreign trade regimes and economic development: Liberalization attempts and consequences*. Cambridge: National Bureau of Economic Research.

Krueger, A. O. (1980). Trade policy as an input to development. *American Economic Review, 70*(2), 288–292.

Krugman, P. (1998). *What happened to Asia?* Retrieved October 28, 2015, from http://web.mit.edu/krugman/www/DISINTER.html.

Kwon, H.-K. (2012). Politics of globalization and national economy: The German experience compared with the U.S. *Politics & Society, 40*(4), 581–607.

Kwon, H.-K. (2013). Politics of institutional change: Evolution of the Irish social concertation model. *Comparative European Politics, 11*(4), 481–510.

Kwon, H.-K. (2014). *Politics of social pacts in the era of globalization: Evolution of the Irish social concertation model*. Seoul: Humanitas.

Lee, S.-J., & Han, T.-J. (2006). The demise of 'Korea, Inc.': Paradigm shift in Korea's developmental state. *Journal of Contemporary Asia, 36*(3), 305–324.

Lee, D. -J. (2009). Woorinara Sahwoihabuijoouiui Hyungsikgwa Siljil ganui Gwoiri [Social Corporatism in Korea: The Evolution of KTC]. *Kyungjewa Sahwoi [Economy and Society], 83*, 143–168.

Lee, Y. H., Lim, Y.-J., & Chung, S.-K. (2002). The rise of the regulatory state and government-business relations in South Korea. *Korean Political Science Review, 36*(3), 199–222.

Lee, Y.-H., Chung, S.-K., & Lim, Y.-J. (2004). A comparative study of 'industrial rationalization' and 'corporate reform'—The Chun Doohwan and the Kim DaeJung government cases. *21st Century Political Science Review, 14*(1), 25–54.

Levy, J. D. (2015). The transformations of the statist model. In S. Leibfried, E. Huber, M. Lange, J. D. Levy, F. Nullmeier, & J. D. Stephens (Eds.), *The Oxford handbook of transformation of the state* (pp. 393-409). Oxford: Oxford University Press.

Levy, J. D., & Samuels, R. J. (1991). Institutions and innovation: Research collaboration as technology strategy in Japan. In L. K. Mytelka (Ed.), *Strategic partnerships: State, firms, and international competition* (pp. 120–148). London: Pinter.

Lim, H.-C., & Jang, J.-H. (2006). Between neo-liberalism and democracy: The transformation of the developmental state in South Korea. *Development and Society, 35*(1), 1–28.

Lim, H.-R., & Lee, H.-N. (2009). Political economy of financial supervisory reform in Korea. *Journal of Korean Politics, 18*(1), 119–146.

Little, I., Scitovsky, T., & Scott, M. (1970). *Industry and trade in some developing countries: A comparative study*. London: Oxford University Press.

Mahoney, J., & Thelen, K. (2010). *Explaining institutional change: Ambiguity, agency, and power*. Cambridge: Cambridge University Press.

Martin, C. J. (2006). Corporatism in the post-industrial age: Employers and social policy in the little land of Denmark. In J. L. Campbell, J. A. Hall, & O. K. Pedersen (Eds.), *National identity and the varieties of capitalism* (pp. 271–294). Montreal: McGill-Queen's University Press.

Mason, E. S., Kim, M.-J., Perkins, D. H., Kim, K.-S., & Cole, D. C. (1980). *The economic and social modernization of the Republic of Korea*. Cambridge, MA and London: Council on East Asian Studies, Harvard University Press.

Moon, C.-I. (1994). Changing state-business relations in South Korea since 1980. In A. MacIntyre (Ed.), *Business and government in industrializing Asia* (pp. 142–166). Ithaca, NY: Cornell University Press.

Moon, C.-I., & Kim, Y.-C. (1996). A cycle of paradox. In A. Leftwich (Ed.), *Democracy and development: Theory and practice* (pp. 139–167). Cambridge: Polity Press.

Noland, M., & Pack, H. (2003). *Industrial policy in an era of globalization: Lessons from Asia*. Washington, DC: International Economic Institute.

Pack, H., & Saggi, K. (2006). *Is there case of industrial policy? A critical survey*. Washington, DC: World Bank Publication.

Park, S.-Y. (2012). Exploring Korea's emerging 'post-developmental' state: Research trends and agendas since the 1990s. *Journal of Contemporary Politics, 5*(1), 63–90.

Pedersen, O. K. (2006). Corporatism and beyond: The negotiated economy. In J. L. Campbell, J. A. Hall, & O. K. Pedersen (Eds.), *National identity and the varieties of capitalism* (pp. 245–270). Montreal: McGill-Queen's University Press.

Pirie, I. (2005). The new Korean state. *New Political Economy, 10*(1), 25–42.

Pirie, I. (2008). *The Korean developmental state: From dirigisme to neo-liberalism*. London: Routledge.

Pisano, G. P., & Shih, W. C. (2012). *Producing prosperity: Why America needs a manufacturing renaissance*. Boston: Harvard Business Review Press.

Samuels, R. J. (1987). *The business of the Japanese state: Energy markets in comparative and historical perspective*. Ithaca, NY and London: Cornell University Press.

Schmidt, V. A. (1996). *From State to Market? The Transformation of French Business and Government*. New York & London: Cambridge University Press.

Schmidt, V. A. (2002). *The futures of European capitalism*. Oxford and New York: Oxford University Press.

Schmidt, V. A. (2008). Discursive institutionalism: The explanatory power of ideas and discourse. *Annual Review of Political Science, 11*, 303–326.

Shin, J.-S., & Chang, H.-J. (2003). *Joosikhwoisa hangookui goojojojung: Moousi moonjeinga* (Restructuring Korea Inc.). Paju: Changbi Publishers.

Shonfield, A. (1965). *Modern capitalism: The changing balance of public and private power*. London and New York: Oxford University Press.

Stiglitz, J. E., Lin, J. Y., & Monga, C. (2013). Introduction: The rejuvenation of industrial policy. In J. E. Stiglitz & J. Y. Lin (Eds.), *The industrial policy revolution I: The role of government beyond ideology* (pp. 1–18). London: Palgrave Macmillan.

Streeck, W., & Thelen, K. (2005). *Beyond continuity: Institutional change in advanced political economies*. Oxford and New York: Oxford University Press.

Stubbs, R. (2011). The East Asian developmental state and the great recession: Evolving contesting coalitions. *Contemporary Politics, 17*(2), 151–166.

Thurbon, E., & Weiss, L. (2006). Investing in openness: The evolution of FDI strategy in South Korea and Taiwan. *New Political Economy, 11*(1), 1–22.

Wade, R. (1990). *Governing the Market: Economic Theory and the Role of Government in East Asian Industrialization*. Princeton: Princeton University Press.

Weiss, L. (2003). Guiding globalization in East Asia: New roles for old developmental states. In L. Weiss (Ed.), *States in the global economy: Bringing domestic institutions back in* (pp. 245–270). New York: Cambridge University Press.

Williams, M. (2014). Introduction & rethinking the developmental state in the twenty-first century. In M. Williams (Ed.), *The end of the developmental state?* (pp. xiii–xxiii, 1–29). London: Routledge.

Witt, M. A. (2015). South Korea: Plutocratic state-led capitalism reconfiguring. In M. A. Witt & C. Redding (Eds.), *The Oxford handbook of Asian business systems* (pp. 216–237). Oxford: Oxford University Press.

Wong, J. (2004). The adaptive developmental state in East Asia. *Journal of East Asian Studies, 4*, 345–362.

Woo, J.-E. (1991). *Race to the swift: State and finance in Korean industrialization*. New York: Columbia University Press.

World Bank. (1993). *The East Asian miracle: Economic growth and public policy*. New York: Oxford University Press.

World Bank. (2012). *Worldwide governance indicator*. Retrieved November 4, 2013, from http://info.worldbank.org/governance/wgi.

Yang, J.-J. (2007). Hankook Sahwoihyubyak Silhumui Choodongryukkwa Hankwe [Social Concertation in South Korea: Could it be Steppingstone to a Coordinated Market Economy?]. *Sahwoikwahakyunkoo, 15*(1), 38–68.

Yoo, J.-H. (2004). *Gwanchisesang: Sijanggyungjemani sal girida*. Seoul: Chaegsesang.

Yoon, S.-W. (2009). Woihwanwigi ihoo Hangookui baljunjoouijuk sinjayoojoouihwa [Internalizing neoliberal globalization in Korea—A case for 'developmental neoliberalization']. *Economy and Society, 83*, 40–68.

Yoon, D.-Y. (2012). *Crisis of export-led development and the politics of industrial policy, 1980–2007: Idea, institution and developmental governance*. Seoul: Yonsei University Dissertation.

Zysman, J. (1983). *Governments, markets and growth: Financial systems and the politics of industrial change*. Ithaca, NY: Cornell University Press.

CHAPTER 3

Characteristics of Korean Economic Growth

This chapter outlines the overall patterns of economic growth in Korea through quantitative indicators from a comparative perspective. It serves as a reference point for analyzing the characteristics and changes of the Korean political economic model presented in Chaps. 4, 5, and 6. Quantitative data show that the Korean economy has transitioned from an input-driven to an innovation-driven economy, which means that the institutional conditions for operating the Korean economy have also changed.

Before examining the institutional changes of the Korean economic development model that has shaped the Korean economy, this chapter explores the distinctive characteristics of Korea's economic growth. First, the rapid and sustained growth of the Korean economy is based on production and exports in manufacturing. Second, the Korean economy has changed its growth driver from the end product assembly industry to the components and materials industry. Third, the Korean economy has shifted from an input-driven to an innovation-driven economy.

Section 1: Economic Growth Based on Manufacturing Exports

The Korean economy has long been of interest to policymakers in many late developing countries, for two reasons. First, South Korea has grown rapidly from the poorest economy to one of the world's top ten

K. M. Kim, *The Korean Developmental State*,
https://doi.org/10.1007/978-981-15-3465-2_3

economies in gross domestic production. Second, Korea's economic growth has been going on for a very long time—over 50 years. To identify how the rapid and sustained growth of the Korean economy was possible, we focus first on the growth engine of the Korean economy: the continuous growth of manufacturing exports.

The development process of the Korean economy underwent rapid industrialization. Yoo (1997) defined industrialization as "the period when the share of employment in the agricultural sector declined from more than 50% to less than 20%." Based on this standard, Korea's industrialization took about 19 years, from 1970 to 1990. Taiwan's industrialization took about 20 years, achieving industrialization in the early 1980s, slightly earlier than Korea. In contrast, early developed countries took a longer time to industrialize: the United States took 54 years, Sweden took 45 years, and Japan 39 years (CCKE 2011a, p. 11).

Since the start of full-scale industrialization in the 1960s, Korea has maintained a high real economic growth rate compared to developed countries. Figure 3.1 shows that Korea's growth rate from 1971 to 2012 is higher than that of the OECD average as well as the United States or Japan for the same period, except for the two years of 1980 and 1998 when Korea experienced severe economic crises. As shown in Table 3.1,

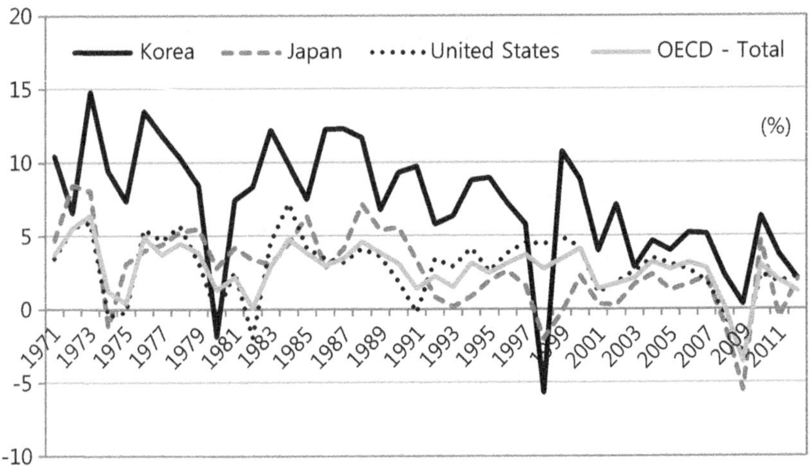

Fig. 3.1 Comparison of real economic growth rate. Source: OECD statistics

Table 3.1 Comparison of real economic growth rate by period (Unit: %)

	1971–2012	*1971–1979*	*1981–1997*	*1999–2012*
Hong Kong	5.8	8.9	6.0	4.1
Taiwan	6.6	10.0	7.3	4.0
Singapore	7.2	8.9	8.0	5.5
Korea	*7.1*	*10.2*	*8.8*	*4.7*
Japan	2.6	4.6	3.4	0.8
Sweden	2.1	2.0	1.7	2.5
United States	2.8	3.6	3.1	2.0
Germany		3.1	2.0/1.8	1.3

Source: UNCTAD statistics

Note: Since Germany was unified in 1990, it was calculated by dividing the period of 1981–1997 into 1981–1989 and 1991–1997. Prior to unification, the data for Germany is only for West Germany

Korea recorded an average growth of 7.1% from 1971 to 2012, similar to Singapore's 7.2%, which in the same period is much higher than growth in other developed countries such as the United States, Japan, Germany, and Sweden, and even higher than those of newly industrializing Asian countries such as Taiwan and Hong Kong. Excluding 1980 and 1998, which had negative growth rates of −1.9% and −5.7%, respectively, the average annual growth rate was 10.2% from 1971 to 1979, and 8.8% from 1981 to 1997, higher than those of Hong Kong, Taiwan, and Singapore or developed countries such as the United States, Japan, Germany, and Sweden. From 1999 to 2012, Korea's growth rate was 4.7%, a little lower than Singapore's 5.5%, but still higher than rates in developed and other emerging economies.

Korea's rapid industrialization and sustained growth have been supported by high export growth rates since the 1960s. As shown in Table 3.2, Korea had an average export growth rate of 19.8% from 1960 to 2010, much higher than that of major export-oriented countries such as Taiwan (16.0%), Hong Kong (14.9%), Singapore (14.0%), and Japan (11.0%). Korea recorded an explosive growth rate of exports for about 20 years during the decades of the 1960s and 1970s, an average of 39.8% and 37.2%. Although the growth rate decreased after the 1980s, Korea's export growth rate (12.5%) is still higher than that of Hong Kong (8.0%), Singapore (12.0%), Germany (10.2%), and other major exporting countries.

Korea's rapid industrialization and dramatic increase in exports was led by the quantitative and qualitative growth of the manufacturing sector.

Table 3.2 Comparison of real export growth rate (Unit: %)

	1960–2010	*1960–1970*	*1970–1980*	*1980–1990*	*1990–2000*	*2000–2010*
Hong Kong	14.9	14.5	22.5	16.6	8.3	8.0
Taiwan	16.0	23.1	28.8	14.8	7.4	7.6
Singapore	14.0	3.3	28.2	9.9	9.9	12.0
Korea	*19.8*	*39.8*	*37.2*	*15.0*	*10.1*	*12.5*
Japan	11.0	17.5	20.8	8.9	4.1	6.3
Sweden	8.8	9.7	16.3	8.0	5.9	8.3
United States	9.2	8.2	18.4	5.7	7.2	6.5
Germany		11.2	19.1		3.7	10.2

Source: UNCTAD statistics

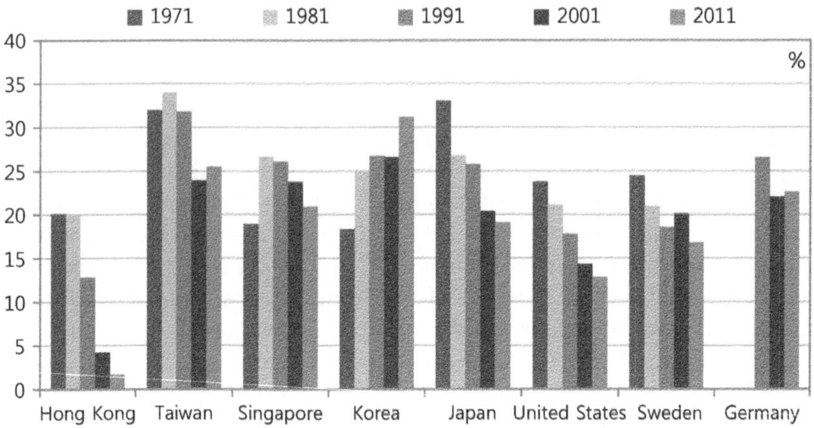

Fig. 3.2 Proportion of manufacturing to GDP. Source: UNCTAD statistics. Note: For Germany, only data after unification are included

Figure 3.2 shows that in all countries except Korea, manufacturing has been in decline since the 1970s or 1980s. In Korea, the GDP share of manufacturing increased from 18.5% in 1971 to 31.2% in 2011. The other major manufacturing countries in the same period that experienced a decrease of manufacturing included Japan (33.7% → 19.1%), the United States (24.4% → 12.8%), Taiwan (29.7% → 25.6%), and Germany (27.1% → 22.6%).

Table 3.3 shows that in 1960, before the start of full-scale industrialization, the number of businesses in Korea was only 15,000, production was

Table 3.3 Trends of the manufacturing industry in South Korea

Period	*Number of businesses*	*Production amount (KRW million)*	*Value added (KRW million)*	*Number of employees*
1960	15,204	59,735	21,866	275,254
1970	24,114	1,334,514	549,793	861,041
1980	30,823	36,279,079	11,856,589	2,014,751
1990	68,872	177,308,768	70,924,547	3,019,816
2000	51,148	534,450,280	205,186,625	2,310,905
2011	63,047	1,502,352,686	480,203,387	2,694,782

Source: KOSIS (http://kosis.kr/index/index.do)

60 billion KRW, added value was 22 billion KRW, and the number of employees was 280,000. In 2011 the scale of manufacturing was as follows: the number of enterprises 63,000, production 1500 trillion KRW, added value 480 trillion KRW, and number of workers 2.7 million, with increases, respectively, of 320%, 2,503,800%, 2,182,600%, and 880%. Employment increased most at the beginning of the 1990s, but industrial restructuring, which started at the end of the 1980s, and the foreign exchange crisis of the late 1990s caused labor-intensive light industries such as textiles and shoes to sharply decline, leading to huge employment reductions in the 2000s but a slight increase afterward. The share of total value added in manufacturing increased from 17% in the 1960s (1961–1970) to 27% in the 2000s (2001–2009).

The quantitative growth of the manufacturing industry was supported by structural changes in the industry. In the 1950s, light industry accounted for 80% and the heavy chemical industry accounted for only 20%, but since the 2000s, the heavy chemical industry accounts for 80%. Even before the industrialization of heavy chemical products in the early 1970s, export ratios in the whole economy were 70% light industry products, 18% primary products, and only 12% heavy chemical products. However, after the 2000s, the proportion of primary products occupies around 18%, and light industrial products around 10%, while heavy chemical products are about 90% (IIT 2010; CCKE 2011a, p. 9).

How did this transformation of industrial structure become possible? As we shall see in detail in Chaps. 4 and 5, the industrial upgrade from labor-intensive light industry to capital-intensive heavy chemical industry, and then to high-tech, has been driven by state-led developmental strategies and policies.

Section 2: From Finished Product Industry to Components and Materials Industry

Korea has traditionally maintained export-oriented growth since the mid-1960s, but the main export items have completely changed. While Korean exports earlier were based on an assembly-oriented industry that relied on imported intermediary goods, a more complete industrial structure has emerged based on growth in the components industry since the 2000s. In this section, we will examine how much the Korean components industry has actually grown through quantitative indicators.

First, looking at Korea's export product structure by item reveals that finished products constituted the bulk of exports by the 1990s. The top ten export items in 1980 included light industry products such as clothing and shoes and heavy industry products such as ships and sound and video devices. The top ten export items in 2000 included traditional heavy chemical industry products, along with electronics, such as computers, wireless communication devices, automobiles, ships, and petroleum products. Of course, components and materials that were strategically developed by the state such as steel, semiconductors, and petroleum products also constitute major export items, but until the late 1990s, finished products, rather than components and materials, comprised most of the major export items. However, after the 2000s, component items largely comprise the major export items. No major change has occurred in the main industries (such as electrical and electronic, automobile, shipbuilding, and petrochemical industries), but each industry's components and component products make up the top export items, such as vessel and marine structures and components, flat panel displays and sensors, and automobile components (IIT 2010, 2015).

Export and import trends in the components and materials industry show better how the national economic status of the components and materials industry in the Korean economy has changed. As seen in Table 3.4, exports in the components and materials industry increased by 8.5 times from $29 billion to $276 billion from 1994 to 2014. This increase outpaces the fivefold increase in exports of the entire industry from $96 billion to $573 billion during the same period. As a result, the proportion of the components and materials industry in total Korean industrial exports increased from 30% in 1994 to 48% in 2014 (Korea Institute for Industrial Economics and Trade [KIET] 2012, p. 17).

Table 3.4 Import and export of parts and materials industry

Year	*Export*			*Import*			*Earning and expense*		
	All industries (A)	*Parts and materials industry (B)*	*(B)/(A)*	*All industries (A)*	*Parts and materials industry (B)*	*(B)/(A)*	*All industries (A)*	*Parts and materials industry (B)*	*(B)/(A)*
	Million USD	*Million USD*	*%*	*Million USD*	*Million USD*	*%*	*Million USD*	*Million USD*	*%*
1994	96,013	29,055	30	102,348	33,950	33	-6335	-4895	77
1995	125,058	42,523	34	135,119	46,479	34	-10,061	-3956	39
1996	129,715	55,300	43	150,339	58,993	39	-20,624	-3693	18
1997	136,164	64,518	47	144,616	61,138	42	-8452	3380	-40
1998	132,313	63,523	48	93,282	44,775	48	39,031	18,749	48
1999	143,685	67,029	47	119,752	57,748	48	23,933	9281	39
2000	172,268	79,915	46	160,481	70,568	44	11,786	9346	79
2001	150,439	61,982	41	141,098	59,250	42	9341	2731	29
2002	162,471	67,815	42	152,126	64,919	43	10,344	2896	28
2003	193,817	82,010	42	178,827	75,843	42	14,991	6167	41
2004	253,845	107,871	42	224,463	92,664	41	29,382	15,207	52
2005	284,419	123,793	44	261,238	101,130	39	23,180	22,663	98
2006	325,465	148,712	46	309,383	113,975	37	16,082	34,736	216
2007	371,489	168,189	45	356,846	131,826	37	14,643	36,363	248
2008	422,007	183,515	43	435,275	148,764	34	-13,267	34,751	-262
2009	363,534	170,957	47	323,085	119,709	37	40,449	51,247	127
2010	466,384	229,038	49	425,212	151,180	36	41,172	77,858	189
2011	555,214	255,297	46	524,413	168,540	32	30,801	86,757	282
2012	547,870	253,411	46	519,584	162,490	31	28,285	90,921	321
2013	559,632	263,042	47	515,585	165,537	32	44,047	97,505	221
2014	572,700	275,900	48	525,500	168,100	32	47,200	107,800	229

Source: Materials & Components Technology Network: MCT-NET

Export growth of the Korean components and materials industry is also remarkable, even when compared to Japan's strong components and materials industry. Korean exports of components and materials increased threefold from $80 billion in 2000 to $229 billion in 2010, doubling the growth rate of Japan, which increased 1.5 times from $270 billion to $405 billion in the same period. Due to rapid growth of the components and materials industry, components and materials accounted for 49.1% of total Korean exports in 2010, almost equal to Japan's 52.7%. These data show that Korea, like Japan, has transformed into a country with strong manufacturing that focuses on components and materials (KIET 2012, p. 35).

The growth of the Korean components industry has been centered on Korea's main industries. In particular, the automobile components industry has seen explosive growth since the mid-1990s. As shown in Fig. 3.3, exports of automobile components increased from $722 million in 1994 to $24 billion in 2014, increasing 3376%, a fourfold increase from the $5.3 billion to $44 billion, or 834% increase of automotive industry exports excluding components for the same period.

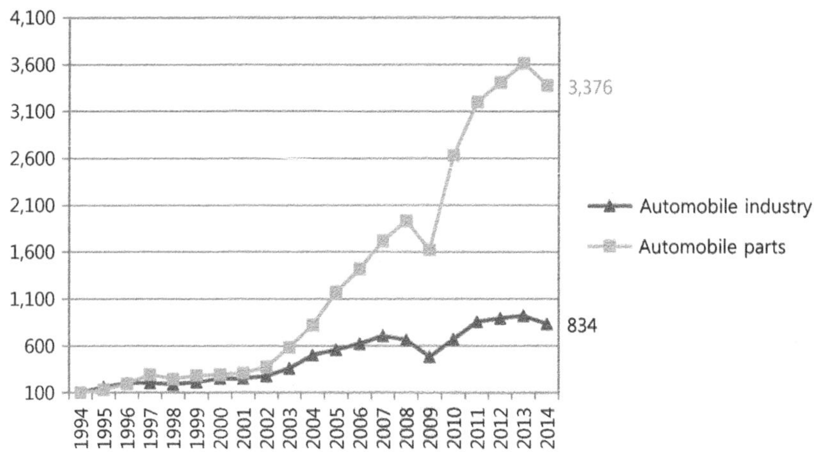

Fig. 3.3 Automobile industry exports in South Korea (values in 1994 = 100). Source: Trade statistics, Korea International Trade Association (http://stat.kita.net/). Note: Refer to Ministry of Trade and Industry code 741 (automobiles, excluding parts) for automobile export statistics, and MTI code 742 (automobile parts) for automobile parts statistics

In the electrical and electronics industry, which is Korea's flagship export industry, the growth of components also surpassed the growth of finished goods. As shown in Fig. 3.4, exports of electrical and electronic products, excluding electronic components, increased from $19 billion in 1994 to $80 billion in 2013, for an increase of 569%, while electronic components increased from $13 billion to about $100 billion, for an increase of 766% in the same period. Electrical and electronic components industry exports do not have as dramatic a growth pattern as the automobile components industry. However, in the electrical and electronics industry, as in the automobile industry, the export growth rate of components is much higher than the overall export growth rate of the electrical and electronics industry. In particular, since 2006, the gap between the export growth rate of electronic components and electrical and electronic products (excluding electronic components) is widening.

Although Korea has maintained a very high export growth rate compared to other countries, as seen in Table 3.2, it had long been in a chronic trade deficit until it faced the foreign exchange crisis in 1997, with the

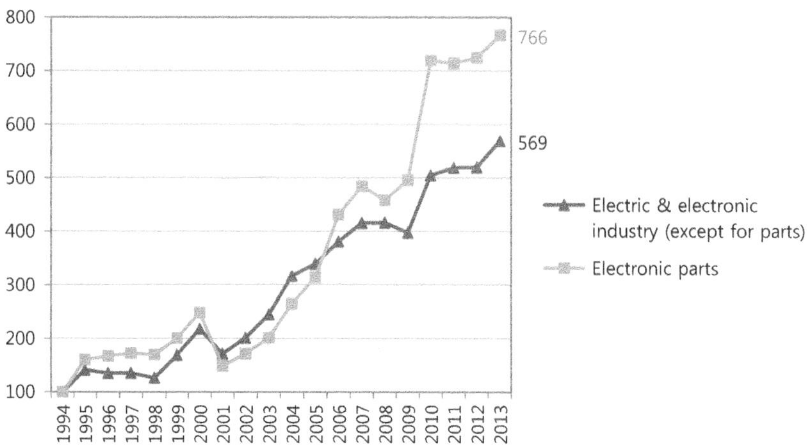

Fig. 3.4 Electrical and electronic industry exports in South Korea (values in 1994 = 100). Source: Trade statistics, Korea International Trade Association (http://stat.kita.net/). Note: Statistics for electrical and electronic product exports were obtained by subtracting MTI code 83 (electronic parts) from MTI code 8 (electrical and electronic products), and statistics for electronic parts are from MTI code 83

deficit widening further in the 1990s. As shown in Fig. 3.5, after Korea began its export-oriented economic policy in 1964, it had been in a trade deficit until the 1997 foreign exchange crisis, with the exception of four years between 1986 and 1989, a period known as the "Boom with Three Lows"—low dollar value, low interest rate, low oil price—due to a favorable international economic environment, boosted by Japan's export reduction after the 1985 Plaza Agreement. During this time, Korea accomplished a surplus in its balance of payments for the first time. However, this surplus, which resulted from external factors, ended in less than four years, and Korea's trade deficit worsened in the 1990s. In 1996 just before the crisis, the Korean trade deficit widened to $21 billion, with much of the trade deficit in the components and materials sector. Of the total trade deficit, the components and materials industry accounted for 18% in 1996.

After the 1997 financial crisis, however, Korea's trade balance turned to a surplus, caused by a surplus in the components and materials industry, which had been the main cause of the trade deficit in the past. The turn to, and expansion of, profit in the components and materials industry has continued since the 2000s, rather than being a temporary phenomenon caused by the low exchange rate effect during the crisis. When the trade balance of the entire industry was a negative $8 billion in 1997, the trade

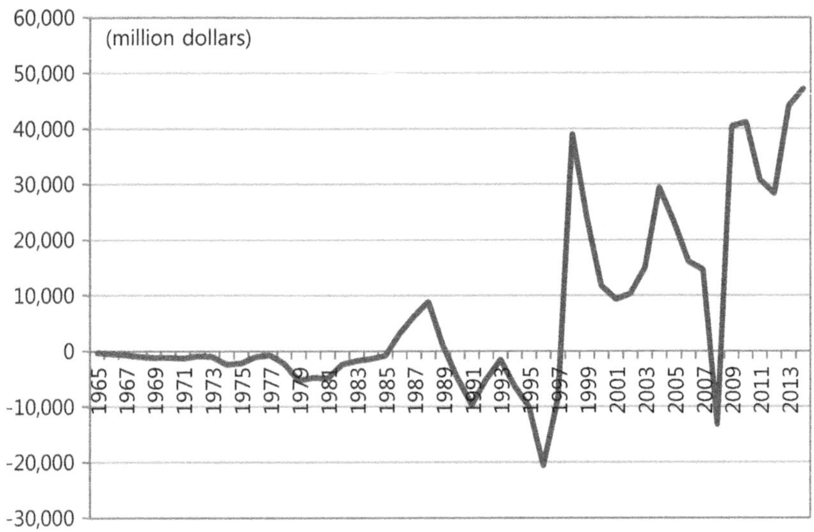

Fig. 3.5 Korea's trade balance. Source: Korea Statistical Information Service (http://kosis.kr/index/index.do)

balance of the components and materials industries was $3 billion in the black. The trade surplus of the components and materials industry, which began at this time, continued to expand. With the global collapse of the IT bubble in 2001, the semiconductor industry was affected, and the industry trade surplus of the components and materials industries decreased to 29% and 28%, respectively, in 2001 and 2002. Nonetheless, exports continued to increase and reached a record 98% in 2005, meaning that the trade surplus reached the point where nearly 100% of the components and materials industry resulted in a surplus. In 2006, the trade surplus of components and materials increased by 216%, meaning that the surplus of the components and materials industry offset the trade deficit of all other industries. This trend has continued to the present; the trade balance of the components and materials industry in 2014 will reach 229% of the entire industry. The rapid growth of the components and materials industry is evident through comparison of shipments to manufacturing. From 1993 when components and materials industry statistics began to be recorded, manufacturing shipments grew 586 times, while the components and materials industry increased 642 times as of 2013.[1]

In addition, Korea's chronic trade deficit with Japan began to decline. The dependence on imports of components and materials from Japan decreased from 28.1% in 2001 to 25.2% in 2010, and the portion of Japan trade deficits to trade deficits in components and materials among all industries in the same period decreased from 103.5% to 67.2%. Most of all, imports of core components such as lithium batteries, printed circuit boards (PCBs), light-emitting diodes (LEDs), section steels, and surface-treated steel sheets, which relied heavily on imports from Japan, fell sharply (KIET 2012, pp. 12–16).

The competitiveness of the Korean components and materials industry has also increased in the world market. The global export market share of the Korean components and materials industry jumped from 3.4% (tenth place) in 2001 to 4.6% (sixth place) in 2009. Excluding Hong Kong, which took fifth place in 2009 as a typical entrepôt trading country, Korea takes fifth place. Meanwhile, Japan's share of the world export market decreased from 9.4% (third place) to 7.7% (fourth place) (KIET 2012, p. 17). Comparing Korea and Japan based on changes in global market share between 2005 and 2009, Korea emerged as a threat to Japan in the

[1] See Statistics Korea, *Mining and manufacturing survey* (8th rev.) and *Mining and manufacturing survey* (9th rev.).

export of components and materials. During this period, only 27% of Korean components and materials items for export were affected by the rising share of Japanese components and materials. On the other hand, 39% of the Korean items for export influenced the decline of Japan's market share. Furthermore, 12% of the Korean export items saw a faster rise in global market share rather than Japan's (KIET 2012, p. 58).

Along with quantitative growth, technological competitiveness of the components and materials industry has greatly increased. According to a 2001 survey by the KIET, design technology, new product development technology, production technology, and quality and reliability level of components and materials were 67.7%, 66.4%, 77.8%, and 85.0%, respectively. However, according to the 2009 Korea Institute for Advancement of Technology, these levels each increased to 91.3%, 91.6%, 94.4%, and 93.1%, respectively. The number of specialized components and materials companies increased from 483 in 2002 to 3353 in 2010 (KIET 2012, pp. 18–27).

The growth of the technology level of Korean components has improved the competitiveness of high-tech components in the world market. Items with a trade balance surplus have been converted from general-purpose products such as chemical synthetic fibers and nonferrous metals to high value-added products such as liquid crystal display (LCD) devices and wireless broadcasting communication devices. The trade balances of 15 high value-added components such as LCD and automobile components increased by more than $1 billion from 2001 levels. The number of world-class products[2] selected for components and materials increased from 8 items in 2001 to 37 items in 2010. In particular, domestic corporations in sectors such as lithium secondary batteries, LCD substrate glass, and sapphire substrates led the global market due to government-supported R&D projects and active investment by the private sector. The lithium secondary battery market share of Samsung SDI increased from 14% in 2006 to 21% in the third quarter of 2010, and LG Chemical's global market share increased from 7% to 12% over the same period. As for the LCD substrate glass, Samsung Corning Precision Materials secured original manufacturing technology, increasing its global market share from

[2] The criteria for the selection of world-class products are that the world market share is 5% or more with less than fifth place, where the world market size is more than $50 million per year and more than twice the domestic market size, or the export market is more than $5 million per year (KIET 2012, p. 22).

20% in 2006 to 40% in 2010, while Sapphire Technology occupies 30% of the world market of sapphire substrate based on its own original technology, 1.5 times higher than its competitors (KIET 2012, pp. 18–24).

Section 3: From Input-Driven Economy to Innovation-Driven Economy

We focus now on the change of drivers leading Korea's economic growth, from an input-oriented economy to an innovation-driven economy. This section reveals the limitation of the static approaches of classical economics and developmental state theory, which explain the growth of the Korean economy with a fixed variable.

The concepts of "input-driven growth" and "innovation-driven growth" are borrowed from economist Paul Krugman's use in analyzing the growth pattern of Asian countries. According to Krugman (1994), economic expansion occurs through two sources of growth: increases in inputs on one side and increases in output per unit of input on the other side. The former refers to the increase in employment, in workers' education levels, and in the stock of physical capital (machinery, buildings, roads, and other infrastructure), while the latter may be achieved by economic policy or better management in the short term, but primarily by improvement of knowledge in the long run (Krugman 1994, p. 66).

Following this concept, this study defines economies in which quantitative input of production factors such as labor and capital significantly contributes to growth as an "input-driven economy," and economies in which the total factor productivity following factor inputs significantly contributes to economic growth as an "innovation-driven economy." Total factor productivity is identified as the Solow residual (Solow 1957), or the remainder after the contribution of labor and capital stock growth in the economic growth rate is excluded. The growth rate of total factor productivity is a comprehensive calculation of productivity including the growth rate of technological progress in a country (Solow 1957). Factors that affect total factor productivity include expansion and increased effectiveness of R&D investment, expansion of human capital, realizing economies of scale, guarantee of markup[3] realization, diffusion of technology among regions and industries, expansion of social overhead capital, advancement

[3] Markup refers to the sale price of a product less the original price, or the profit gained after the exclusion of the original price.

of economic systems, and advancement of industrial relations (Pai and Kim 2004, pp. 2, 7). These conceptualizations are not new. Similar conceptualizations have appeared in policy reports written by the KIET or the Bank of Korea. "Transition to the innovation-driven economy" also has been adopted as an official goal of industrial policy since the Roh Moo-hyun government in the mid-2000s (Cho et al. 2012; Shim 2005; Kim and Bae 2004; Kim and Kim 2008).

According to Krugman's growth accounting analysis, East Asian countries including South Korea developed on the basis of a typical input-driven growth strategy. In the mid-1990s, Krugman insisted that the astonishing economic growth in Asia was due to an unusual increase in input, such as labor and capital, rather than an increase in productivity, through a paper entitled "The Myth of Asia's Miracle" (Krugman 1994). According to the article:

> Sustained growth in a nation's per capita income can only occur if there is a rise in output per unit of input. Mere increases in inputs, without an increase in the efficiency with which those inputs are used—investing in more machinery and infrastructure—must run into diminishing returns; input-driven growth is inevitably limited. … The newly industrializing countries of Asia, like the Soviet Union of the 1950s, have achieved rapid growth in large part through an astonishing mobilization of resources. Once one accounts for the role of rapidly growing inputs in these countries' growth, one finds little left to explain. Asian growth, like that of the Soviet Union in its high-growth era, seems to be driven by extraordinary growth in inputs like labor and capital rather than by gains in efficiency. (Krugman 1994, pp. 67, 70)

Indeed, Korea's economic growth strategy during the industrialization period of the 1960s and 1970s was the input-driven strategy that relied on inputs of labor or capital. As we will discuss in more detail in Chap. 4, the important work at this time was to quickly build up the mass production system by importing technologies developed in advanced countries. Korea's technological innovation system at this time depended on the imitation of foreign technology through reverse engineering and turn-key capital goods imports (Yoon 2006; Kim 1997b/2000; Hemmert 2007, p. 13; Hillebrand 1996). The total amount of national R&D increased only from 0.2% of GDP in 1964 to 0.57% in 1979, with approximately 170 billion KRW as the total amount in 1979. The percentage of government spending in the gross national R&D investment decreased from 96%

in 1964 to 54% in 1979, but the state still had been responsible for at least half of the gross national R&D until the 1970s. In other words, the private sector had little interest in R&D, coupled with low rates of R&D investment in the whole national economy. During this period, patent registration by Koreans was hardly active, and only registration by foreigners was on an increasing trend. The number of patent registrations in Korea was only 99 in 1962 but increased to 1419 in 1979. However, foreigners accounted for 82% of all patent registrations during the same period (Yoon 2006, pp. 123–127).

Since the 2000s, however, the pattern of the Korean economy has transformed. Now the improvement of total factor productivity (TFP), based on the innovation of production processes, plays an important role in economic growth since the 2000s. As shown in Table 3.5, the contribution of capital stock to economic growth reached 57.1% in the 1970s, but this figure dropped to 33.6% in the 2000s, while the contribution of TFP to economic growth was only 8.5% in the 1970s, but up to 61.7% in the 2000s.

Table 3.6 shows the contribution of factor input and productivity to real income growth. It also reveals that productivity contribution has outstripped factor input contribution since the mid-2000s. As shown in the table, even during the period of 2001–2005, the factor input contribution was 93.5% of the real income growth rate, and the productivity contribution of the real income increase was much lower, at 39.0%. However, in the period of 2006–2010, the contribution of productivity was 79.4%, which surpassed the contribution of factor input at 65.4%. These results suggest that the Korean economy has been moving from input-driven to

Table 3.5 Changes in economic growth contribution by factor (Unit: %)

		1971–1980	*1981–1990*	*1991–1995*	*1996–2000*	*2001–2006*
GDP growth rate		7.0	8.4	7.5	4.3	4.5
Growth rate	Capital input	13.0	10.8	13.0	8.1	5.3
	Labor input	3.5	2.1	2.2	0.6	0.3
	Total factor productivity	0.6	4.0	2.5	1.8	2.8
Contribution to GDP growth rate	Capital stock	57.1	34.2	44.8	47.8	33.6
	Labor input	34.4	18.3	21.9	9.9	4.7
	Total factor productivity	8.5	47.4	33.3	42.3	61.7

Source: Kim and Kim (2008, p. 3)

Table 3.6 Contribution by factor to real net income growth (Unit: Growth rate and contribution rate %; contribution %p)

		1981–2010	*1981–1990*	*1991–2000*	*2001–2010*	*2001–2005*	*2006–2010*
Net real income (%)		6.02	9.99	4.51	3.57	4.02	3.11
Real depreciation effect (%p)		−1.26 (−20.9)	−1.58 (−15.8)	−1.25 (−27.7)	-0.94 (−26.3)	−0.83 (−20.8)	−1.04 (−33.4)
Real price effect (%p)		-0.45 (-7.4)	0.88 (8.8)	−1.81 (−40.1)	-0.41 (−11.5)	-0.47 (−11.7)	−0.36 (−11.4)
Factor input effect (%p)	Subtotal	4.56 (75.8)	6.12 (61.2)	4.68 (103.7)	2.90 (81.2)	3.75 (93.5)	2.04 (65.4)
	Capital input	2.34	2.56	2.66	1.79	1.97	1.61
	Labor input	2.23	3.56	2.01	1.11	1.79	0.42
Productivity (%p)		3.16 (52.5)	4.58 (45.8)	2.89 (64.0)	2.02 (56.6)	1.57 (39.0)	2.47 (79.4)

Source: Cho et al. (2012, p. 9)

Note: () represents contribution rate (%) to real gross income growth rate

productivity-driven in both production and income. These results are in line with that of Pyo et al. (2009), which looked at the starting point of the productivity-driven growth pattern in the late 1990s (Pyo et al. 2009; Cho et al. 2012, p. 6).

Several national innovation indices explain qualitative changes in the Korean economy. Korea's total R&D expenditure as a percentage of GDP remained around 1% until the 1980s (Yoon 2006, pp. 124, 136). However, Korea's national R&D relative to GDP is currently the highest in the world. As of 2014, Korea's total R&D expenditure as a percentage of GDP is 4.3%, ranking number one in the world, surpassing second place Israel's 4.1%. This change in Korea's national innovation index is even more impressive when compared with other countries. As shown in Fig. 3.6, Korea's total R&D share of GDP increased from 1.7% in 1991 to

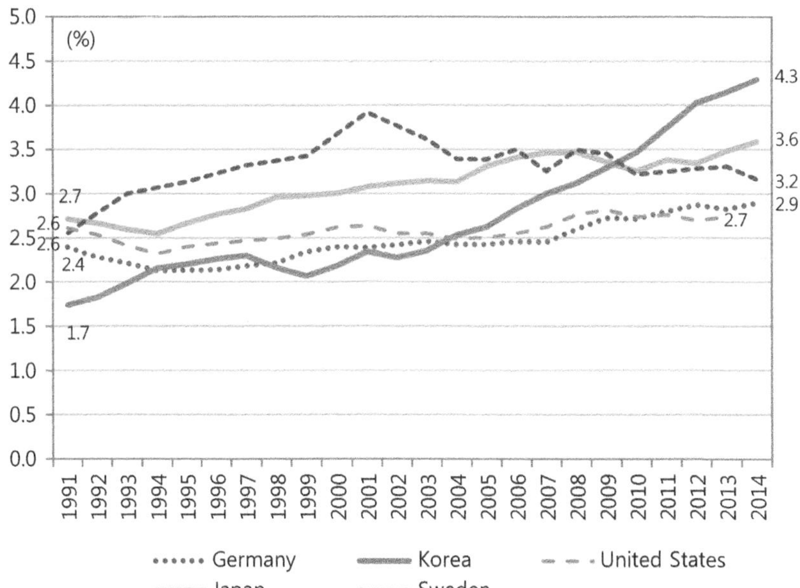

Fig. 3.6 National total R&D expenditure relative to GDP. Source: OECD statistics, Main Science and Technology Indicators. Note: Data from the United States are available until 2013

4.3% in 2014. However, in the same period, Germany's increased only slightly from 2.5% to 2.9%, Japan's from 2.7% to 3.6%, Sweden's from 2.6% to 3.2%, and the United States' from 2.6% to only 2.8%. Clearly the growth rate of Korea's R&D expenditure overwhelms that of other nations.

With the increase in R&D spending, the number of researchers also increased; the ratio of researchers per thousand persons in Korea in 2011 was 11.51, ranking as the world's fourth largest, with Finland (14.8), Denmark (13.08), and Taiwan (11.97) comprising the world's top three. Korea's researcher ratio is higher than the United States (9.1), Japan (10), and Germany (7.8). In addition, the number[4] of Korean patents increased greatly so that the number of triadic patent families increased to 1709 in 2011, ranking fifth in the world after Japan (13,705), the United States (12,649), Germany (4982), and France (2053). In particular, the number of information and communication technology (ICT) patents granted by the Patent Cooperation Treaty (PCT)[5] is 4394, the fourth largest after Japan (17,044), the United States (16,548), and China (8097). According to IMD World Competitiveness Ranking 2013, Korea ranked fourth in the number of patent applications and registrations by applicant nationality (IMD 2013).

Korea's growth of high-tech industries is impressive. The proportion of high-tech industries[6] in Korean manufacturing exports has reached the highest level worldwide since the 2000s. After reaching second place in 2006, it achieved top rank worldwide in 2012. The trade balance in the high-tech industry also increased from $18,178 million in 2002 to $66,859 million in 2010, much higher than Japan's $18,023 million surplus and the United States' $109,209 million deficit. Korea's global market share of high-tech industries is also world class. In 2011, the Korean electronics industry (ISIC Rev. 3 Code 32) accounted for 6.86% of global exports, occupying fifth position following China (22.8%), Singapore (7.6%), the United States (7.3%), and Taiwan (7.2%). The Korean share of medical precision and optical instruments and watches and clocks industry

[4] Refers to a patent registered at the United States Patent and Trademark Office (USPTO), the Japanese Patent Office (JPO), and the European Patent Office (EPO; OECD 2013, p. 10).

[5] This international treaty calls out the fact that patent applications applied simultaneously to many countries come with large financial and time burdens (OECD 2013, p. 10).

[6] High-tech industries include aerospace, electronics, computer and office equipment, pharmaceuticals, and machinery industries (OECD 2012).

(ISIC Rev. 3 Code 33) in the world export market is 6.21% at sixth place, following the United States (13.88%), Germany (11.92%), China (11.22%), Japan (8.22%), and Switzerland (6.43%).[7]

The expansion of Korean high-tech industries is related to Korea's R&D investment in high-tech industries. First, the proportion of high-tech industries in Korean manufacturing R&D expenditure was 53.4% in 2010, similar to the United States' 51.9% as of 2008, and is much higher than other major countries: Japan at 34.6% in 2010, Germany at 27.6% in 2008, France at 42.5% in 2007, and the United Kingdom at 45.8% in 2009 (Ministry of Education, Science and Technology & National Science and Technology Commission 2013, p. 27). Notably, the proportion of electronic components, computers, video, sound, and communication equipment in manufacturing R&D expenditure reached 47.1% in 2011. Furthermore, the share of R&D expenditure to sales in Korea's high-tech industries is much higher than the overall manufacturing average. The R&D shares to sales in Korean high-tech industries are 9.01% in the "medical, precision, optical and watch industry" and 6.74% in "electronic components, computer, video, sound and communication equipment manufacturing," which is far higher than the manufacturing average 2.99% in 2011 (National Science and Technology Commission 2013, p. 254).

How was Korea's transition to an innovation-driven economy possible? It seems related to the shift of direction of Korea's industrial policy from supply of capital to R&D investment. Since the 1997 financial crisis, government expenditure in R&D has been strengthened, and the policy transition to an innovation-driven economy has taken root. After 1997, government R&D expenditure increased dramatically, and since 2002 the annual growth rate of Korea's R&D budget has reached 10.1%. The proportion of Korea's R&D budget to GDP in 2011 was 1.05%, ranking higher than 1.03% in the United States in 2010, 0.91% in Germany in 2011, and 0.78% in Japan in 2011 (National Science and Technology Commission 2012, p. 34).

More important, Korea's R&D expenditure is strategic and selective. The Korean government's R&D investment policies, unlike US or European R&D policies, place economic development as a priority. According to the *2014 Government-supported R&D Project Research and Analysis Report* ("2014nyundo Gukgayungugaibalsaup Josa Bunseokbogoseo") published by the Ministry of Science, ICT and Future

[7] See OECD (2012).

Planning, the R&D expenditures of 33 ministries of the Korean government totaled 17.64 trillion KRW in 2014, including 7732 billion KRW in the economic development sector that comprised 43.8% of total government R&D expenditure, while the proportion spent on the health-care sector was only 11.8% (Ministry of Science, ICT and Future Planning, and Korea Institute of S&T Evaluation and Planning 2015, p. 20). In contrast, the United States has the highest budget at 60% of total government R&D expenditure for the health-care sector, while R&D expenditure for the economic development budget was about 15%. In the United Kingdom, the government R&D share for health care was also high, at 30%, while government R&D share for economic development was not even 10%. Japan (about 40%) and Germany (about 32%) had the highest R&D expenditures for university promotion funds with expenditure for economic development at about 25%, higher than the United States and the United Kingdom but much lower than Korea.[8]

Furthermore, as of 2014, 34.2% of Korean state R&D expenditures (6352.2 billion KRW) were invested in the industrial sector (65.8% in the public sector). By industry, 18.4% of industrial R&D, or 1112.6 billion KRW, was invested in electronic components, computer, video, sound, and communication equipment. And 10.5% of industrial R&D, or 632 billion KRW, was invested in electrical and mechanical equipment. Investment in automobile and transportation equipment amounted to 577.4 billion KRW, or 92.3% of industrial R&D funded by the government. In other words, 38.1% of R&D expenditure in the industrial sector was invested in the electrical and electronics industry and automobile industry, main industries in the Korean economy (Ministry of Science, ICT and Future Planning, and Korea Institute of S&T Evaluation and Planning 2015, pp. 17–19).

Finally, a remarkable characteristic of the Korean innovation system since the end of the 1990s is the increase in SME R&D. As shown in Fig. 3.7, the ratio of SMEs in total business R&D in the manufacturing sector[9] started to increase significantly around 2000. The share of SMEs

[8] This report analyzes the government R&D budgets of six countries—Korea, United States, United Kingdom, Japan, Germany, and France—based on OECD Main Science and Technology Indicators (Ministry of Science, ICT and Future Planning, and Korea Institute of S&T Evaluation and Planning 2013, p. 25).

[9] In total business R&D, the manufacturing sector's share accounted for more than 80% of total industrial R&D in 2011, about 88%. See Ministry of Science, ICT and Future Planning, *Survey of Research and Development in Korea* (n.d.).

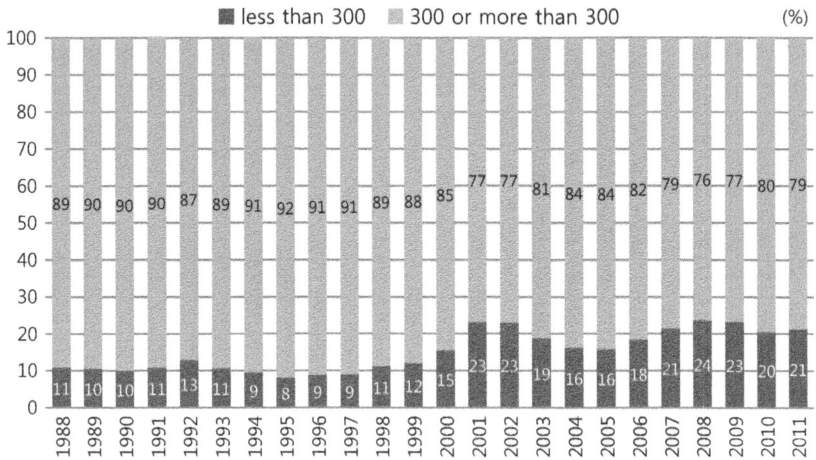

Fig. 3.7 Proportion of private R&D by employee size (manufacturing). Source: Ministry of Science, ICT and Future Planning, *Survey of Research and Development in Korea* (each year)

in total business R&D maintained an average of 10.3% between 1988 and 1999 but increased to an average of 20% between 2000 and 2011. The R&D gap between large firms and SMEs has eased somewhat because the growth rate of R&D investment by SMEs has surpassed the growth rate of R&D investment by large corporations. From 1998 to 2011, the annual growth rate of SME R&D investment remained at 16.5%, while the annual growth rate of R&D investment in large enterprises was only 10.3%. In particular, from 1998 to 2007, before the 2008 global financial crisis, the annual growth rate of SME R&D investment reached 19.1%. In the same period, large corporations maintained a growth rate of just 8.4%.

The increase in SME R&D is also related to the state's policy to nurture SMEs following the financial crisis, such as the Act on Special Measures for the Promotion of Venture Businesses. As shown in Fig. 3.8, the share of SMEs in government and public sector R&D occupies an annual average of 47.5% during the period of 1998–2011, while it was only 26.5% per year during the 1987–1997 period. In addition, since the venture bubble collapse in 2000, the number has consistently remained at more than 50%, accounting for an annual average of about 55% during the period from 2003 to 2011.

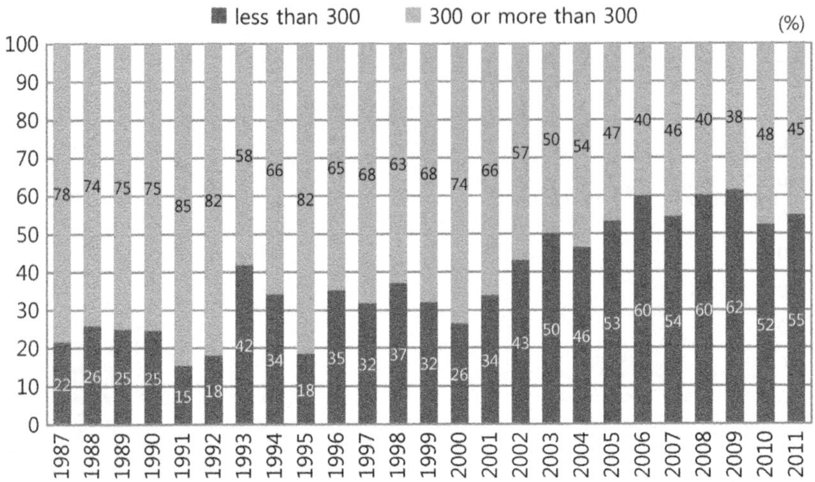

Fig. 3.8 Proportion of government and public R&D by employee size. Source: Ministry of Science, ICT and Future Planning (annual)

In short, the Korean economy has shifted from an input-driven economy to an innovation-driven economy, and a sharp increase in business R&D investment has been at the center of this transition. The private sector could actively invest in technology development with high uncertainty because of the state's selective and strategic industrial policy. In the following chapters, we will look specifically at how Korea has transitioned from an input-driven economy to an innovation-driven economy and how state intervention could still work effectively despite the pressures of change. Chapter 4 looks at the traditional characteristics of the Korean political economic model in the 1960s and 1970s.

References

CCKE (The Compilation Committee for the Korean Economy for 60 Years). (2011a). *The Korean economy: Six decades of growth and development: Summary*. Seoul: Korea Development Institute.

Cho, T.-H., Kim, J.-H., & Schreyer, P. (2012). *Woorinara 2000nyundai joongban ihoo sangsansungjoodohyung kyungjero ihang*. BOK issue paper series, no. 2012-2, 1–12.

Hemmert, M. (2007). The Korean innovation system: From industrial catch-up to technological leadership? In J. Mahlich & W. Pascha (Eds.), *Innovation and technology in Korea: Challenges of a newly advanced economy* (pp. 11–32). Heidelberg: Physica-Verlag.

Hillebrand, W. (1996). *Shaping competitive advantages: Conceptual framework and the Korean approach*. London: Routledge.

IMD. (2013). *IMD world competitiveness yearbook 2013*. Lausanne: IMD International.

Institute for International Trade. (2010). *Jooyo mooyukdonghyangjipyo* [Main trade indicators]. Seoul: Korea International Trade Association.

Institute for International Trade. (2015). *Jooyo mooyukdonghyangjipyo* [Main trade indicators]. Seoul: Korea International Trade Association.

Jo, T.-H, Kim, J.-H., & Schreyer, P. (2012). *Woorinara 2000nyundae joongban ihoo saengsansungjoodohyung kyungjero ihaeng*. BOK issue paper series no. 2012-2. Bank of Korea. Retrieved July 3, 2014, from https://www.bok.or.kr/portal/bbs/P0002353/view.do?nttId=181021&menuNo=200433.

Kim, L.-S. (1997b). *Imitation to innovation: The dynamics of Korea's technological learning*. Boston: Harvard Business School Press. Korean edition: Kim, L.-S. (2000). *Mobangesu hyuksineuro* (Y.-C. Lim & H.-S. Lee, Trans.). Seoul: Sigma Insight.

Kim, W.-K., & Bae, M.-K. (2004). Hyuksinjoodohyung kyungjewa chongyo-sosengsansung. *e-KIET Sanupkyungjejungbo*, 214.

Kim, W.-K., & Kim, I.-C. (2008). Hangook sanupjungchekui gwaguwa hyunje geurigo Mire. *e-KIET Sanupkyungjejungbo, 379*, 1–6.

Korea Institute for Industrial Economics & Trade. (2012). *Boopoom·sojae miraebi-jun soorip yungoo*. Seoul: The Korea Institute for Advancement of Technology.

Krugman, P. (1994). The myth of Asia's miracle. *Foreign Affairs, 73*(6), 62–78.

Ministry of Science, ICT and Future Planning & Korea Institute of S&T Evaluation and Planning. (2013). *2012nyundo Kookgayungoogaebalsaup josa·boonsukbogosu* [2012 Analysis Report on Government R&D]. Seoul: Ministry of Science, ICT and Future Planning.

Ministry of Science, ICT and Future Planning & Korea Institute of S&T Evaluation and Planning. (2015). *2014nyundo Kookgayungoogaebalsaup josa·boonsukbogosu* [2014 Analysis Report on Government R&D]. Seoul: Ministry of Science, ICT and Future Planning.

Ministry of Science, ICT and Future Planning & Korea Institute of S&T Evaluation and Planning. (n.d.). *Survey of research and development in Korea*. Seoul: Ministry of Science, ICT and Future Planning.

National Science and Technology Commission. (2012). *2012 White paper of science technology statistics*. Seoul: National Science & Technology Commission and Korea Institute of S&T Evaluation and Planning.

National Science and Technology Commission. (2013). *2012 Kwahakgisoolyungam* [2012 almanac of science and technology]. Seoul: National Science & Technology Commission and Korea Institute of S&T Evaluation and Planning.

OECD. (2012). *Main science and technology indicators, 2012(1)*. Retrieved October 11, 2013, from https://www.oecd-ilibrary.org/science-and-technology/main-science-and-technology-indicators_2304277x.

OECD. (2013). *Main science and technology indicators, 2013(1)*. Retrieved October 11, 2013, from https://www.oecd-ilibrary.org/science-and-technology/main-science-and-technology-indicators_2304277x.

Pai, M.-K., & Kim, W.-K. (2004). Chongyososangsansungui Yoin Boonsukgwa Sisajum. *e-KIET Sanupgyungjejungbo, 218*, 1–12.

Pyo, H.-K., Kim, W.-C., & Jun, E.-K. (2009). *Hangookui sanupbyul sooiknyool mit sayongja biyong choogye (1970–2006)*. Seoul: Korea Institute for Public Finance.

Shim, S.-Y. (2005). Kwagu sungjangjunryakui kyungrouijonsunggwa hyukshinjoodo dongbansungjangui gwajee daehan yungoo [A study on the path-dependency of old growth model and the tasks of innovation-driven accompanied growth model]. *Hangookjungchekhakhwoibo* [Korean Policy Studies Review], *14*(4), 223–248.

Solow, R. M. (1957). Technical change and the aggregate production function. *Review of Economics and Statistics, 39*(3), 312–320.

Yoo, J.-H. (1997). Konguphwa Sokdoe Daehan Segyesijang Kyoomoui Younghyang. *KDI Jungchekyungoo* [KDI Journal of Economic Policy], *19*(2), 73–157.

Yoon, J.-H. (2006). *Hangookgisooljungchaekron: Hangook hisoolneungryuk baljun 40nyunsa*. Seoul: Gyeongmunsa.

CHAPTER 4

The Traditional Korean Political Economic Model

Before we look at how and why the Korean political economic model changed, we will first analyze the traditional characteristics of the Korean development model in the 1960s and 1970s.

Korea's traditional model can be defined as a type of state-led capitalism based on a developmental system. In the traditional regime, the state relied on an input-driven development strategy centered on assembly-centered conglomerates to establish and promote export-oriented economic growth. Under the input-driven development strategy, the state mobilized all resources internationally as well as domestically to foster large enterprises with economies of scale for export competitiveness in strategic industries.

Such an input-driven growth strategy based on large assembly-centered corporations formed state-business relations based on a closed developmental alliance between state and large conglomerates and played a crucial role in forming characteristics of Korea's business relations. Typical Korean business relations are characterized by short-term contract practices and exploitative relations between small- and medium-sized component companies and lead corporations, which caused the marginalization and underdevelopment of small and medium component companies. These characteristics resulted from fostering large corporations to realize economies of scale.

In this chapter, we examine typical characteristics of the Korean economic development model, paying attention to state-business relations and interfirm relations.

K. M. Kim, *The Korean Developmental State*,
https://doi.org/10.1007/978-981-15-3465-2_4

Section 1: State-Business Relations

State-led capitalism, as seen in East Asia and France, applies different methods, means, and extent of intervention, but is distinguished from liberal capitalism, in that the state intervenes in the market with a vision for the industrial development of the national economy.

State-business relations in the traditional Korean political economic model feature top-down dirigisme, applied in four steps. First, the state builds a development strategy with a vision for growth of the national economy. Second, it focuses on fostering specific industries and specific companies selectively. Third, it mobilizes the resources needed for economic development. Fourth, it fosters large companies through the protection and regulation of the domestic market.

Establishment of State-Led Economic Development Strategy

In the traditional Korean political economic model, the state presents the development direction of the entire national economy and establishes concrete action plans. This model is distinguished from Anglo-American market liberalism, in that the direction of economic development is deliberately discussed and coordinated by a specific group, and not determined by the laws of supply and demand of the market. However, it is far from corporatist capitalism, in which the direction of development of the national economy is determined through organized participation of business and labor and their coordination of interests, and the role of the state is limited to coordinating macroeconomic policy. Despite state intervention to the market, the Korean model also differs from a socialist planned economy, in that the method of profit-seeking and the manner of management are left to the autonomy of the corporation, and private property rights are protected.

From 1962 to 1996, the Korean government established seven sets of the Five-Year Economic Development Plan. The First Five-Year Economic Development Plan was completed by the EPB, which revised and supplemented the Comprehensive Economic Recovery Plan (Jonghapjegeongyehwoik) based on the previous government's Five-Year Economic Development Plan (Kim 1999b, pp. 55–56). Although the specific contents changed over time, the basic goal of the economic development plans through the first four phases during the Park Chung-hee government gave priority to "growth" (Kang 2000b).

In fact, it is hard to say that the economic development plan served as a concrete business plan. However, the planning process clarified Korea's economic situation as a whole to policymakers and businessmen and educated them by establishing a place for discussion among bureaucrats and politicians and communicating the government's vision to firms (CCKE 2011a, p. 46). The Seventh Five-Year Economic Development Plan was the last. Yet the unique role of the Korean state was established in suggesting the development direction of the national economy and setting economic development plans. The state's role remains in economic ministries through processes of decentralization, specialization, and systemization.

While the Five-Year Economic Development Plans played important roles in suggesting a national vision, it was actually specific industrial policies that carried out state-led development, in particular, using exports as a specific strategy for economic growth. In 1964, the Korean government abandoned its existing import substitution strategy for a full-fledged export-oriented strategy. Here, the government focused on labor-intensive light industry and enacted policies to quantitatively expand exports in the 1960s and fostered the heavy chemical industry to advance export industries in the 1970s (CCKE 2011a, pp. 30–31).

The export promotion policy established in 1964 and 1965 included various benefits favorable to exports, such as a high exchange rate policy, export-friendly policy finance, and tax benefits, all backed by an administrative support system to promote exports (Amsden 1989, pp. 67–68; Lee 2004, pp. 146–149; CCKE 2011a, pp. 31–37).

First, the government increased the exchange rate from 130 KRW to 255 KRW per USD in May 1964 and changed the previous fixed exchange rate system to the single floating exchange rate system. As a result, labor costs decreased, while Korean exports became price competitive. In early 1964, the average hourly wage was USD 56 cents in Japan, 19 cents in Taiwan, and 16 cents in Korea. With the exchange rate hike, Korea's wage fell to about 10 cents per hour, making Korean labor cheaper than Thailand's and the Philippines' in the international market (Oh 2006, pp. 78–79). Given Korea's history with heavy foreign debt burden, the change in the exchange rate policy was a difficult decision, which meant the beginning of an aggressive export strategy (Kim 1999b, p. 145).

Second, the interest rate on trade finance, set at half of the rate on general loans, induced private business to export sectors. Despite the overall interest rate increase by the government in September 1965, the trade finance rate still was lower than the market (commercial) rate, increasing the difference between general loan rates and trade finance rates. Hence the upper limit on interest went from 20% to 40% annually, and the deposit interest rate of financial institutions doubled from 15% to 30% annually for fixed deposits, while loan interest rates increased from 15% to 26% per year. As a result, the average lending rate was 23.2% during the 1966–1972 period, while the export finance rate remained at only 6.1%, maintaining about a 17.1%p difference (Kim 1993a, p. 125).

Third, various tax benefits went to export companies. In the case of imports of intermediate goods for production of export items, nontariff or tariff reduction (tariff refund) was applied. Additional tax incentives included exemption of indirect taxes on input of intermediate goods for production and sales of export goods, exemption of direct taxes on export income (abolished in 1973), reduction of tariffs and indirect taxes for domestic suppliers of intermediate goods for export, and allowance for accelerated depreciation of fixed assets in major export industries (CCKE 2011a, p. 36).

Finally, the incentive system for export promotion was reinforced by the government's administrative support system. First, the president held monthly export expansion meetings where ministers and representatives of the export industrial associations and organizations examined whether they achieved export targets and sought countermeasures in cases of poor performance. Second, an export targeting system compiled export forecasts for individual companies and set annual national export targets. Third, the Korea International Trade Association (KITA) was established to encourage export expansion at the business level, and the Korea Trade Promotion Corporation (KOTRA) was established to form overseas networks, promote export marketing, and collect market information. As a result, exports in the 1960s increased sharply (CCKE 2011a, p. 37).

The heavy chemicals industrialization policy of the 1970s also promoted exports. Policies for heavy and chemical industries were already included in the First Five-Year Economic Development Plan (1962–1966) and in the Second (1967–1971). However, during these two periods, major export industries were limited to light industries such as cotton textiles, and the heavy and chemical industry development plan focused on the expansion of basic industries and import substitution of intermediate and capital goods, not on export. Although exports started to increase sharply in the mid-1960s, the balance of payments remained in deficit as imports of intermediate and capital goods surged. However, according to the "Heavy Chemical Industry Promotion Plan" established in 1973, the government proposed the goal of increasing the proportion of heavy chemical industry in the industrial production from 35% in 1972 to 51% in 1981, and the share of heavy industrial products in the export industry from 27% in 1972 to 65% in 1981 (CCKE 2011a, pp. 38–39, 2011c, pp. 77–78).

Support for heavy chemicals industrialization policy in the 1970s exceeded support for the export promotion policy in the 1960s. The government established the National Investment Fund to finance the heavy chemical industry. From 1974 to 1979, the National Investment Fund financed about 61% of investment in targeted heavy and chemical industries (CCKM 2013, p. 105; Cho 1995).[1] Receiving a hint from the accounts[2] of the Treasury Department of the Japanese Colonial Government, Minister of Finance Nam Duck-woo raised the National Investment Fund. The government issued bonds for the deposit of public funds from the pension funds for government employees, military and private school teachers, and from funds for industrial accident compensation insurance, family planning research, export insurance, and national savings, and funneled them into the National Investment Fund (Nam 2009, pp. 110–112). In addition, to supplement insufficient capital, the finance minister earmarked a portion of the bank's savings deposits and the insurance company's profits. According to the National Investment Fund Act, 10–39% of bank deposit amounts, 40–50% of insurance premiums, and about 90% of extra money in public funds would purchase National Investment Bonds to raise the fund. Foreign capital was actively used to finance heavy and chemical industries. In the latter half of the 1970s, 46% of commercial loans were used to purchase foreign equipment for heavy chemical industries. In addition to financial support, tax privileges were granted by the Tax Reduction Act of 1975. Due to these tax privileges, the gap in the effective marginal tax rates of corporations was

[1] The National Investment Fund established by the Ministry of Finance was intended for only heavy chemical industries such as steel, shipbuilding, machinery, electronics, and chemical. However, in the course of deliberation by the National Assembly, lawmakers of the ruling and opposition parties demanded that legislative support for food production be officially designated, so support was given to food aid projects and other projects, which decreased the proportion of heavy chemical industries (CCKM 2013, p. 105; Cho 1995).

[2] The Japanese government used a certain percentage of public funds, such as public servant pensions, as bonds, and absorbed them for industrial development or social welfare projects (Nam 2009, p. 110).

30%–35%p between light industry and heavy chemical industry from 1975 to 1981 (CCKE 2011a, pp. 40–41).

In summary, in the traditional Korean model, the state fostered industrialization through economic development plans, a new growth strategy, and building new industries. All policies by the Korean state were imbalanced and selective.

Selective Industrial Policy

From the perspective of classical economics, the Korean economy gained rapid growth by relying on market-friendly macroeconomic policies such as exchange and interest rates (World Bank 1993; Yoo 2004). However, Korea's export promotion policy in the 1960s went beyond "market competition" and included a wide range of selective microeconomic policies as well, to foster specific industries and firms. Korea's 1960s policy selected industries that could expand exports rapidly and intensively supported a few large companies in the industries (Kim 1990, p. 119, 1994b, p. 23; Ha 2006, p. 136). A policymaker who led the industrial policy at the time said:

> Under the constraints of finances, financing, foreign exchange, and foreign loan, we selected and nurtured industries that we thought would be most appropriate and effective for the Korean economy at the time, and then when the first target was completed, we re-selected and nurtured other strategic industries. Repeating it again and again was regarded as a shortcut of export-oriented industrialization. This so-called "selection and focus" strategy is based on the unbalanced growth theory that focuses on investment on industries with the greatest ripple effect. (Kim 1990, p. 119)

The imbalanced growth theory at the time held that all industries should not be supported evenly because economies of scale were thought to be necessary for international competition. Selection and concentration ensured that items with the greatest ripple effects were given priority. Imbalanced growth theory held that even a selected industry should not be given full support. Supporting selected individual companies rather than an entire industry allowed for performance evaluation. Firms with good export performance received more support, while underperforming firms and those who did not cooperate with the policy were excluded from support. Only if a selected company showed successful export performance would the state give more support. Support by the state covered all aspects including facility investment, operating funds, tariff exemption for export equipment, low-interest finance, technical guidance, and foreign inspection. Finally, when a firm reached its export target, the government recognized it officially and awarded a medal to further motivate export practices (O 1992).

As exports increased sharply due to Korea's export promotion policy, the government started to build a more systematic industry promotion system. In 1967, the government announced plans for the construction of heavy chemical industries such as steel, various machinery industries, and petrochemical in the Second Five-Year Economic Development Plan (1967–1971). In 1967, the government legislated the Machinery and Shipbuilding Industry Promotion Acts and Textile Industry Modernization Promotion Act, in 1969 the Electronic and Steel Industry Promotion Acts, in 1970 the Petrochemical Industry Promotion Act, and in 1971 the Nonferrous Metals Industry Act. This legislation established tax and financial support for these industries (CCKE 2011a, pp. 38–39).

The 1973 heavy chemicals industrialization policy exemplifies the most systematized type of selective industrial policy in the traditional Korean model. The 1960s general industrial policy favored industries, which helped to achieve the national export goals, unlike long-term selective plans designed to promote particular industries. The heavy chemicals industrialization policy of 1970 enabled the state to select and cultivate strategic industries with a long-term goal of advancing industrial structure (Kim 2014, p. 244).

Korea's Heavy Chemical Industry Promotion Plan (Joonghwahakgongupyooksunggyehwoik), which was established after the presidential declaration of heavy chemicals industrialization in 1973, selected six core industries to foster: steel, nonferrous metals, machinery, shipbuilding, electronics, and chemical industries. Support for the heavy chemical industry included, first, providing long-term policy finance and tax incentives to selected industries; second, expanding professional and vocational institutions to supply new technical expertise needed for heavy and chemical industries; third, establishing and expanding a government-funded research institute that will be responsible for R&D for technological development of the heavy and chemical industry (CCKE 2011a, p. 40; Kim 1994a, pp. 347–348, 2014, pp. 243–244; An and Kim 1995, p. 330).

The heavy chemicals industrialization policy of the 1970s supported selective firms intensively. The government determined the structure of the domestic market by selecting companies that would participate, according to the detailed business plan of each industry. The government excluded minor companies by restricting entry into the market through business licenses and enabled effective competition by allocating more than one company to an industry. The state entrusted low-profitability business to companies in high-profitability industries. By restricting other firms' participation in the market, the government protected firms exposed to investment risks. This plan intentionally sought to enhance industrial linkages and engineering perspective of industrial development (CCKM 2013).

The heavy chemicals industrialization policy fostered large firms in order to promote those industries as the main export industries, by nurturing internationally compatible corporations with economy of scale. As a result, the traditional Korean model's principle in establishing a factory was to build the least competitive unit internationally, rather than adjusting factory scale to the demand, and then to look for demand in accordance with the scale of production (Ha 2006, p. 131).

The government fostered export-led industries by emphasizing efficiency rather than fair market competition as a concrete way to realize economies of scale. The government selected large conglomerates as heavy chemical industry operators to take over insolvent companies, providing them with tax exemptions and financial preference. Thus, Hyundai Group acquired Incheon Steel and Korea Aluminum, and Samsung Group acquired Korea Engineering, Daesung Heavy Industries, Woojin Shipbuilding, Tongil Construction, and Korea Semiconductor. Daewoo Group acquired Korea Machinery, Okpo Shipbuilding, and Saehan Motors and shifted the group's focus to heavy chemical industry. Many chaebols based on commercial capital shifted their focus to industrial capital through acquisition of insolvent companies. As companies' competitive participation raised concerns about overinvestment, the government allowed market oligopoly by restricting the number of companies to produce finished goods by main industries. For example, as shown in Table 4.1, engine manufacturing was given only to Hyundai Shipbuilding, Ssangyong Heavy Industries, and Daewoo Heavy Industries; automobiles only to Hyundai Motors, Saehan, and Kia; and color TVs only to Goldstar, Samsung, and Taihan Electric (Lee 2004, p. 237).

Large corporations grew rapidly as they actively participated in government policies and gained chaebol status. The growth rate of the top ten

Table 4.1 Major corporations participating in heavy chemical industry development plan

Industry	*Specific industry*	*Major participating companies*
Steel	Iron manufacturing	Kookje
Machinery	Automobile	Hyundai, Daewoo, Kia
	Locomotive	Daewoo, Hyundai
	Automobile engine	Hyundai, Daewoo, Kia
	Machinery	Hyundai, Hyosung, Kookje, Sunkyung (current SK)
	Heavy machinery	Hyundai, Samsung, Daewoo
	Heavy equipment for construction	Hyundai, Daewoo
Shipbuilding	Shipbuilding	Hyundai, Samsung, Daewoo
	Marine engine	Hyundai, SSangyong, Daewoo
Electric and electronics	Electronic	Samsung, Lucky-Goldstar (current LG), Taihan Electric Wire
	Heavy electric machine	Hyosung, Ssangyong
	Electric generation	Hyundai, Samsung, Daewoo, Hyosung
Chemical	Chemical	Lucky-Goldstar, Sunkyung
	Synthetic fiber	Lucky-Goldstar, Ssangyong, Hanhwa
	Oil refining	Lucky-Goldstar
	Cement	Ssangyong

Source: Kim (2012b, p. 149) and Lee (2004, p. 237)

chaebols reached five to ten times the growth rate of the whole Korean economy (Kim 2014, p. 244). As shown in Table 4.2, major corporations greatly expanded the number of affiliates during the 1970s. Hyundai's affiliates increased from 6 in 1972 to 31 in 1979; LG's increased from 18 to 43, Samsung's from 16 to 33, Daewoo's affiliates from 2 to 34, and Hyosung's from 4 to 24. One characteristic of Korean conglomerates is diversification into businesses that are not related to their main business. For example, the number of industries that LG and Samsung were involved in reached 24 and 26, respectively, in 1979, while Daewoo was involved in 20 different industries, and Hyundai in 15 industries, with the remaining major chaebols participating in an average of 15–16 industries each. Among the top ten chaebols of the 1970s, the remaining groups, except for the disbanded Kookje and Daewoo Groups, have maintained highest ranking in the hierarchy to date.

Table 4.2 Changes in the affiliates of the 10 largest chaebols in the 1970s

Name	*Owner*	*Number of affiliate companies in 1971*	*Number of affiliate companies in 1979*
Hyundai	Chung, Ju-yung	6 (5)	31 (15)
Lucky-Goldstar	Koo, In-Hwoi	18 (14)	43 (24)
Samsung	Lee, Byung-chul	16 (15)	33 (26)
Daewoo	Kim, Woo-Choong	2 (3)	34 (20)
Hyosung	Cho, Hong-je	4 (4)	24 (15)
Kookje	Yang, Jeong-mo	3 (5)	22 (16)
Hanjin	Cho, Joong-hoon	8 (10)	15 (15)
Ssangyong	Kim, Seong-gon	6 (7)	20 (13)
Hanhwa	Kim, Chong-hee	7 (8)	18 (16)
SK	Choi, Jong-Hyun	5 (6)	14 (16)

Source: Lee (2004, p. 244)

Note: The numbers within parenthesis refer to the number of involved industries

Capacity of Developmental States: Policy Instruments

As seen in Chap. 3, growth factors of the traditional Korean model were based on an input-driven strategy, realization of economy of scale, and concentration of capital for export competitiveness. The question is: How could the state mobilize and concentrate capital with a long-term perspective on the national economy? The implementation of policies needs a means to realize it. In order to actualize selective industrial policies such as South Korea's, it was necessary to concentrate domestic capital and foreign loans as well as financial assistance from the state in strategic industries to achieve economies of scale. Korea's strong state-led industrial policies during the industrialization period were effective because of the government's exclusive right to allocate resources.

The Korean government in the 1960s and 1970s directly supplied financial resources for economic development through the mobilization of domestic capital and procurement of foreign funds, as seen in the 1960s export finance policy and the 1970s National Investment Fund for the heavy chemicals industrialization. To this end, the Korean government mobilized all means including financial, fiscal, and monetary policy and foreign loans. The Korean state attracted corporations to its government-led economic development process through policy finance and foreign commercial loan guarantees, provided at interest rates significantly lower than general interest rates. During the 1960s and 1970s, the portion of policy loans in Korea's total loans reached 60% on average, and the total amount of foreign loans introduced from 1966 to 1979 reached about 5% of GDP.[3] The average interest rate of policy finance in the 1970s was 6–9% for export finance and 12–16% for the National Investment Fund, which was 3–10%p lower than that of the general loan rate. The average interest rate of foreign commercial loans then was only 5.7–7.5%, at least 11%p lower than the domestic lending rate. In the latter half of the 1960s when commercial loans were actively introduced, the gap with the domestic lending rate was approximately 20%p (Choi 1995, Tables 5-23, 5-24; Bank of Korea n.d.-a; Lee 2005, p. 118).

Domestic Capital Mobilization

Financial, fiscal, and currency policy all were used for mobilizing domestic capital. First, the financial policy was fundamentally based on financial repression, especially through the government's regulations on deposit and lending interest rates and on new bond issues. The method for keeping the legal interest rate lower than the market interest rate was commonly used in state-led developmental states such as Japan or Taiwan, but Korea's financial repression was the most severe. During the 1960s and 1970s, the gap between the Taiwanese legal interest rate and market interest rate was about 10–15%p, and the real interest rate remained positive. The gap between Japan's legal interest rates and market interest rates remained at 5–10%p by the mid-1970s, after which the interest rate ceiling was abolished. Real interest rates also remained positive. During the 1960s and 1970s, the difference between Korea's legal interest rate and market interest rate reached 15–25%p, while the real interest rate remained negative (Patrick 1994, pp. 4–35).

In addition to general loans, Korea operated a wide range of policy finance, far lower than the general lending rate. As shown in Table 4.3, the interest rate difference between export finance (a traditional policy finance) and private money market reached almost 30–40%p, with the export finance interest rate at less than half the general lending rate. In addition, the interest rates of machinery funds and the National Investment Fund, mainly invested in the heavy chemical industry, remained at 12–16% throughout the 1970s. They were 3–3.5%p lower than the general loan

[3] See data from the Economic Statistics System of the Bank of Korea.

Table 4.3 Loan interest rate and inflation rate (1971–1985) (Unit: %)

Year	*General loan interest rate*	*Policy loan rate*			*Private loan interest rate*	*GNP deflator*
		Export	*Machinery funds*	*National Investment Fund*		
1971	22.0	6.0	n.a.	n.a.	46.4	12.9
1972	15.5	6.0	n.a.	n.a.	37.0	16.3
1973	15.5	7.0	10.0	n.a.	33.4	12.1
1974	15.5	9.0	12.0	12.0	40.6	30.4
1975	15.5	9.0	12.0	12.0	41.3	24.6
1976	18.0	8.0	13.0	14.0	40.5	21.2
1977	16.0	8.0	13.0	14.0	38.1	16.6
1978	19.0	9.0	15.0	16.0	39.3	22.8
1979	19.0	9.0	15.0	16.0	42.4	19.6
1980	20.0	15.0	20.0	22.0	44.9	24.0
1981	17.0	15.0	11.0	16.5–17.5	35.3	16.4
1982	10.0	10.0	10.0	10.0	32.8	7.1
1983	10.0	10.0	10.0	10.0	25.8	5.0
1984	10.0–11.5	10.0	10.0–11.5	10.0–11.5	24.8	3.9
1985	10.0–11.5	10.0	10.0–11.5	10.0–11.5	24.0	4.2

Source: Sakong (1993, p. 244) and Kang (2000, p. 37)

Note: n.a. refers to not applicable

rate of 15.5–19% in the same period and 24–38%p lower than the private money market rate. As shown in Fig. 4.1, the percentage of policy finance with such low interest rates as a percentage of the total loan amount from the 1960s to the mid-1980s was a minimum of 44% and a maximum of 70%. In terms of time, averages were 57% in the 1960s (1962–1969), 53% in the 1970s (1970–1979), and 67% in the first half of the 1980s (1980–1984). This means that during the period of high growth from the 1960s to 1980s, the state procured more than half of total domestic loans as policy finance at low interest rates to preferential industries and companies.

In the 1960s and 1970s, fiscal policy depended on deficit financing. As shown in Fig. 4.2, the deficit worsened until the early 1980s. In the 1960s it was −1 to −2% of GDP, and in the 1970s it was −2 to −5%. However, the figures improved from the early 1980s, reaching a surplus in 1987. Government debt remained at 10–20% of GDP during the 1960s and 1970s, but continued to decline after the 1980s, until the 1997 financial crisis, declining to 5% in the mid-1990s. In the 1970s, the portion of economic development expenditure in the general government budget

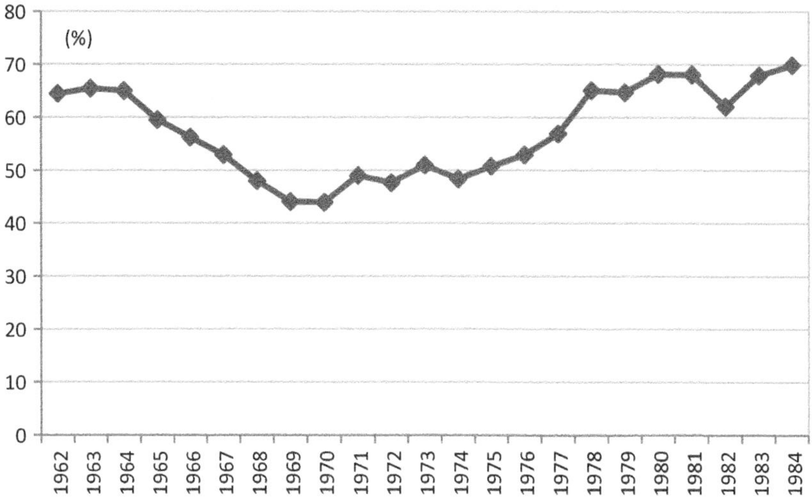

Fig. 4.1 Proportion of policy finance to total loans. Source: Kim (1986, p. 54)

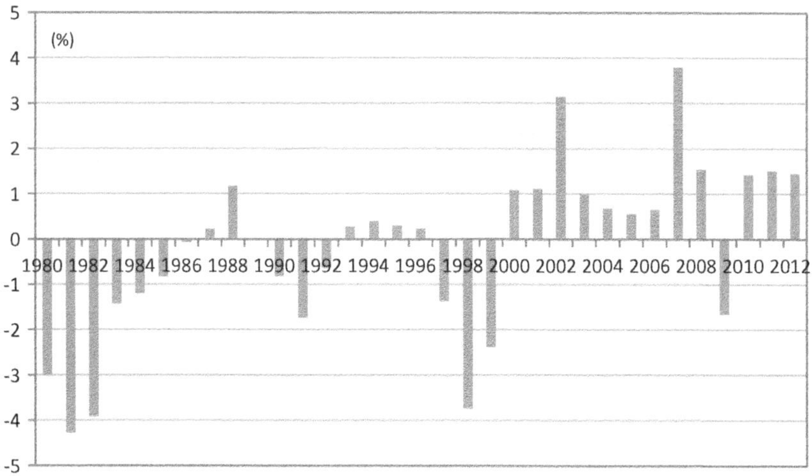

Fig. 4.2 Consolidated budget balance to GDP. Source: KOSIS

remained around 23%.[4] The share of financial investments and loans in the government's general finance reached 31% spanning ten years, from 1967 to 1976.[5]

However, the Korean government's fiscal soundness has remained strong compared to the government's deep involvement in economic development, since the government relied on policy finance rather than direct financial investment. However, policy financing was backed by the Bank of Korea's lending to deposit banks (reappreciation), which resulted in the increased issue of currency. As a result, the soundness of the financial sector had been maintained on the basis of inflationary monetary policy and inflation tax (CCKE 2011b, p. 175).

Monetary policy maintained its expansionary character due to low interest rates and large-scale policy financing. As shown in Table 4.4, the monetary base's growth rate was very high, reaching 49.0% in 1951–1964, 39.3% in 1965–1972, and 25.1% in 1973–1981. While the main reason for the increase of the monetary base until the early 1960s was monetization of the fiscal deficit, from then until the end of the 1960s, the Bank of Korea's lending to deposit banks was the main source of currency evaporation. Due to the chronic demand for excess funds resulting from policy fund lending and the shortage of deposit banks' reserves, the government abolished the ceiling on total rediscount in 1968 and shifted to a method that automatically rediscounted all policy funds excluding liquidity adjustment funds at a certain rate. As a result, during the period 1973–1981, 20.2% of the 25.1% of currency growth rate was due to borrowing by deposit banks from the Bank of Korea (CCKE 2011b, pp. 60–61).

Raising Foreign Capital

The government's financing role was not limited to domestic capital mobilization. As shown in Fig. 4.3, at the beginning of Korea's industrialization, the domestic savings rate was below 15%, and even during the high growth of 1966–1979, the domestic savings rate was on average 6%p lower than the domestic investment rate. As a result, the government had actively sought overseas loans to supplement lacking domestic investment funds. On July 18, 1962, the government enacted a law on the

[4] See Ministry of Economy and Finance, annual, *Report on Settlement of Account for Governmental Finance* (Jungbojaejung Gyulsanbogosu).

[5] See Ministry of Economy and Finance, *1976 Report on Settlement of Account for Governmental Finance* (Jungbojaejung Gyulsanbogosu).

Table 4.4 Contribution to the increase in monetary base

	1951–1964	*1965–1972*	*1973–1981*	*1982–1986*	*1987–1993*	*1994–2001*	*2002–2009*
Loan from Government	29.7	1.1	6.0	−1.8	−7.0	−1.6	2.9
Loan from deposit banks	12.7	9.5	20.2	32.0	6.7	−3.1	0.4
Foreign net assets	–	1.5	5.8	4.5	22.1	62.0	45.0
Sterilization	0.0	−3.8	−8.6	−28.8	−30.7	−29.8	−21.1
Others	6.6	31.0	1.6	17.2	34.0	−21.8	−17.5
Monetary base growth rate	49.0	39.3	25.1	13.0	25.0	5.7	9.7

Source: For 1950–1969, see data from *Kyungjetonggyeyunbo*, the Bank of Korea; data for thereafter are from the Bank of Korea, Economic Statistics System (http://ecos.bok.or.kr); CCKE (2011b, p. 61)

Note: (1) Contribution to monetary base growth = year-on-year growth × percentage of monetary base in previous year. (2) Net loan from government = loan and national debt from government − government deposit from Bank of Korea. (3) Sterilization means sterilization using monetary securities and foreign exchange bonds (in KRW)

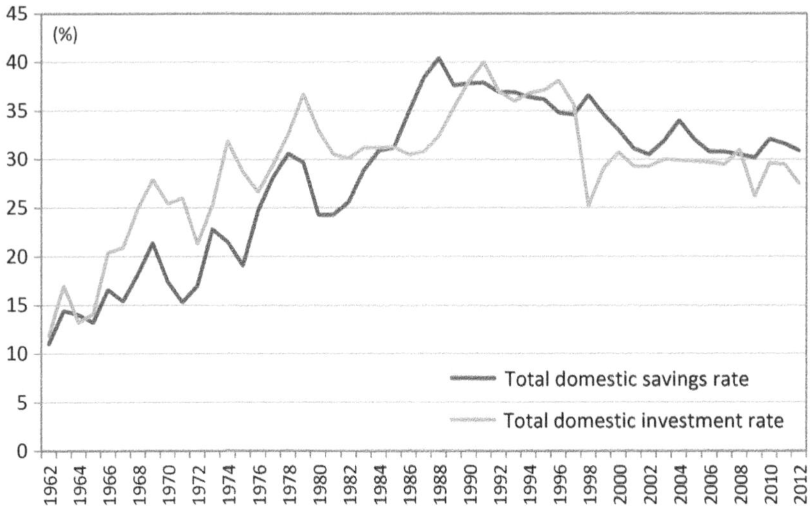

Fig. 4.3 Savings rate and total domestic investment. Source: Bank of Korea

introduction of capital goods through long-term settlement methods and a law on government-guaranteed loans. At that time, foreign banks and companies were reluctant to funding Korean companies. With the government guarantee system, the Korean government took the unprecedented step of assuming responsibility for repaying debts when private enterprise defaulted (Kim 1999b, pp. 75–76).

Foreign loan introduction became full-fledged after the inauguration of Deputy Prime Minister Chang Ki-young in 1964. He drove the aggressive policy of introducing foreign capital and contributed to the normalization of diplomatic relations with Japan in 1965. After that, the total amount of foreign loans introduced from 1966 to 1979 was about $15 billion, approximately 5% of GDP at the time.[6] According to Table 4.5, out of Korea's total investment rate of 23.5% during the 1960s, domestic savings were 14.0%, while overseas savings accounted for 9.4%, with overseas savings accounting for about 40% of the total domestic investment. Despite the rapid accumulation of capital due to rapid export growth in the 1960s, the proportion of domestic savings accounted only for 24.4% of the total

[6] See data from the Economic Statistics System of the Bank of Korea.

Table 4.5 Ratio of investment resources (Unit: %)

Period	*Total investment rate (A)*	*Domestic savings rate (B)*	*Foreign savings rate*	*Contribution of domestic resources to investment (B/A)*
1954–1961	12.2	3.2	8.4	26.3
1962–1970	23.5	14.0	9.4	59.6
1971–1980	30.6	24.4	6.2	79.7
1981–1985	26.1	23.0	3.1	88.1
1962–1985	*27.5*	*23.3*	*4.2*	*84.7*

Source: Ministry of Finance (1986), The Bank of Korea (1984), and Kim (1986, p. 50)

investment rate of 30.6% even in the 1970s, and the share of overseas savings accounted for 6.2%, with reliance on overseas savings at about 20%. The average interest rate of commercial loans was only 5.68–7.5% at the time, at least 11%p lower than the domestic lending rate. In the latter half of the 1960s when commercial loans were actively promoted, the difference between domestic and foreign lending rates reached up to 20%p (Choi 1995, Tables 5-23, 5-24; Bank of Korea n.d.; Lee 2005, p. 118).

Since that time the financing system of Korean corporations characterized by a high debt ratio has become fixed. In particular, an unusual structure was formed in which larger corporations had a higher debt ratio, a result of policies in which the Korean government supplied low interest policy loans and preferred foreign loan introduction rather than foreign direct investment. Korean corporations' high debt ratio intensified their reliance on the state.

As shown in Fig. 4.4, the Korean manufacturing sector's debt-to-equity ratio increased sharply from 100% in 1965 to 400% in 1970 and to close to 500% in the early 1980s. Comparing the average debt-to-equity ratio by period in Table 4.6, the debt ratio of the manufacturing industry was 155% per annum in the 1960s and remained above 300% per annum from the 1970s to the 1990s, due to reliance on external borrowing rather than raising funds through equity capital. The share of equity capital versus the share of external borrowings in total assets of manufacturing firms was 41% and 32%, respectively, in the 1960s. The share of equity fell to 20% between the 1970s and the 1990s, with external borrowing rising to nearly 50%. Patterns in all industries remained close to those in the manufacturing sector.

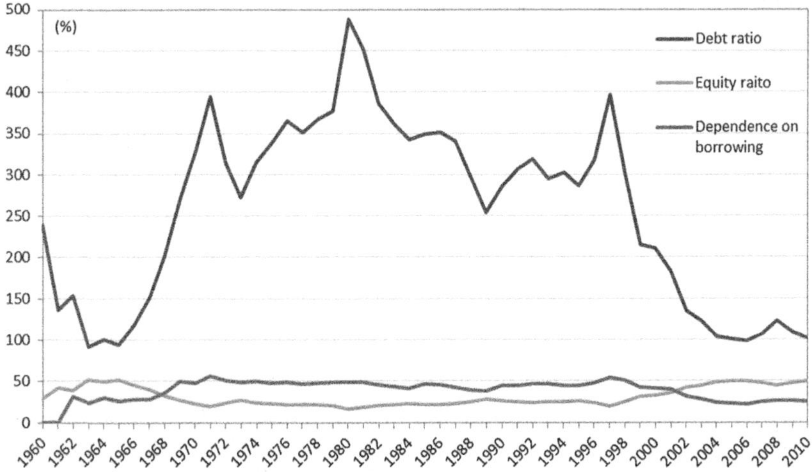

Fig. 4.4 Debt-to-equity ratio and financing structure of the manufacturing industry. Source: Bank of Korea, Economic Statistics System, Corporate Management Analysis Index. Note: (a) Debt ratio = debt/equity × 100. (b) Equity ratio = equity capital/total capital × 100, equity includes stocks. (c) Dependence on borrowing = (short-term debt + corporate bond)/total capital × 100. (d) Average of 1963–1969 values. (e) Average of 1971–1979 values. (f) Average of 1962–1969 values

Table 4.6 Debt ratio and financing structure of Korean companies (Unit: %)

		1960–1969	*1970–1979*	*1980–1989*	*1990–1999*	*2000–2010*
All industries	Debt ratio[a]	128[b]	318	357	320	137
	Equity ratio[c]	46[b]	24	22	24	43
	Debt dependence[d]		49[e]	44	44	29
Manufacturing	Debt ratio	155	342	362	303	127
	Equity ratio	41	23	22	25	45
	Debt dependence	32[f]	49	44	47	28

Source: Bank of Korea, Economic Statistics System, Corporate Management Analysis Index

[a]Debt ratio = debt/equity × 100

[b]Average of 1963–1969 values

[c]Equity ratio = equity/total capital × 100; equity includes stocks

[d]Debt dependence = (short-term debt + corporate bond)/total capital × 100

[e]Average of 1971–1979 values

[f]Average of 1962–1969 values

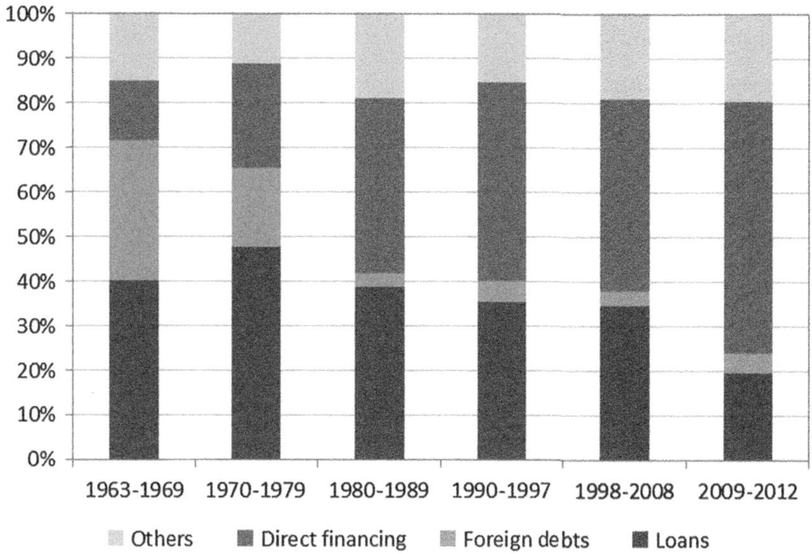

Fig. 4.5 External financing sources of non-financial companies. Source: The Bank of Korea, Economic Statistics System. Note: (1) Direct financing: government bonds, corporate bill, corporate bonds, foreign currency bonds, stocks/investments. (2) Foreign debts: direct investments, other external debt obligations (loan). (3) Loans: bank and non-bank loans. (4) Others: commerce credit (corporate credit), other financial assets debt, call loan/call money, government loan

Of particular note during the 1960s and 1970s, reliance on borrowing from domestic financial institutions or foreign sources (external debt) was absolutely higher than the proportion of direct financing from external corporate funds. As shown in Fig. 4.5 and Table 4.7, the portion of loans from external financial institutions in the 1960s and 1970s accounted for 40% and 48%, respectively, while the ratio of foreign debt reached 31% in the 1960s and 18% in the 1970s. Indirect financing combined with loans from financial institutions and foreign debt reached 71.6% in the 1960s and 65.6% in the 1970s. Meanwhile, dependence on direct financing such as corporate bonds and stocks was very low, 13% in the 1960s and 23% in the 1970s.

Korean firms' high dependence on external funds and high reliance on external loans are more prominent when compared to other countries. As shown in Table 4.8, external funds accounted for 74.8% of Korean

Table 4.7 External financing resources of Korean companies (non-financial companies) (Unit: %)

Proportion	*1963–1969*	*1970–1979*	*1980–1989*	*1990–1997*	*1998–2008*	*2009–2012*
External funds	100.0	100.0	100.0	100.0	100.0	100.0
Loans	40.2	47.8	38.2	35.5	34.9	19.7
Bank[a]	31.4	31.2	20.0	15.5	36.1	8.9
Non-bank[b]	8.7	16.6	18.1	19.9	−1.1	10.8
Foreign bonds/debt[c]	31.4	17.8	2.9	4.8	3.5	4.4
Direct finance	13.3	23.2	38.4	44.5	43.4	56.4
Government bonds	0.0	0.0	1.8	1.2	0.1	0.5
Corporate bills	0.0	2.1	6.1	8.9	4.5	4.4
Corporate bonds	0.4	4.8	10.2	18.0	9.2	28.8
Foreign currency bonds	0.0	0.0	0.0	2.0	2.0	3.1
Stocks/investments	12.8	16.2	20.4	14.3	30.2	19.7
Others[d]	15.1	11.3	18.6	15.4	19.0	19.4

Source: The Bank of Korea, Economic Statistics System Timeline of Financial Transactions during Funds Circulation

[a]Banks: depositories

[b]Non-bank: Bank of Korea, insurance, credit agencies, public finance, others

[c]Foreign bonds/debt: direct investment, other foreign debts

[d]Others: commerce credit (corporate credit), other financial asset debts, call loan/call money, government loan

Table 4.8 Financing structure of non-financial companies (average of 1970–1985, net basis) (Unit: %)

	Korea	*Japan*	*France*	*Germany*	*United Kingdom*	*United States*
Total funds	100.0	100.0	100.0	100.0	100.0	100.0
Internal funds	25.2	33.7	44.1	55.2	72.0	66.9
External funds	74.8	66.3	55.9	44.8	28.0	33.1
Short-term securities	2.6	n.a.	0.0	0.0	2.9	1.4
Loans	44.5	40.7	41.5	21.1	21.4	23.1
Commerce credit	n.a.	18.3	4.7	2.2	2.8	8.4
Private loan	7.2	3.1	2.3	0.7	0.8	9.7
Stock	11.1	3.5	10.6	2.1	4.9	0.8
Others	9.4	0.7	−4.7	11.9	−7.2	−10.2

Source: Lee (2005, p. 108)

companies' financing system from 1970 to 1985, a rate much higher compared to liberal market economies, with the United Kingdom at 28.0% and the United States at 33.1%, but still higher than Germany at 44.8%, France at 55.9%, and Japan at 66.3%—countries with relatively high dependency on banks' long-term financing (patient capital). In addition, the dependency rate on loans of external funds was also highest in Korea. In the same period, the dependency ratio on loans of Korean companies was 44.5%, while only 21.1% for German companies, 21.4% for British companies, 23.1% for American companies, 40.7% for Japanese companies, and 41.5% for French companies.

Finally, in the 1960s and 1970s, the larger the firm size, the higher the debt ratio while lower the borrowing cost. During the industrialization period, the trend in debt ratio of the Korean manufacturing sector by firm size shows that the traditional Korean developmental state's policies gave priority to large corporations. As shown in Fig. 4.6, the debt ratio of large corporations and SMEs does not differ much until the mid-1960s. From the end of the 1960s, however, a noticeable difference emerges. In the 1970s, the debt ratio of large corporations averaged 349%, while the debt ratio of SMEs averaged 236%. As shown in Table 4.9, the liability dependency ratio of large corporations in the 1970s was 50%, while that of SMEs was only 39%.

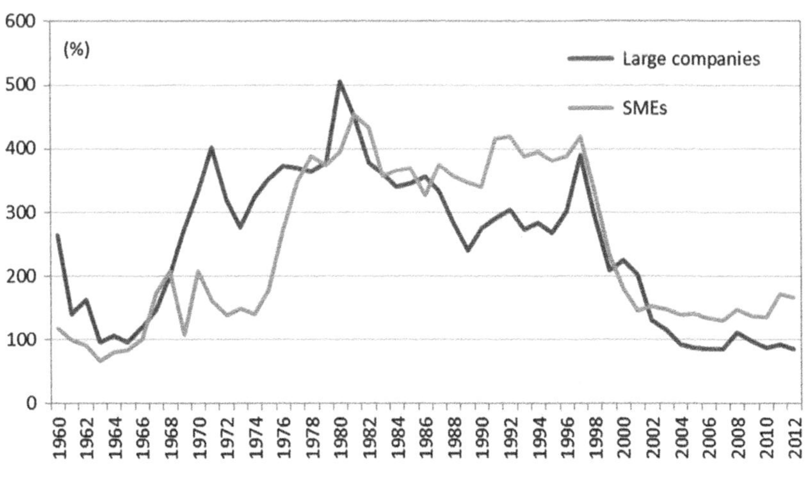

Fig. 4.6 Trend of debt ratio by firm size in manufacturing industry. Source: The Bank of Korea, Financial Statement Analysis (years)

Table 4.9 Changes in funding structure by firm size in manufacturing industry (Unit: %)

		1960–1969	*1970–1979*	*1980–1989*	*1990–1999*	*2000–2012*
Debt ratio	Large corporations	160.4	348.6	359.1	288.9	114.6
	SMEs	112.3	235.6	378.1	371.0	147.7
Equity ratio	Large corporations	40.4	22.4	22.3	26.0	48.2
	SMEs	48.7	32.0	21.0	21.6	40.5
Debt dependence	Large corporations	33.2	50.0	45.2	47.9	24.7
	SMEs	26.2	38.6	39.5	42.2	34.0

Source: The Bank of Korea, Financial Statement Analysis (years)

In addition, as shown in Table 4.10, long-term debt accounted for a large portion of the overall debt of large corporations, while short-term debt showed little difference between large corporations and SMEs. The large portion of long-term debt among large corporations resulted from the high dependency ratio of large corporations on foreign loans. SMEs had little opportunity to procure foreign loans because the government provided payment guarantees only for large corporations. As a result, foreign loans accounted for 9.3% of financing in large companies during the period of 1969–1980, while similar loans accounted for only 1.3% of financing for SMEs. According to one survey, most chaebol conglomerates initiated foreign loans of more than $500 billion or more than $100 million by the mid-1970s.[7]

The difference in loan composition led to a difference in borrowing costs between large enterprises and SMEs. As shown in Table 4.11, the ratio of borrowing cost to turnover was 1.9%p higher for SMEs than for large enterprises during the 1970s. Moreover, the ratio of borrowing cost to turnover was 1.4%p higher in non-exporting companies than in exporting, and the ratio of borrowing cost to turnover was 2.8%p higher in light industry than in heavy chemical industry. Clearly, the state's policy benefits were concentrated on large exporting companies in heavy chemical industry.

[7] For specific firms that introduce loans, see Lee (2004, pp. 143–144).

Table 4.10 Detailed financing structure by firm size in manufacturing industry (1969–1980) (Unit: %)

		1969	*1970*	*1971*	*1972*	*1973*	*1974*	*1975*	*1976*	*1977*	*1978*	*1979*	*1980*	*1969–1980*
Large corporations	Self-financing	32.1	24.3	17	51.6	39.4	28.5	26.9	36.6	31.4	31.6	27.2	16.2	30.2
	Financing by others	67.9	75.7	83	48.4	60.6	71.5	73.1	63.4	68.6	68.4	72.8	83.8	69.8
	Long-term loan	22.5	13.5	37.5	41.7	17.1	22.9	23.6	21.3	26.3	22.7	21.2	29.9	25.0
	Bank loan	6.7	16.3	14	23.1	13.7	8.7	1.4	10.4	10.5	11.1	9.9	8.9	11.2
	Foreign loan	13.2	−4	21.7	9.7	3.8	13.4	14.9	6.2	11.7	5.8	2.8	12.5	9.3
	Other long-term	2.5	1.2	1.9	8.9	−0.4	0.8	7.3	4.6	4.1	5.8	8.3	8.5	4.5
	Short-term loan	26	19.6	22.8	11.7	19.3	25.5	10.6	20.3	16.9	21.6	22.4	22.2	19.9
	Account payables	10.4	8.7	12.8	9.2	5.9	12.9	19.4	5.8	10.6	4	14.3	19.7	11.1
	Other	8.9	33.8	9.8	9.3	18.3	10.3	19.5	16	14.8	19.1	15	12.1	15.6
SMEs	Self-financing	46.5	40	57.8	62.3	45.5	50.4	33	29.1	28.3	30.4	27.5	22.5	39.4
	Financing by others	53.5	60	42.2	37.7	54.5	49.6	67	70.9	71.7	69.6	72.5	77.5	60.6
	Long-term loan	11.4	18.9	5.2	18.7	8.3	12.5	11.1	14.6	17.6	26.4	24.7	13	15.2
	Bank loan	5.3	25.3	−1.7	14.7	6.3	8.9	5.2	10	13.6	21.6	25.2	11.5	12.2
	Foreign loan	5.5	1.3	1.7	−1.3	−0.2	−0.2	4.5	1.2	1.1	1.7	−1.5	1.6	1.3
	Other long-term	0.6	−7.7	5.2	5.3	2.3	3.8	1.5	3.3	3	3.1	0.9	−0.1	1.8
	Short-term loan	20.9	14.8	20.2	22.2	19.6	14.3	20.5	23.5	24.5	18.4	21.1	24.9	20.4
	Account payables	9.1	13.2	12.6	−1.5	8.1	11.8	20.3	19.5	15.9	10.6	14	27.1	13.4
	Other	12.1	13.1	4.3	−1.8	18.5	11	15.1	13.3	13.6	14.2	12.7	12.4	11.5

Source: Bank of Korea, Financial Statement Analysis (years)

Notes: (1) Self-finance: Stock (or capital increase), internal reserves (surplus, net profit), depreciation expense. (2) Other long-term borrowings: Corporate bonds and other long-term borrowings. (3) Short-term Loans: Short-term bank borrowings, other short-term borrowings

Table 4.11 Difference in average borrowing cost by manufacturing sector (Unit: %, %p)

	1973–1981	*1982–1986*	*1987–1999*	*1991–1994*	*1995–1997*
Large corporations (A) (%)	13.0	14.0	12.6	14.0	10.9
SMEs (B) (%)	14.9	14.2	14.3	16.1	12.1
(A–B) (%p)	−1.9	−0.2	−1.7	−2.1	−1.2
Export firm (C) (%)	12.6	12.7	12.6	14.0	10.8
Domestic firm (D) (%)	14.0	14.8	13.2	14.6	11.3
(C–D) (%p)	−1.4	−2.1	−0.6	−0.6	−0.5
Heavy chemical industry (E) (%)	12.1	13.5	12.7	14.0	10.8
Light industry (F) (%)	14.9	14.9	13.5	15.4	12.4
(E–F) (%p)	−2.8	−1.4	−0.8	−1.4	−1.6

Source: Bank of Korea, Corporate Management Analysis, each volume; Lee (2005, p. 123)

Closed and Centralized Policy Decision-Making

In the 1960s and 1970s, the Korean government's economic policy governance was notably centralized. First, decisions on important development strategies involved the presidential staff of the Blue House, and, if necessary, key officials and external experts in the field were brought in. Second, the establishment and implementation of specific policies were carried out by an institutionalized bureaucracy. The Ministry of Commerce and Industry and the Ministry of Finance, led by the EPB, set detailed implementation plans of policies, mobilized necessary resources to enact policy, and sought continuous feedback to ensure that policy objectives would be achieved. Third, in the early 1960s, the Korean government established a domestic capital mobilization system by centralizing control over currency and monetary policy.

Exclusiveness and Non-institutionalization of the Decision-Making Process

The most prominent feature of the policy governance system of the traditional Korean developmental state was the reliance on the president-centered top-down policy decision process. Primary development strategies during the Park Chung-hee government were set and promoted mainly by presidential staffs at the Blue House (Kim 2014, p. 241). With the mid-1960s shift to export-led strategy, the role of the deputy prime minister for economic affairs, who exercised control over economic policy as chief of the EPB, was significant until the late 1960s. After the 1970s, however, the economic minister was excluded from important decisions such as the decision to freeze private loans in 1972 and the declaration of heavy chemicals industrialization in 1973 (CCKM 2013, pp. 391–397; Kim 1999b, pp. 97–98, 115–119, 206–217).

Such president-centered policy decisions not only undermined the policy autonomy and expertise of ministries of economic affairs in the decision-making process but also created competition between ministries to get the president's trust and authority. For example, conflicts emerged between the Ministry of Commerce and Industry and the EPB over export policy and heavy chemical industry policy.[8] Conflicts and differences of opinions between ministries were managed vertically by the president, not through horizontal coordination. In addition, agents such as the Cabinet, Minister of Finance, vice ministers, Economic Science Council, and National Security Council, whose participation in policymaking was legally guaranteed, were often alienated (Ha 2006, pp. 142–154; Lee 1969, pp. 405–406; Chung 1987, 1988, pp. 509–516). In short, president-centered dirigisme prevented institutionalized and systematized policy-making in Korean industrialization (Kim 1999b, pp. 213–215).

Role of the Economic Planning Board

The coup government, which took over in 1961, established the Economic Planning Board (EPB) and prepared the basic institutional structure for state-led economic development. The Korean EPB was similar to Japan's Economic Planning Agency or India's Planning Commission but was much stronger in terms of function and status. The EPB was formed by absorbing the Ministry of Finance's Budget Bureau and the Ministry of Home Affairs' Statistics Bureau into the existing Ministry of Economic Revival. In addition, with the transfer of power to civil government in 1963, the chair of the EPB was given the position of Economic Deputy Prime Minister, giving the Board higher status than other ministries. In addition, President Park Chung-hee gave absolute authority to the Economic Deputy Prime Minister after the transfer of power to civil

[8] "(Economy Cocktail) Soochoolmokpyojungchek Sanggongbooui Uiyoke 'Ukje' Woomjikim," *The Chosun Ilbo*, December 29, 1978, p. 2; "(Economy Cocktail) Choongwhahak, Sanggongboojjoke Kaljaroo," *The Chosun Ilbo*, 1975/05/29, p. 2; "(Economy Cocktail) Soochoolguemyoong Manuenya Jukuenya Yisaeknonjaeng," *The Chosun Ilbo*, 1978/07/04, p. 2; "(Economy Cocktail) Soochoolguemyoongsago Gyungjaeboochuuigyn Daerip," *The Chosun Ilbo*, 1979/06/26, p. 2.

government and firmly established the lead role of the EPB in economic development (Kim 1999b; CCKM 2013).

The three main functions of the EPB were planning, budgeting, and cooperation. The planning function enabled the EPB to set mid- and long-term economic plans and develop policy instruments. In addition, since setting economic policy required coordination with other economic ministries, planning also included coordination. The budget function (internal financing) and the cooperation function (foreign financing), which corresponded to the resource mobilization function, served as "both wings" to support the coordination efforts of the EPB. Although planning in principle was at the center of the EPB, the center of real power lay in the budget and cooperation functions. Since foreign capital financing played an important role at the start of Korea's industrialization, the cooperative function was at the center of power, but as the economic scale expanded, the focus of power transferred to the budget function. Cooperation was mainly concerned with the introduction of foreign loans and basic projects, requiring frequent contact with firms and foreigners, and prioritizing political decisions rather than economic logic. The budget function, meanwhile, maintained a relatively conservative stance. If the budget bureau had the characteristics of the Ministry of Finance, then the loan introduction bureau was closer to the characteristics of the Ministry of Commerce and Industry (Kim 1999b, pp. 91–94).

Governance of Monetary and Financial Policy

The coup government that came to power in the early 1960s took institutional measures to control commercial banks and the flows of funds to secure the domestic capital mobilization infrastructure for economic development. First, the Park Chung-hee government enacted two amendments to the Banking Law and renationalized commercial banks. In 1961, the government enacted the Provisional Measures against Financial Institutions Act to limit the voting rights of banks' major shareholders. Through the Unfair Stock Processing Act (Boojungchookjaechuribup), most of the chaebol-owned bank shares were transferred to the government. Second, measures were introduced to limit the independence of the Bank of Korea. The Bank of Korea Act was amended to vest the Ministry of Finance with final authority and responsibility for the Bank's monetary policy. The Monetary Policy Board was renamed the Monetary Policy Operating Board, with its function downgraded only to operate and manage monetary policy. Third, various special banks were established to intervene in financial markets. In 1961, the Small and Medium Business Bank was established, and in 1962, Kookmin Bank was established by merging existing mutual loan companies to support small-loan finance. In addition, the National Federation of Fisheries Cooperatives, Korea Exchange Bank, and Korea Housing Bank were established to provide special financial support, and local banks were established to stimulate regional finance. Fourth, the National Investment Fund[9] was created in December 1973 to raise funds for heavy chemicals industrialization. In 1974, main creditor banks were introduced for the management and support of financing to large corporations, and in 1976 the Export-Import Bank of Korea was established for financing facility investment and for mid- to long-term export of heavy and chemical industries. In the traditional Korean model, the functions of special banks were strengthened in order to vitalize policy finance; even general banks were required to carry some part of policy finance (Amsden 1989, p. 73; CCKE 2011b, pp. 124–130; Kim 2014, p. 240).

Economic Nationalism

The most distinctive feature of Korea's traditional political economic model, which distinguishes from other late industrialized countries such as Latin American countries, Europe's Ireland, and Asia's Taiwan, is a model dependent on domestic large corporations (Amsden 1989, p. 21). For a late developing country with no accumulated capital and skills, industrialization through foreign direct investment may prove most effective. For this reason, many late industrializing countries have taken strategies to utilize foreign direct investment, such as Latin American countries, or to supply OEM products or components to advanced foreign companies, as in the case of Taiwan, instead of adopting a method of fostering indigenous brands that might lack competitiveness. In particular, Taiwan has actively promoted foreign direct investment since the end of the 1960s, with its active cultivation of the IT industry (Breznitz 2007, p. 37).

[9] The National Investment Fund lends funds financed by the issuance of national investment bonds and the receipt of deposits from the government to financial institutions and finances the important industries set forth in the Act. Major industries include heavy chemical industries such as steel, nonferrous metals, shipbuilding, machinery, chemical, electronics industries, mining, and the Saemaul Factory.

But in Korea, foreign firms have not become major economic actors. From 1966 to 1979, Korea's cumulative foreign direct investment amounted to $2.2 billion (standard of reporting), less than 1% of GDP. Foreign direct investment has been welcomed by the export-oriented sector in light industry, but it was restricted in national strategic industries such as heavy and chemical industries or the pharmaceutical industry (Koo 1981; Amsden 1989, pp. 74–76).

As a late industrializing country lacking capital and technology, the Korean government in the 1960s enacted the Foreign Capital Inducement Act (Woijadoipbup) and began the introduction of foreign investment. The Foreign Capital Inducement Promotion Act (Woijadoipchokjinbup), introduced in 1960, included tax and customs benefits to attract foreign capital. The later Foreign Capital Inducement Act, enacted in 1966, abolished the minimum rate of foreign direct investment (25%) and limitations on repatriation of profit (Ministry of Finance and Korea Development Bank 1993, pp. 54–57, 99). Moreover, in 1970 the Korean government became more active in attracting foreign investment by establishing the Masan Free Trade Zone and setting up a temporary special law to restrict activities of unions in foreign-invested companies (Lee 1986, pp. 792–793; No 1986, p. 567).

However, foreign direct investment remained low until the 1997 financial crisis. Prior to the crisis, the Korean capital market had been closed to foreign capital inflows except for selectively allowed loans and limited foreign direct investment. Despite the Foreign Capital Inducement Act and aggressive foreign investment promotion policies, Korea's approach in the 1960s and 1970s basically restricted foreign capital. Despite preferential provisions for attracting foreign capital, the government disallowed full-scale opening to foreign direct investment by adding ambiguous regulations and restrictions. According to the 1960 Foreign Capital Inducement Promotion Act, investment was prohibited in nuclear power-related, defense-related, coastal vessel, and domestic airline industries, along with government monopoly business. The Act also allowed the government to prohibit foreign investment that could prove harmful to foreign exchange or that could disturb monetary stability, cause overproduction, or lead to speculation (Ministry of Finance and Korea Development Bank 1993, p. 59).

Thus, regulations designed to restrict foreign direct investment served to protect domestic industries' production base. For example, in the electronics industry, foreign-invested companies were allowed to invest on the condition that their products would be exported. Domestic sales of foreign investors were not permitted due to the opposition of domestic companies in the industry. In 1968, domestic electronic companies, at the initiative of Korean Electronic Industries Cooperative, filed a proposal with the government to restrict domestic sales of foreign companies. The government adopted this policy, thus protecting the domestic production base in the early stages of the electronics industry (Korea Electronics Association [KEA] 1999, p. 98).

While the Korean government took a cautious stance on foreign direct investment, it maintained a generous policy on the introduction of foreign technology, thus treating capital and technology separately. This strategy enabled indigenous companies to maximize the effects of importing foreign technologies and skills (Lee 1989; Yoon 2006, p. 121).

The Korean government wanted to keep private companies under strict control of the state, restricting foreign direct investment. This economic nationalism of the Korean government is distinguished from the practice in Latin American countries. For example, in the Mexican automobile industry, it has been impossible for the state to control private companies, as multinational corporations from the United States entered the country from the very start of industrialization (Samuels 1990; Shapiro 1994; Kronish and Mericle 1984). The Korean government, on the other hand, managed its economy by keeping private enterprises under control, making it easier to implement upgrades to new industries.

The Korean government's nationalistic economic policies were based on economic self-reliance rather than economic efficiency. Economic self-reliance for Korea meant building an economically viable economy without foreign aid following the Korean War (Amsden 1989, p. 72). According to Kimiya Tadashi, the Park Chung-hee government's inclusive industrialization strategy emphasized the internal integration of the national economy. The core of this inclusive industrialization strategy was to mobilize investment resources domestically to alleviate external dependency (Kimiya 2008).

However, since industrialization began in earnest in the 1960s and the industrialization strategy shifted from import substitution to export-oriented, the meaning of "self-reliant economy" began to change from one that receives less foreign aid to an economy with a full-fledged and self-sufficient industry structure (Amsden 1989, pp. 164–165). Having a complete industrial structure domestically meant that the economic development strategy put long-term industrial construction above short-term economic efficiency. Indeed, Korea's industrialization strategy insisted that even if it is cheaper to bring in foreign technology, it must invest in domestic skills for "self-reliance" (Amsden 1989, p. 21).

The establishment of Pohang Iron and Steel Co., Ltd (POSCO) in the 1960s illustrates the characteristics of the Korean development strategy. From the perspective of economic efficiency, the establishment of integrated steelworks in the 1960s would not have been possible. At the time, economic experts at home and abroad had a negative stance on such a strategy. Steel mills require large-scale capital, but Korea lacked capital and could not ensure economic viability, given Korea's small domestic market, even if a factory were constructed. Thus, when the government sought the opinions of foreign financial institutions on loans to construct factories, they all expressed negative viewpoints, advising that it was more economical for Korea to import steel from nearby Japanese steel companies. Even domestically, many economic experts including economists at the EPB held a negative position on establishing the steel mill.

However, the president's intent to build integrated steelworks in Korea was firm in view of the forward and backward linkages of this domestic strategic industry and the competitiveness of entire national industries. He and his supporters found it necessary to construct the steelworks in order to enhance long-term competitiveness of domestic strategic industries, as Japanese steel companies were selling steel to foreign companies at high prices. Ultimately, the Korean government inaugurated Pohang Iron and Steel Co., Ltd in 1968 and began full-scale operation in 1973. POSCO has played a major role in strengthening the competitiveness of Korean companies in strategic industries such as automobile, shipbuilding, and construction industries by supplying them steel at relatively low prices (Amsden 1989, pp. 291–317; CCKM 2013).

In short, Korean economic nationalism was based on the idea to build an economy with a full-fledged and self-sufficient structure of industry and led by indigenous corporations. This strong nationalistic characteristic of the Korean government emerged from strong resistance to foreign capital based on experiences of the colonial period and the aid economy following the Korean War and the political motivation of an authoritarian government to control the private economy and promote state-led economic development (Evans 1985; Yoon 2006, pp. 78, 120).

Section 2: Traditional Interfirm Relations in Korea

In Korea's traditional business model established in the 1960s and 1970s, Korean assembly conglomerates developed an innovation system that relied on internal resources and imported components rather than creating efficiency through business relations with domestic component companies. This was possible because large-scale conglomerates were internally equipped with a self-sufficient system through extensive diversification following the state-led heavy chemicals industrialization of the 1970s. The self-sufficient system, based on ownership of large conglomerates in Korea, differed from Japanese big business groups (Kaisha), which relied on relational networks of independent companies (Whitley 1992, p. 46; Hamilton et al. 1990; Witt 2015, p. 218).

Accordingly, the traditional business model in Korea is similar to that of the United States, which is characterized by arms-length relations between conglomerates and subcontractors, and distinct from Germany's horizontal and cooperative interfirm relations or Japan, which has vertical but cooperative interfirm relations. Whitley's (1992) comparative analysis of business systems of main East Asian countries such as Japan, Korea, Hong Kong, and Taiwan found that the structure in which Korean companies are organized in the market reveals relatively low interdependence and cooperation, compared to Japan. According to Whitley's analysis, Korean firms showed weaker vertical integration, shorter business relations, and weaker commitment than Japanese firms (Whitley 1992, p. 46; Amsden 1989, p. 183; Wade 1990, pp. 315–316).

Indeed, Korea's subcontracting did not establish long-lasting trade relations in the 1970s. According to the *1976 Survey Report of Small and Medium Enterprises* by the Ministry of Commerce and Industry and the Small and Medium Business Bank, only 46.2% of subcontractors had long-term exclusive subcontracts, while 53.8% had irregular or uncertain temporary subcontracts (Lee 1979, pp. 12–13; Korea International Trade Association [KITA] 1977, p. 125).

The arm's-length characteristics of Korean firms' relations persisted until the mid-1990s, despite the quantitative growth of subcontracting transactions since the early 1980s. According to a study by Dyer and Chu (2000) that analyzed the determinants of "trust" between lead firms and components suppliers in the US, Japanese, and Korean automobile industries based on surveys conducted in 1992–1994, the degree of trust in interfirm relationships in the Korean automobile industry was lower than in Japan and the United States. Compared to Japan, Korea rated lower on the indicators that influence trust such as length, closeness, and continuity of transactions, and participation by capital, and was similar or slightly higher than the United States (Dyer and Chu 2000, pp. 271–272).

Interfirm relations characterized by short-term contracts and exploitative relations between large conglomerates and small- and medium-sized component companies resulted from the input-driven growth strategy of the traditional Korean model to focus on fostering large corporations with economies of scale, causing underdevelopment of the components and materials industry. This section examines the traditional characteristics of Korean business relations.

Characteristics of the Korean Components Procurement System

Large Firms' Strategies: Internalization and Import of Core Components

Characteristics of interfirm relations in the traditional Korean economic development model were influenced by large conglomerates' strategies that were highly dependent on internal resources. Large corporations have primarily relied on import or in-house production to procure components for their export competitiveness. In the 1970s, by diversification chaebol conglomerates established a vertically integrated system for core businesses and formed a system for supplying core components from subsidiary companies within the group. Core technologies and components that could not be quickly internalized relied on imports based on their capabilities to mobilize capital (Amsden 1989, p. 177; Han 1988, pp. 104–105).

For example, in 1985, when ten years had passed since Hyundai Motors developed the first Korean car model, Pony, it had been still subcontracting only about 40% of its value. Core components were procured through subcontractors with close ties to the Hyundai Group, while simple components were procured through about 185 SMEs (Amsden 1989, p. 184).

Until the 1970s, core components, materials, and machinery equipment depended on the introduction of overseas technology. For example, in the automobile industry, core component technologies such as engine, carburetor, steering, transmission, and axle still relied on foreign technology (Korea Development Institute [KDI] 1980, pp. 43–46). In fact, looking at the cost structure of components and materials of domestic passenger cars in the late 1970s, 48.7% and 67.8%, respectively, of material costs of Hyundai's Cortina and Saehan Motors' Royale Record constituted exported components, except for Hyundai's Pony, which followed the government's components localization policy (KDI 1981, p. 64). Material costs of Hyundai's Pony consisted of 92.0% for domestic components, but the high rate of localization was achieved through domestic suppliers importing, assembling, and supplying foreign components to Hyundai, so it could not actually be called the localization of component technologies (A professor at the KAIST Graduate School of Technology Management, personal communication, June 3, 2001).

When the heavy and chemical industries began to be promoted with the declaration of heavy chemicals industrialization in 1973, subcontract relations in the Korean industry did not exist. The number of subcontracting SMEs in 1976 was only 19.4% of all SMEs. In particular, the proportions in the general machinery and electric machinery sectors, which are typical assembling industries and require integration of enterprises, are not high, 35.1% and 49.6%, respectively, compared with the proportion of subcontractors in the same industries in Japan at 75.8% and 78.9%, respectively, in 1975 (Lee 1979, pp. 11–12; Junkyungryunhwoibo, October 21, 1977). According to the *Survey Report of SMEs* in 1979, the average proportion of subcontractors in Korea was 37.7%, with 44.7% in general machinery, 57.7% in electric machinery, and 57.7% in transportation equipment, which showed a growing trend but still low. In addition, the proportion of companies that depended on subcontracting for 80% or more of their sales was not high. In 1979, it was 62% in all industries, with 71.6% in the machinery sector, 66.7% in the electric machinery sector, and 50.8% in the transport equipment sector (Small and Medium Business Cooperative Federation 1979).

Even 20 years after a full-fledged domestic car model of Pony was developed, the economic status of independent component companies in the Korean automobile industry was not high. As shown in Table 4.12, the proportion of components suppliers' delivery costs to total production costs among Korea's three main car makers was 65.6% in 1995. This percentage is considerably higher than in the United States or the United Kingdom, but lower than Japan's 70% in 1985 (Mitsubishi Research Institute 1987; KIET 1994). However, excluding the components procurement cost from car makers' subsidiaries and related companies,[10] the

[10] "Subsidiary" refers to a company designated by the Fair Trade Commission as a member of a large-scale enterprise group as of April 1, 1996, under the "Act on Monopoly Regulation and Fair Trade." Therefore, "subsidiary" here can be understood as the minimum value of the capital subsidiaries of the car makers. Related companies include capital participating companies that are not included in affiliates or companies owned and managed by relatives. However, due to the lack of relevant data, the figures presented here can be understood as the minimum value of affiliated companies (KIET 1997a, p. 6).

real rate of outsourcing is much lower compared to Japan. As shown in Table 4.12, excluding the costs of components procured by subsidiaries from the components delivery cost of the three car makers in 1995, the outsourcing ratio is about 56%, and excluding costs of components procured from both subsidiaries and related companies, the ratio is reduced to 43% (KIET 1997a, pp. 5–7).

The reason that the outsourcing ratio of Korean and Japanese automakers is higher than that of U.S. or European automakers is that they have the higher ratio of capital participation with components suppliers and procure main components and materials from them. U.S. automakers tend to internalize the development and manufacture of main components within their companies rather than work with affiliates (KIET 1997a, p. 7).

However, relations between a lead firm and its subsidiaries in Japan differ qualitatively from those in Korea. Japanese relations between lead firms and subsidiaries are based on cooperation or partnership rather than ownership. The vertical integrated system in Japan consists mainly of affiliates invested in by the lead firm. The share ratio of lead firm to affiliates varies from high to less than 10%; companies with less than 20% share ratio account for more than 70% of affiliates in the integrated system. Relations between a lead firm and its affiliated components suppliers in Japan are relatively more independent than in Korea, even though the capital participation of a lead firm with its suppliers is widespread. On the other hand, relations between a lead firm and its subsidiaries in Korea are divided into relations with subsidiaries with capital investment by the lead firm and relations with independent components companies that have no capital investment by the lead firm. The former, Japanese-style affiliated companies with capital investment constitute only a small part of subcontractors in the Korean vertically integrated system. Most subsidiaries of a lead firm also have a share ratio of more than 50% by the lead firm, but even if the ratio is less than half, the management is not independent of the lead firm, unlike Japan (KIET 1997a, p. 7).

The vertical integration system in Japan was developed based on close cooperation and interdependence between large companies and their subcontractors because the system was established, thanks to the considerably developed components industry. When heavy industries, including the automobile industries, began to develop in Japan in the 1920s, the components industry was already capable of independent exports. Conversely, in Korea the components industry was not well developed at the start of

Table 4.12 Outsourcing ratio of three finished-car companies (1995) (Unit: 100 million KRW, %)

	Sales (A)	*Manufacturing cost (B)*	*Delivery cost (I)*	*Delivery cost to subsidiaries (D)*	*Delivery cost to affiliate (E)*	*C/A*	*C/B*	*(C-D)/A*	*(C-D)/B*	*(C-D-E)/A*	*(C-D-E)/B*
Hyundai Motors	103,392	84,106	56,248	3440	15,543	54.4	66.9	51.1	62.8	36.0	44.3
Kia Motors	56,885	37,001	26,818	4677	3313	47.1	72.5	38.9	59.8	33.1	50.9
Daewoo Motors	34,705	27,731	14,622	4848	861	42.1	52.7	28.2	35.2	25.7	32.1
Total	194,982	148,838	97,688	12,965	19,717	50.1	65.6	43.5	56.0	33.3	43.7

Source: Korea Automobile Industry Coop. Association (1996)

industrialization of the heavy chemical industry in the 1970s, so lead companies in the industries relied on imports or internalization of main components. In Korea's vertical integration system, domestic components suppliers were able to grow to some extent, with limited support from large assembly companies, but their growth was restricted to the level allowed by their lead companies.

Limited Role of Component Companies

Large assembly companies in Korea had a components procurement structure in which they were dependent on internal development and production or import from advanced foreign companies for core components and materials and procured only general components from subcontractors or the market. Until the 1980s, domestic subcontractors in the automobile industry were mainly in charge of processing such as press, casting, forging, machining, heat treatment, and assembly, while the six major functional components such as engines, electronic systems, power transmissions, braking devices, steering devices, and shock absorbers were manufactured internally or supplied by components-specialized manufacturers, which were mainly subsidiaries or related companies of automakers (KIET 1987).

Similarly, the electronics and electrical devices industry had a structure in which core components were procured through internal production or import, while only general-purpose components were procured from the market. In the production of TVs in the 1980s, active high-tech components such as cathode-ray tubes and semiconductors, tuners, switches, and capacitors were produced internally or by subsidiaries. Production of general electronic components such as resistors, coils, and PCBs was procured from small and medium components suppliers. Although some active components were supplied by the vertically integrated system, core components and materials still depended on imports from Japan. Only general electronic components were procured from the market or subcontractors. According to a survey of subcontracting transactions in 1979, the percentage of assembly companies purchasing components in the market exceeded 80% (Han 1988, pp. 99–101).

Even limited subcontracting transactions were based on the division of labor for the production process rather than for technology. Korean large corporations' outsourcing motivation was not the development and production of specialized components but mainly to reduce costs of capital investment and labor by using subcontracting companies, streamlining their management for any downturn. According to a 1982 survey of large manufacturing corporations in Busan, the most important reason large corporations felt the need for vertical integration was to "save in facility investment" (41%), while the "use of professional technology" was only 12%. Japanese subcontracting, conversely, depended on specialized skills and technologies of components companies. According to the *1979 Survey of SMEs* by the Small and Medium Enterprise Agency of Japan, the most important reason Japanese lead companies want to subcontract is because they can "use the specialized technology and special facilities that the subcontracting firms have" (47.0%; Choi 1983, pp. 146–147).

In the Korean components supply system, components companies were at most limited to mass production of existing products and improvement of production quality and precision, rather than the development of new products and technologies. According to a mid-1980s survey on what is required for subcontractors' qualitative growth in the electronics industry, "improvements in quality and precision," "reduction of production costs," and "improvement of production technology" received the highest responses at 67.5%, 52.5%, and 50.8%, respectively, while a focus on the "development of new products" scored only 27.5% of the responses (Yoon and Hong 1989, pp. 128–130). Moreover, in a 1990 survey on improvements of components companies in the automobile industry, 75% of participating components companies responded that "improvement of quality and precision" was required for their improvement, but firms that emphasized "strengthening of technological development" scored only 39% (Kim and Cho 1991, p. 220).

Limited Interfirm Cooperation

Although the extent to which large corporations depended on subcontracting with components companies was limited, efforts have been made since the mid-1970s to develop domestic subcontracting systems by some large corporations. Consequently, the form of the Korean vertical integration system began to be established at this time. However, interfirm subcontracting relations in Korea at this time cannot be compared to bilateral cooperative relations like Japan's. Although Japanese companies' vertical integration systems also depend on hierarchical coordination by the lead company, Japanese components manufacturers develop and produce components with their own expertise in the system. In contrast, the vertical integration structure of Korean firms established in the 1970s and 1980s relied on unilateral knowledge transfer from lead firms to components suppliers, as well as top-down coordination by lead firms. In return for unilateral support, the relationship between lead firms and their subcontractors was exclusive and dependent. Under this structure, the growth of Korean components suppliers was limited to the extent allowed by their lead firms.

For example, as Hyundai Motors increased its production, it further developed its subcontracting network and expanded financial and technical support for subcontractors, working closely with components suppliers ranging from product development to quality control. As quality problems became serious following the sale and export of Pony in 1976, Hyundai Motors established a Components Development Department in 1980–1981 to increase the production skills of the components suppliers. About 150 Components Development Department engineers were dispatched to the components companies in small groups to supervise components suppliers' production process (Amsden 1989, pp. 184–185, 280).

> MIC (Myongdo Industrial Co.) gets some financial assistance from HMC (Hyundai Motors Co.). In the case of a new investment at MIC, HMC gives it advance payment. HMC also gives it credit to buy new machinery from Hyundai Heavy Industries. Most of MIC's finance, however, comes from the Small and Medium Industrial Bank. MIC gets technical assistance from HMC. When MIC starts to make a new part, HMC's people work together with MIC's. But HMC cannot give specialized technical assistance because it does not have the know-how. MIC had to ask a Japanese equipment maker to supervise it for a while. MIC gets assistance for quality control from HMC. HMC taught it about inspection standards and how to develop quality. MIC and HMC meet to discuss quality. Usually HMC people don't come to MIC's factory unless there are problems with quality. In the case of a new part, HMC people stay at the factory, check the specifications with MIC people, and discuss how to troubleshoot. They test together and after the test report, HMC sends MIC feedback. HMC does random inspections of MIC's deliveries. (Amsden 1989, pp. 185–186)

However, as in the case of Myongdo Co., some large companies like Hyundai Motors were providing technical assistance to subcontractors, but the scale and scope of their support remained narrow. In fact, according to the *1976 Survey Report of Small and Medium Enterprises*, only 31.0% of subcontractors were supported by their lead company. In addition, since cooperative relations between large companies and subcontractors depended on unilateral support from large enterprises, the level of support was restricted to meeting the quality level desired by large companies, but not to the level that allowed subcontracting companies to have their own independent product development technologies. Furthermore, large assembly corporations did not guarantee enough profit to allow subcontracting firms to invest in technology development relative to their market power. According to a late 1970s survey by the Ministry of Commerce and Industry, the pretax profit per employee of SMEs was only 54.9% of that of large enterprises. In fact, the survey found that subcontractors had difficulty with the low order price, delayed payments, and excessive competition (Son 1978, p. 170). According to the 1997 KITA survey, more than 40% of lead companies unilaterally decided the delivery price; payment of lead firms by cash settlement was only 25.6%; and a payment period of less than 30 days was only 22.4%. As a result of these financing problems, SMEs struggled to invest in improvements in technology, equipment, and productivity (Lee 1979, pp. 11–13; Choi 1983, p. 159). Actually, unlike large corporations, small- and medium-sized components companies lacked financial and organizational resources to introduce foreign technology and engineers directly, so they had to rely at best on reverse engineering (Kim 1993b, pp. 364–366).

Relative Underdevelopment of the Components Industry

Interfirm relations remained marginal, while the state's strategic choice focused on fostering export-led large enterprises. While the assembly industry grew rapidly in the 1960s and 1970s, due to government policy support, the growth of the components industry lagged.

The Korean components industry was not competitive in terms of facilities and economies of scale. In the mid-1980s, finished-car corporations succeeded in exporting to the U.S. market to establish a substantial mass production system based on economies of scale. Yet components companies did not exceed their small size until the mid-1990s, lacking access to economies of scale. Looking at trends in delivery cost of first-tier automobile industry suppliers, the scale of components delivery per supplier was 3.3 billion KRW in 1988, growing to 10.2 billion in 1995. Yet despite this trend, components manufacturers did not benefit from economies of scale. According to a 1996 survey conducted by the KIET, 87.2% of respondents said that production should be increased to achieve economies of scale, while only 12.8% of respondents said that they were currently experiencing economies of scale (KIET 1997a, pp. 18–19).

More problematic than size was component companies' low technical ability. The quality of small- and medium-sized components makers in the mid-1970s, when Korea began heavy chemicals industrialization, was far below international standards. According to a 1976 Korea Automobile Industry Association survey, only 10% of the 1200 small- and medium-sized company respondents were able to produce components meeting international standards, and 60% were far below standard (KDI 1980, pp. 43–47; Kim and Lee 1980; Amsden 1989, p. 164).

The relative low growth of the Korean components industry continued for a considerable period of time beyond the 1970s. According to a survey on the technology level of subcontractors in the electronics industry by Yoon and Hong in the late 1980s, only 34.2% of companies answered that their technology level was "the same or better than that of the parent company (the lead company)." In contrast, during the same period, 52% of Japanese subcontractors in the manufacturing sector indicated that their technology level was the same or better than that of the parent company; for subcontractors in advanced countries, the proportion of companies that indicated that their technology level was same or better was 48.4%, compared with Korean companies' 34.2% (Yoon and Hong 1989, pp. 96–102).

In terms of product design capability, which indicates a firm's technology level, the level of Korean components companies in this period was very limited. The same 1989 survey of component firms in the electronics industry found that when a lead company orders a new product from a subcontractor, 73% of new orders were designed entirely by the lead company, with only 24% of subcontractors involved in new product design (Yoon and Hong 1989, pp. 105–106).

The low technology level of the Korean automobile components industry becomes especially evident when compared to Japan's during that period. In the early 1990s, according to a survey on components procurement methods for finished-car firms in the Korean automobile industry, 51% of the components design relied on black box drawing, or the method of developing and producing components based on design instructions by the lead firm. In contrast, approved drawing, or the method of developing and producing based on the component company's own design, was only 36%. In contrast, Japanese finished-car firms had 39% black box drawing method, with 55% approved drawing method. Moreover, participation in new vehicle development by components companies was 38% in Korea, much lower than Japan's 45% (KIET 1997a, pp. 72–73).

Given Korea's traditional industrialization strategy of fostering large enterprises with economies of scale in strategic industries, by mobilizing policy instruments such as credit rationing, bank system control, tax systems, control of business license, and other administrative devices, the Korean state artificially promoted national strategic industries, especially forming the oligopolistic domestic market in the heavy chemical industry (Whitley 1992, pp. 46–47; Zeile 1989).

This strategy marginalized small and medium components companies. From 1960 to 1980, the government's investment allocation was 70% for large corporations and 30% for SMEs (Ministry of Commerce 1982, p. 5). SMEs grew by 218 times, while large corporations grew by 928 times, in terms of output during that period. In terms of added value, SMEs grew by 226 times, while large corporations grew by 820 times (Choi 1983, pp. 143–144).

This study focuses not only on the traditional strategy of the Korean model but also on how that strategy has changed. As we saw in this chapter, traditional Korean interfirm relations were formed by state strategy, but those relations could also be transformed by change in state strategy, a change which enables state-led capitalism in Korea to survive and continue.

References

Amsden, A. H. (1989). *Asia's next giant: South Korea and late industrialization*. New York: Oxford University Press.

An, C.-Y., & Kim, J.-H. (1995). Daewoijihyang mooyukjungchaekgwa sanupbaljun. In D.-S. Cha & K.-S. Kim (Eds.), *Hangookgyungje bansegi: 21Segi yeoksajuk pyonggawha 21segi vision* (pp. 321–369). Seoul: KDI.

Breznitz, D. (2007). *Innovation and the state: Political choice and strategies for growth in Israel, Taiwan, and Ireland*. New Haven and London: Yale University Press.

CCKE (The Compilation Committee for the Korean Economy for 60 Years). (2011a). *The Korean economy: Six decades of growth and development: Summary*. Seoul: Korea Development Institute.

CCKE (The Compilation Committee for the Korean Economy for 60 Years). (2011b). *The Korean economy: Six decades of growth and development: Economy*. Seoul: Korea Development Institute.

CCKE (The Compilation Committee for the Korean Economy for 60 Years). (2011c). *The Korean economy: Six decades of growth and development: Industry*. Seoul: Korea Development Institute.

CCKM (The Compilation Committee for the Korean Miracle). (2013). *The Korean miracle I.* Paju: Nanam.
Cho, Y.-J. (1995). Kwangbok ihoo woorinaraui geumyoongjungchaeke daehan pyungga mit apeuroui jungchaekgwaje. In Korea Institute for Public Finance (Ed.), *Kwangbok Hoo 50nyunganui Jose Mit Keumyoongjungchekui Baljungwa Jungcheckbanghyang* (pp. 11–89). Seoul: Korea Institute for Public Finance.
Choi, D.-K. (1983). A study on the systematization of medium & small enterprises. *Kyungyungnonchong, 6*, 143–161.
Choi, J.-B. (1995). *Haebang ihoo hangookui geumyoongjungchaek.* Busan: Kyungsung University Press.
Chung, C.-K. (1987). Jungchaekgwajung. In Jo, Suk-joon et al. (Eds.), *Hangookhaengjungui yuksajuk boonsuk, 1968–1984* (pp. 504–521). Seoul: Seoul National University Press.
Chung, C.-K. (1988). Kyungjejanggwanhwoiuiwa jungchaekgyuljung. *Korean Journal of Public Administration, 26*(2), 370–380.
Dyer, J. H., & Chu, W.-J. (2000). The determinants of trust in supplier-automaker relationships in the U.S., Japan, and Korea. *Journal of International Business Studies, 31*(2), 259–285.
Evans, P. B. (1985). Transnational linkage and the economic role of the state. In P. Evans, D. Rueschemeyer, & T. Skocpol (Eds.), *Bringing the state back in* (pp. 44–77). Cambridge and New York: Cambridge University Press.
Ha, Y.-C. (2006). *Late industrialization and the dynamics of the strong state in South Korea: Debureaucratization and hollowing out.* Seoul: Seoul National University Press.
Hamilton, G., Zeile, W., & Kim, W. J. (1990). The network structures of East Asian economies. In S. Clegg & G. Redding (Eds.), *Capitalism in contrasting cultures* (pp. 105–130). Berlin and New York: de Gruyter.
Han, S.-H. (1988). Hangook jejoupui gyeyulhwa goojo hyunhwanggwa gyeyulhwajungchaek: Saengsangongjung mit boopoomgooksanhwawa gwanryunhayu. *Jungchaekdonghyang, 6*(1), 94–112.
Kang, E. C. S. (2000). Segyehwa reform of the South Korean developmental state. In S. Kim (Ed.), *Korea's globalization* (pp. 76–101). New York: Cambridge University Press.
Kim, J.-W. (1986). Sanupbaljungwa jungchaekgeuyoong. *KDI Journal of Economic Policy, 8*(1), 43–76.
Kim, C.-Y. (1990). *Hangook kyungjejungchek 30nyunsa: Kim Chungyum hwoigorok.* Seoul: JoongAng Ilbo.
Kim, J.-K. (1993a). Jungchaekgeumyoongui jaewonjosunggwa gaesunbangan. In D.-H. Song & H.-P. Moon (Eds.), *Kookgayesangwa jungchaekmokpyo: 1993nyundo* (pp. 113–176). Seoul: KDI.
Kim, L.-S. (1993b). National system of industrial innovation: Dynamics of capability building in Korea. In R. R. Nelson (Ed.), *National innovation system: A comparative analysis.* New York: Oxford University Press.

Kim, K.-S. (1994a). Trade and industrialization policies in Korea: An overview. In G. K. Helleiner (Ed.), *Trade policy and industrialization in turbulent times* (pp. 317–363). London and New York: Routledge.
Kim, S.-J. (Ed.). (1994b). *Park Chung-hee side: Geugusun wooriege moousiut-neunga*. Seoul: Chosun Ilbo Co.
Kim, H.-K. (Ed.). (1999b). *Youngyokui hangookgyungje: Bisa kyungjegihwoikwon 33nyun*. Seoul: Maeil Business Newspaper Co.
Kim, Y.-T. (2012b). *Hangookui chaebolgwa baljungookga: Hangookui chebol2* [Chaebol and the developmental state in Korea: High growth, dictatorship and the making of a dominant class]. Paju: Nanam.
Kim, E. M. (2014). The South Korean developmental alliance between business, labor and government. In I.-C. Yi & T. Mkandawire (Eds.), *Learning from the South Korean developmental success: Effective developmental cooperation and synergistic institutions and policies* (pp. 235–258). New York: Palgrave Macmillan.
Kim, J.-H., & Cho, K.-H. (1991). *Gaebanghwawa hadogeupchejeui gaepyun*. Seoul: KDI.
Kim, C.-K., & Lee, C.-H. (1980). *Ancillary firm development in the Korean automotive industry*. Seoul: Korea International Economics Institute.
Kimiya, T. (2008). *Park Jung-hee jungbooui suntek* [The park government's choice]. Seoul: Humanitas.
Koo, B.-Y. (1981). *Role of foreign direct investment in recent Korean economic growth*. Working paper no. 8104. Seoul: KDI.
Korea Automobile Industries Cooperative Association. (1996). *Jadongchagonguppyunram*. Seoul: Korea Automobile Industries Cooperative Association.
Korea Development Institute. (1980). *Hangookui jadongchagongup*. Seoul: Korea Development Institute.
Korea Development Institute. (1981). *Jadongchagongupui baljunbanghyanggwa jungchaek*. Seoul: Korea Development Institute.
Korea Electronics Association. (1999). *Junjasanup40nyunsa: 1959~1999*. Seoul: Korea Electronics Association.
Korea Federation of SMEs. (1979). *1979 SMEs poll report*. Seoul: Korea Federation of SMEs.
Korea Institute for Industrial Economics & Trade. (1987). *Korea·the United States·Japan·Brazil Jadongchaboopoomgongupboonupchegyeui bigyoboonsuk – dogeupguruesiltaereul joongsimeuro*. Seoul: Korea Institute for Industrial Economics & Trade.
Korea Institute for Industrial Economics & Trade. (1994). *21segireul hyanghan Hangook jadongchasanupui baljunbanghyang*. Seoul: Korea Institute for Industrial Economics & Trade.
Korea Institute for Industrial Economics & Trade. (1997a). *Hangook jadongchasansubui dogeupchegyewa hwalsunghwa bangan*. Seoul: Korea Institute for Industrial Economics & Trade.

Korea International Trade Association. (1977). *Joongsosoochoolsanupui gyeyulhwa yooksungbangan*. Seoul: Korea International Trade Association.

Kronish, R., & Mericle, K. S. (Eds.). (1984). *The political economy of the Latin American motor vehicle industry*. Cambridge, MA: MIT Press.

Lee, H.-B. (1969). Choigo gwanli. In H.-B. Lee et al. (Eds.), *Hangookhaengjungui yuksajuk boonsuk, 1948~1967* (pp. 393–407). Seoul: Hangookhaengjungmoonjeyungooso.

Lee, S.-Y. (1979). Joongsogiup gyeyulhwabangane gwanhan yungoo. *Kyungjukyungsangjunmoondaehaknonmoonjip*, 2.

Lee, K.-J. (1986). Gongupgibanui goochookgwa gookjegyungjaengryuk jego (1967~70). *Hangookgyungjejungchaek40nynsa*. Seoul: The Federation of Korean Industries.

Lee, W.-Y. (1989). *Direct foreign investment and technology transfer*. Industrial policies of Korea and the Republic of China. Korea Development Institute, Conference Series 89-01.

Lee, H.-G. (2004). *Hangookchaebolsa*. Seoul: Daemyungchoolpansa.

Lee, Y.-H. (2005). *Chaebolui jaemoogoojowa jageumjodal: Hangookui chaebol2*. Paju: Nanam.

Lee, Y.-H., Chung, S.-K., & Lim, Y.-J. (2004). A comparative study of 'industrial rationalization' and 'corporate reform'—The Chun Doohwan and the Kim DaeJung government cases. *21st Century Political Science Review, 14*(1), 25–54.

Ministry of Commerce and Industry. (1982). *Joongsogiupjinheungjanggigyehwoik soojungbowan yungoobogosu 1982–1991*. Seoul: Small & Medium Business Corporation.

Ministry of Finance. (1986, January). *Jaejunggeumyoongtonggye*. Seoul: Ministry of Finance.

Ministry of Finance and Korea Development Bank. (1993). *Hangookwoijadoip 30nyunsa*. Seoul: Ministry of Finance and Korea Development Bank.

Mitsubishi Research Institute. (1987). *The relationship between Japanese auto and auto parts makers*. Washington, DC: Japan Automobile Manufactures Association.

Nam, D.-W. (2009). *Kyungjegaebalui gilmokesu: Jiam Nam Duck-woo hwoigorok*. Seoul: Samsung Economic Research Institute.

No, I.-H. (1986). Daenaewoihwangyungui geupbyungwa kyunghyuppaetunui godohwa (Chongsul). In The Federation of Korean Industries (Ed.), *Hangookgyongjejungchaek40nyunsa* (pp. 560–570). Seoul: The Federation of Korean Industries.

O, W.-C. (1992, September 17). Sanupjyunlyakgoondansa. *The Korea Economic Daily*.

O, W.-C. (2006). *Parkchung-heeneun udduke kyungjeganggook mandeulutna: Boolgoolui dojun hanganguí gijuk*. Seoul: Dongsumoonhwasa.

Patrick, H. (1994). Comparisons, contrasts and implications. In H. T. Patrick & Y. C. Park (Eds.), *The financial development of Japan, Korea, and Taiwan: Growth, repression, and liberalization* (pp. 325–372). New York: Oxford University Press.
Sakong, I. (1993). *Korea in the world economy*. Washington, DC: Institute for International Economics.
Samuels, B. C. (1990). *Managing risk in developing countries: National demands and multinational response*. Princeton: Princeton University Press.
Shapiro, H. (1994). *Engines of growth: The state and transnational auto companies in Brazil*. Cambridge and New York: Cambridge University Press.
Son, G.-S. (1978, September). Yoomyungmoosilhan joongsogiupui gyeyulhwa. *Sedae*.
The Bank of Korea. (n.d.). *Kiupgyungyoungboonsuk* [Financial statement analysis]. Seoul: The Bank of Korea.
The Bank of Korea. (1984). *National income account*. Retrieved October 21, 2013, from http://ecos.bok.or.kr/flex/ClassSearch.jsp?langGubun=K&topCode=102Y002.
The Federation of Korean Industries. (1977, October 21). *Junkyungryunhwoibo*. Seoul: The Federation of Korean Industries.
Wade, R. (1990). *Governing the Market: Economic Theory and the Role of Government in East Asian Industrialization*. Princeton: Princeton University Press.
Whitley, R. (1992). *Business systems in East Asia: Firms, markets and societies*. London and New Bury Park: Sage Publications.
Witt, M. A. (2015). South Korea: Plutocratic state-led capitalism reconfiguring. In M. A. Witt & C. Redding (Eds.), *The Oxford handbook of Asian business systems* (pp. 216–237). Oxford: Oxford University Press.
World Bank. (1993). *The East Asian miracle: Economic growth and public policy*. New York: Oxford University Press.
Yoo, J.-H. (2004). *Gwanchisesang: Sijanggyungjemani sal girida*. Seoul: Chaegsesang.
Yoon, J.-H. (2006). *Hangookgisooljungchaekron: Hangook hisoolneungryuk baljun 40nyunsa*. Seoul: Gyeongmunsa.
Yoon, C.-B., & Hong, J.-K. (1989). *Hangookgwa ilbonui junjasanup hadogeupgoojo bigyoboonsuk – gajunsanupeul joongsimeuro*. Seoul: Korean Institute for Industrial Economics & Trade.
Zeile, W. (1989). *Industrial policy and organizational efficiency: The Korean chaebol examined*. Program in East Asian business and development research working paper no. 30. Institute of Governmental Affairs, University of California, Davis.

CHAPTER 5

Change and Continuity of the Korean Developmental Model

Following the 1997 crisis, the Korean economy continued to grow in the 2000s, making it a subject of constant interest of policymakers and political economists. However, the growth beyond the 2000s is based on an innovation-led growth strategy, different from traditional development based on the input-driven growth strategies discussed in Chap. 4. The objective of this chapter is to examine the difference between traditional developmental states of the past and new developmental systems developed since the 2000s.

Section 1: State-Firm Relations

Chapter 3 examined Korea's growth engine that changed from input-driven to innovation-driven. This shift was possible due to state-led intervention, not market intervention. In Korea, the developmental state has not been abolished, but the goals, means, and objects of policy have changed. The policy goal has shifted from achieving economy of scale to accumulating independent capabilities of technology development. Policy means have transformed from supplying physical resources, such as capital and labor, to the private sector to organizing an innovative ecosystem and providing opportunities for R&D of technologies. Objects of policy have changed from exclusive to inclusive, increasing the number of actors participating in the state's development policy. These shifts have been accompanied by a qualitative change in Korea's state-firm relations. This section

K. M. Kim, *The Korean Developmental State*,
https://doi.org/10.1007/978-981-15-3465-2_5

examines specifically what has changed, and what has continued, in Korea's state-firm relations.

Changes in Industrial Policy Strategies and Means

The Korean development model's greatest changes were in terms of policy instruments. Specifically, policy instruments that relied on credit allocation and discretionary orders through existing financial controls became weaker or reduced. However, policy instruments such as R&D support, regulation, and tax benefits remain valid. Under the past input-driven growth strategy, capital concentration for economy of scale was important, so financial support through direct control was the most important policy means of the state. Now, the growth strategy itself has changed to an innovation-driven strategy, so that policy means through R&D incentives are being used effectively.

Change in Growth Strategy: From Input-Driven to Innovation-Driven

The priority in Korea's previous growth strategy was to achieve economies of scale through large-scale facility investment and to secure price competitiveness in export markets. Now the goal of Korean industrial policy is to secure technological competitiveness through R&D support (Amsden 2013, p. 2; Yoon 2012, p. 249; Kang and Chang 1989, pp. 99–126; Kim 1997b/2000, p. 64).

In Korea's industrial strategy until the 1970s, R&D capabilities and infrastructure did not play a significant role. The priority, rather, was to establish a system to import mature technologies from developed countries, build factories, and export products. The Korean government was not disinterested in technology localization, but in its fervor to export products quickly, technology development, with its long lead time and high uncertainly, was not a priority. Large enterprises with financial capability mainly introduced technology through turnkey technology transfer from abroad, while SMEs, lacking capital power, acquired mature technology at most through reverse engineering. In short, there was little interest in establishing infrastructure for developing new technologies, whether by large corporations or by SMEs (Kim 1993b, pp. 364–366).

However, as shown in Chap. 3, Korean companies have upgraded to transition to innovation-led, high value-added industries. In addition, change occurred through cooperative relations between large assembly companies and components companies. This has not been a natural transition by the market, but rather a state-led industrial policy.

At present, the priority of the Korean government's industrial policy has completely changed and is now fully inclined to support R&D. R&D expenses are government-supported for technological development. If this development succeeds, the government will take measures to support facility investment and supply operating funds needed by the company until the business becomes established. Unless technology development supported by the government is achieved, the system cannot progress to the next step. To promote R&D by firms, the Korean government mobilizes all policy measures such as subsidies, policy finance, and tax benefits that were used to foster external growth until the 1970s (Kim 1993b, pp. 372–374).

As of 2014, the Korean government has invested a total of 17.6 trillion KRW in 53,493 R&D projects, accounting for 6% of 291 trillion KRW in government expenditures (by general accounting standards). This investment is in contrast to the government's 1991 public sector R&D expenditure of 79 billion KRW, which was only 0.25% of the total government spending, at 31.28 trillion KRW. The proportion of R&D projects through the government's consolidated finance is steadily increasing. In a recent five-year span (2010–2014), the government's investment in national R&D projects increased by 6.6% per annum, 1.2 times higher than the annual average growth rate of 5.3% in the government's consolidated budget (Ministry of Science, ICT and Future & Korea Institute of S&T Evaluation and Planning 2015). By 2014, major Korean government economic departments spent the following on R&D projects: Ministry of Science, ICT and Future Planning: 6.0 trillion KRW out of a total 12.6 trillion KRW (or 48%); Ministry of Trade, Industry and Energy: 3.2 trillion KRW out of a total 9.5 billion KRW (or 43%); and the Small and Medium Business Government: 900 billion KRW out of a total 2.9 trillion KRW (or 31%).[1]

The Korean government's R&D policy is part of a thoroughly selective industrial policy conducted under the goal of industrial structure

[1] See summary of settlement of accounts of each fiscal year of the Ministry of Strategy and Finance. National R&D expenditure refers to the National Research and Development Industry Survey and Analysis Report jointly published each year by the Ministry of Science, ICT and Future Planning and the Korea Institute of Science and Technology Evaluation and Planning.

advancement, and far from simply being support for SMEs from the social justice dimension or noneconomic activity such as creation of basic knowledge. Most of the major policies of the Ministry of Trade, Industry and Energy and Ministry of Science, ICT and Future Planning, which currently lead the Korean government's industrial policy, are comprised of programs designed to secure future advanced technology and policies for building R&D infrastructure. The Creative Economy Industrial Engine Project, a major industry policy of the Ministry of Trade, Industry and Energy, aims to achieve $2 trillion of trade in 2020 by exploring and supporting 13 sectors, Industrial Engines, in order to upgrade the main industry and create a new industrial ecosystem. The project consists of 13 projects including autonomous vehicles, wearable smart devices, smart-bio production systems, and supercritical CO_2 generation system in four industries: systems industry, materials and components industry, creative industry, and energy industry. Since the 1990s, the Ministry of Trade, Industry and Energy has been exploring, supporting, and cultivating future high-tech industries through the G7 project, Chasedesungjangdongryuk (the next-generation growth engine) project, Shinsungjangdongryuk (the new growth engine) project, and so on. Moreover, the K-ICT's 9 Strategic Program, which is the main policy program of the Ministry of Science, ICT and Future Planning, selects and supports nine strategic technologies such as software, contents, IoT, big data, cloud, 5G, UHD, information security, and smart device, with a budget allocation of 1.308 trillion KRW in 2016 alone.[2]

The difference between these policy programs and previous heavy chemical industry policies lies in the fact that they focus on industry innovation and technology development, which explains why the effects of government industrial policies in Korea are more difficult to feel compared to the past. The previous method of industry cultivation omitted the time-consuming technology development process and led more quickly to tangible results. However, industrial policy that focuses on technology development, rather than technology import, takes much time before results can appear. If technology development is successful, even more time is required to achieve industrialization.

[2] See the Ministry of Trade, Industry and Energy and the Ministry of Science, ICT and Future Planning homepages.

Expansion of Policy Partners

The target of state industrial policy expanded from the previous narrow focus on large corporations to SMEs and from finished goods assembly to the components and materials industry. First, rather than simply protecting and fostering subcontractors of large companies, SME policy shifted to securing the competitiveness of the SMEs themselves, making SMEs major partners in the new version of the Korean developmental state, where innovative capabilities and domestic large corporations are now used for the competitiveness of SMEs. Second, the focus of industrial policy has shifted to nurturing the components and materials industry rather than the finished goods industry. And third, the components and materials development policy and the SME policy have been synergistic since 2000 and have led the rapid growth of the components and materials industry.

Industrial policies in the new version of Korean developmental state center on SME support (Amsden 2013, p. 23). With the establishment of Small and Medium Business Administration (SMBA) in 1996, an institutional structure was prepared for the independent management of SME policies. Previously, SME policies had been managed in the Small and Medium Business Bureau of the Ministry of Commerce and Industry. However, the Small and Medium Business Bureau expanded into the SMBA, an independent organization under the Ministry of Commerce and Industry, in 1996.[3]

As of 2016, SMBA has a total budget of 1.85 trillion KRW, including 1.58 trillion KRW for general accounts and 270 billion KRW for special accounts.[4] Support for SMEs is widely implemented by SMBA and other economic departments. The 2014 budget shows that SME policy finance alone amounted to 2.9 trillion KRW; including all SME supports through loans, guarantees, and insurance, it reached 95 trillion KRW. It increased by 11.7%, compared to 2.6 trillion KRW (total amount 82 trillion KRW including loans, guarantees, insurance, etc.) in the 2013 budget (Ministry of Strategy and Finance 2013, p. 22).

With the high growth rate of SME support by the government, the share of government and public sector support in SME R&D expenditure in the manufacturing sector increased from 4.5% in 1991 to 15.7% in 2009, while the share of government and public sector support in large

[3] The Small and Medium Business Administration expanded into the Ministry of SMEs and Startups in 2017.

[4] See the Financial Statistics database of the Ministry of Strategy and Finance.

corporation R&D expenditure in the manufacturing sector has remained unchanged at 3% in 1991 and 2009. The fact that the government and public sector support had a higher share in SME R&D compared to large corporation R&D in 1991 does not signify that the amount of the fund supported by the government and public sector was higher in SMEs rather than in large corporations. In terms of value, government and public sector funding for SME R&D was only 12 billion KRW in 1991, accounting only for 18% of 67 billion KRW of large corporation R&D from the government and public sector. But in 2009, government and public sector funding to SME R&D increased to 883 billion KRW, far surpassing government and public sector funding to large corporation R&D at 552 billion KRW.[5] Government and public sector support to SMEs has increased dramatically since the 1990s.

The Korean government's SME policies existed marginally in the 1960s and 1970s. The SME credit guarantee system is a typical example. However, the necessity of SME policies has been unmistakably clear since the 1980s, when large conglomerates grew rapidly during the 1960s and 1970s, while SME growth slowed, giving rise to serious imbalances.

However, despite expanded SME support from the 1980s through the 1990s, Korea's SME policy had focused on supporting the competitiveness of lead companies representing the Korean economy, not on raising the competitiveness of SMEs themselves. SMEs were protected rather than cultivated. The 1975 Promotion of Alliance between Small and Medium Enterprises Act (Joongsogiupgyeyulhwachokjinbup) focuses on establishing subcontracting practices led by large companies rather than nurturing technology-specialized SMEs, maximizing the interests and efficiency of large companies (Han 1988, p. 109). Since the end of 1979, the SME Priority Business System (Joongsogiupwoosunupjongjedo) was formally designed to encourage specialized SMEs but, in reality, was limited to protecting SMEs from large companies with market power rather than boost their competitiveness. The Promotion of Alliance between Small and Medium Enterprises Act and SME Priority Business System were integrated into Act on the Protection of the Business Sphere of Small and Medium Enterprises and Promotion of Their Cooperation of 1995 (Baik et al. 1995, p. 6).

[5] See each issue of the National Research and Development Project Survey and Analysis Report.

However, since 1997, SME policy has begun to change qualitatively, with the combination of the Korean government's policy turn to technological innovation and components and materials sector promotion. Since the 1997 financial crisis, SME policy's focus has been to enhance the competitiveness of SMEs themselves, rather than protect them. The Special Law for Promoting Venture Businesses, which was in effect since October 1997, guaranteed various benefits such as tax benefits, corporate regulation exemptions, R&D support, and policy financing. In addition, the Korean government established an infrastructure to legalize the KOSDAQ market and establish a joint government-private venture investment company to finance small- and medium-sized venture firms (Kwon 2010, pp. 234–235; Weiss 2003, p. 257).

As a result, SMEs have become major partners in industrial policies since the late 1990s. Researchers and managers from the Electronics and Telecommunications Research Institute (ETRI), a leading government-funded research organization, observed:

> In the past, there were many big projects. Even though in a few cases SMEs participated in such projects, in a dominant number of cases, large companies launched joint ventures of development and commercialization—for example, CDMA, TDX, Automatic Electronic Exchangers, and memory chip businesses. However, as large corporations increasingly built their own research capabilities, the public R&D projects went to small and medium-sized enterprises (SMEs). In recent state-funded R&D projects, the state research centers focused on transferring their technology after collaborating with their SMEs. ... Even in the cases in which SMEs did not participate in the state-funded research projects, they often received technology transfer. This change occurred in the late 1990s. From that time on, the center for strengthening SMEs was built in our organization. The policy priority of our organization has changed. (ETRI researchers and managers, personal communication, April 18, 2013)

Another characteristic of the Korean industrial policy lies in the focus on components and materials industries, which had been marginalized in the previous Korean developmental state. As we saw in Chap. 3, the Korean components and materials industry's status in domestic and international economies has greatly increased since the 2000s. During that decade since 2001, components and materials have led the increase in exports and trade surplus in all industries, and the global export market share of the Korean components and materials industry also rose from tenth place in 2001 to sixth place in 2009. Along with quantitative growth, technological competitiveness of the components and materials industry has greatly increased (KIET 2012, pp. 12–27).

This growth of the Korean components and materials industry since the 2000s has been mainly due to the shift in focus of industrial policies from the finished product assembling industry to the components and materials industry. In February 2001, the Korean government enacted the Special Measures for Components and Materials Act as a law in force for ten years (expired on December 31, 2011) to reduce Korea's trade deficit with Japan and to expedite the development of domestic components and materials industries. Based on this act, MCT-2010 (Material and Component Technology, 2010) was established. MCT-2010, first, invested R&D funding of 1.5 trillion KRW for ten years (2000–2010) in order to localize the development of core components and materials. Second, MCT-2010 invested a total of 363 billion KRW for ten years to improve the reliability of domestic components and materials to the level of advanced countries. Third, MCT-2010 encouraged large-scale specialization of components and materials companies and supported global market entry through global partnership projects. Since 2007, the government has supported 21 merger and acquisition deals (427.5 billion KRW) of domestic and overseas companies and has promoted export contracts of $640 million through a total of 47 export conferences since 2004 (KIET 2012, pp. 10–12; Lee 2001).

To further promote the development of the materials industry, the Korean government revealed a vision for materials industry development in 2007, established a second basic plan for materials and components in 2009, and has been implementing the World Premier Materials (WPM) to provide 1 trillion KRW in development of ten core materials during 2010–2018. The project is to develop the world's top ten core materials that can generate sales of more than $1 billion in global markets by 2018 and achieve market share of over 30%. In 2011, the Korean government announced its Future Vision of the Components and Materials Industry 2020, to extend by ten years the Special Measures for Components and Materials Act that was scheduled to expire on December 31, 2011 (KIET 2012, pp. summary–1, 10).

In addition, the Ministry of Trade, Industry and Energy has redesigned its organizational system, composed of industry-specific support systems, into a functional support system and formed the Materials and Components Policy Division that would take full charge of the technology development of the materials and components industry. In 2016, the Materials and Components Policy Division's budget was 626 billion KRW, almost equivalent to the 710.5 billion KRW used by the System Industry Policy Division that oversees all of the key industries (Ministry of Trade, Industry and Energy 2015).

The policy to promote components and materials has become and could become a major industrial policy of the Korean government since the 2000s because it connects with the policy of fostering SMEs while supporting the existing economic structure centered on large corporations. If the agenda of fostering SMEs emerged as a major point of government policy since the 1980s and drifted from the economic structure centered on large corporations, the policy of promoting the components and materials industry, which emerged in 2000, created a new turning point in SME policy. In addition, the agenda to promote SMEs is also showing synergistic effects that make policy for components and materials development more important. A former Minister of Trade, Industry and Energy noted that as the need to cultivate components and materials increased, policies to foster SMEs have been unintentionally strengthened:

> Even though Korea did more export of final products compared with other countries, the profits that went to Korea were too small because many parts were imported from foreign countries. The added value in Korea was small compared with the growth of total export volume. In this situation, the government supported development of parts and materials. But the policy to support parts development was identified as policy to promote SMEs, because most parts suppliers were small and medium-sized firms. When I was the Minister of Trade, Industry and Energy (MTIE), I paid special attention to the policy for exporting T50 airplanes as a means to promote parts and material firms, because the T50 airplane contained 200,000 components. By exporting the final T50 product, we attempted to promote domestic parts suppliers. The policy to promote SMEs meant nurturing parts and material industries. (Former Minister of Trade, Industry and Energy, personal communication, April 23, 2013)

Changes in Policy Governance: Authoritarian to Comprehensive/Democratic

Korea's policy governance methods have dramatically changed since the authoritarian system of the 1960s and 1970s, when policy formulation, decision-making, and enforcement were centralized, closed, and one-sided. Korea's industrial policy governance has transformed in three ways.

First, the process of policy formulation, decision, and enforcement no longer depends on the discretionary order of the supreme commander, the president, but on the legal and institutional framework. Second, the government has established a co-governance system to create, decide on, and enforce industrial policies, involving all relevant stakeholders in the industry, government-funded research institutes, and academia. The government expresses this approach as "civilian-led industrial policy." Third, policy enforcement is not based on unilateral goal setting and support, but on a system that resolves problems through a continuous feedback process, with policy agencies and firms working together.

Former president-centered, top-down practices left formal economic ministries out of policy decisions. Differences of opinions between the ministries were not horizontally coordinated but rather vertically adjusted by the president (Ha 2006, pp. 142–154; Lee 1969, pp. 405–406; Chung 1987, 1988, pp. 509–516). However, these closed, unilateral, and arbitrary forms of policymaking no longer worked.

First, the Korean developmental state established a legal and institutional system to replace policymaking and promotion functions that had been dependent on the charisma of the supreme commander until the 1970s. According to Yoon (2012), the Korean government gave institutional discretion to the government through legislation beginning in the 1980s. At the same time, the government has expanded its policy research institutes and industrial and scientific technology research institutes, thus institutionalizing state-centered policy governance. The role of the state has been institutionalized as the subject of industrial structure advancement and supplier of science and technology. This broader and more inclusive institutionalized policy governance has shaped both a physical condition of the state's policy capacity and its ability to reinforce and reproduce policy ideology (Yoon 2012, pp. 4, 166).

Since the 1980s, the state has replaced its state-centered policy practices with a broader policy network. To this end, it established several government-funded research institutes that would complement functions of policymaking and implementation. The institutes responsible for policy research functions established in the 1980s were the Korea Institute for Industrial Economics and Trade (1981), the Korea Information Society Development Institute (1985), the Science and Technology Policy Institute (1987), the Korea Energy Economics Institute (1986), the Korea Labor Institute (1988), and the Korea Institute for International Economic Policy (1987). The institutes responsible for industrial technology R&D functions were the Korea Institute of Construction Technology (1983), the Korea Electronics and Telecommunications Research Institute (1985), the Korea Electrotechnology Research Institute (1985), the Korea Institute of Machinery and Materials (1986), the Korea Food Research Institute (1987), and the Korea Institute of Industrial Technology (1988). The institutes responsible for basic scientific technology research were the Korea Research Institute for Bioscience and Biotechnology (1985), the Korea Basic Science Institute (1988), the Korea Research Institute (1986), the Korea Aerospace Research Institute (1989), and the Korea Polar Research Institute (1987). Since then, more government-funded research institutes have been established as needed (Yoon 2012, p. 164).

In addition, the state institutionalized broader participation of the private sector in the scope of the policy network. Even though several industrial trade associations such as the Korea Automobile Industries Cooperative Association (KAICA), Korea Electronic Industries Cooperative, and the Korea Electronics Association (KEA) were established under government leadership in the 1970s, the state have formed and legalized more associations by industry since then. Twenty-seven trade associations were legally established between the 1980s and 1990s, including the Korea Automobile Manufacturers Association (KAMA, 1987), the Korea Automotive Technology Institute (1990), and the Korea Electronics Technology Institute (1991; Yoon 2012, pp. 177–178).

Second, institutionalization of the policy process was accompanied by decentralization of authority. Forming a new co-governance system, the Korean government began to engage all relevant stakeholders such as industry, government-affiliated research institutes, and academia in the process of establishing and implementing policies through policymaking agencies and private industrial associations—all a shift toward a "civilian-led" economy.[6]

[6] The stabilization policy announced in 1979 came to light under the new military regime that ruled after the assassination of President Park Chung-hee. The 5th Five-Year Economic Development Plan, established under the new military government, reflected the keystone of the stabilization policy. The direction of the 5th plan was set as "stability, autonomy, openness." In this case, "stability" meant that policy was centered on growth from price stability; "autonomy" was the shift from government-led economic management to a civilian-led market economy; and "openness" meant that the framework of economic policy fundamentally changed from protection to opening up imports and promotion of competition (Kang 2003b,

For policy formation, the government involved civilian experts in industries, academics, and research institutes. For example, in the early 1980s, the electronics industry development initiative, led by the Blue House Economic Secretariat, was made up of experts from business, academia and research institutes, government officials, and Blue House officials, who presented alternatives and eliminated contradictions to make a policy for the growth of the electronics industry. Headed by the economic secretariat team of Myung Oh and Seong-won Hong, the work was carried out by government officials from related government offices such as the communications department of the Ministry of Commerce and Industry, the Ministry of Communication, and the Ministry of Science and Technology, along with businessmen, researchers, and academic experts. The electronics industry promotion plan, formed in March 1981, was a breakthrough in the ways of governance at the time, presupposing the harmony of government support and regulation (Jung 2003, pp. 122–129). This measure was historically significant, as the way the state and private actors worked and cooperated with each other began to change from one-sided and hierarchical to interactive and horizontal.

This way of civilian participation policy formulation was institutionalized through the 1986 Industrial Development Act. The Industrial Policy Council and Industrial Development Council served as policy review bodies under the Act. If the bureaucracy-led Industrial Policy Council was led by the EPB composed of ministerial-level personnel, the Industrial Development Council was a civilian-led deliberative body comprised of 30 private experts. The Industrial Development Council was the first institutionalized body to collect extensive opinions from the civil sector such as university professors, journalists, and businessmen. Later, it accepted more bureaucrats from the Ministry of Commerce and Industry, related central administrative agencies, and the Fair Trade Commission, by revising the enforcement decree of the Industrial Development Act (Kim 2006, pp. 12–14).

Decentralization of policy governance intensified in the 1990s. After democratization in 1987, Kim Young-sam served as head of South Korea's first "civilian government." In the mid-1990s, the government reorganized the EPB, which oversaw Korea's developmental system, and consolidated the board with the Ministry of Finance to form the Ministry of

pp. 105–106). From this point on, the term "civilian-led" was reflected in the overall policy of the government.

Finance and Economy. At the time, the dissolution of the EPB was seen as a symbol of the dissolution of Korea's state-led developmentalism.

However, the consolidation was not a dismantling of the developmental state, but a decentralization. The main functional change brought on by the absorption and integration of the EPB into the Ministry of Finance and Economy was that planning, which was the main function of the EPB, was distributed to other ministries, and in return, its functions of policy coordination and budget establishment were combined with tax and finance governance functions of the Ministry of Finance. According to a former member of the EPB who later served as Minister of Commerce, Industry and Energy, the EPB was dismantled since its planning function had weakened while its coordination function grew. However, the weakening of planning by the EPB did not mean that the planning function itself of Korean developmentalism had weakened, but that the planning functions of other ministries had strengthened.

> In the early stage of development when the Economic Planning Board (EPB) led other departments within governments, departments except the EPB had few foreign-trained Ph.Ds. They did not have planning capabilities. In the early stage of EPB, there were excellent economic bureaucrats, such as Nam Duckwoo and Kim Jaeik. However, as time went on, other departments also came to have planning capabilities. Indeed, EPB experienced more difficulty in leading other departments. In addition, the meaning of the Five-year Economic Development Plans began to change. In the old days, say, the Park Chung-hee era, the Five-year Plans were regarded as significant implementation plans. However, as time passed, the significance of the Five-year Plans as a real implementation plan was tapering, becoming insignificant by the 1990s. Similarly, EPB's authority was also declining. EPB began to change its role from economic planner to coordinator among diverse and capable departments. In the past, the development tasks were simple, and a single pilot department could plan its development. However, as time went, even a single development project needed many different departments' involvement. For example, in the past, if the government planned to develop an industrial complex, the Ministry of Industry alone did it. Now we need Ministry of Environment, Ministry of Defense, and Ministry of Agriculture, as well as Ministry of Industry. More conflicts occurred among different departments. Initially, the key function of EPB was economic development planning, but later it began to focus on policy coordination as the planning function weakened. (Former Minister of Commerce, Industry and Energy, personal communication, April 23, 2013)

Third, in policy implementation as well as formation, the Korean government constructed a system that allowed policy enforcement agencies and firms to resolve problems together, establishing a co-governance system of government, government affiliates, and private sector with a continuous feedback process, which is different from the past way of presenting a goal unilaterally and supporting firms to achieve the goal.

However, this decentralization of private participation did not lessen the characteristic of state-led capitalism or lead to a transition to an Anglo-American free market or corporatist regime based on horizontal negotiations between private organizations. Korea's state-led developmental system continues; the state still initiates and leads national industrial development.

Changes in Policy Instruments

Most studies that claim the dissolution of the Korean state-led development model focus on the change in policy instruments. As stated earlier, the policy instruments of Korea's developmental state in the 1960s and 1970s lay in its ability to control and allocate resources and protection. The state equipped the mobilization system of domestic capital by centralizing control over the means of currency, finances, and banking and introduced foreign investment to supplement Korea's scarce domestic savings. Protectionism applied to both foreign and domestic markets. The state protected the domestic market from foreign companies by selectively limiting imports and foreign investments and protected selective large corporations from other companies by directly creating oligopolistic dominance in the domestic market. Through these policy measures, the state nurtured a small number of large corporations in strategic industries.

However, policy instruments that relied on direct and physical supports such as financial and tax benefits have transformed to more indirect ways based on the national innovation system. They include formal policy instruments such as government-funded technology development programs and informal networks among policy agencies, firms, trade associations, colleges, and other innovation organizations. Rather than direct market protection measures such as business licenses and tariff barriers as before, informal ways such as favorable policy support for technologically innovative companies and domestic companies also limit excessive market competition in the domestic market and protect domestic companies from foreign competition.

Through the 1980s and 1990s, most policy instruments of the previous two decades weakened and disappeared. Financial reform measures in the early 1980s privatized some commercial banks, moderating the interest gap between policy finance and commercial banks. In addition, financial deregulation measures were fully applied during the Kim Young-sam government. Gradual interest rate liberalization was achieved, and policy finance began to decline due to reforms. Control of banks was relaxed, and capital markets gradually opened (Hart-Landsberg and Burkett 2001, p. 411).

By 1992, policy financing accounted for more than 50% of annual financial loans and played a crucial role in corporate financing. However, due to Kim Young-sam's policy finance reform and reform measures following the financial crisis, industrial policy finance in commercial banks almost disappeared. Companies today are less dependent on policy finance than financing directly from the financial market or internal reserves, thus avoiding loan-oriented management (Yoon 2012, p. 256).

Protectionist policy has gradually moderated since the early 1980s. The import liberalization policy, prepared by Jae-ik Kim of the EPB in the late 1970s, was temporarily suspended with the second oil crisis in 1979, but began to be implemented in earnest as the balance of payments improved in 1982. Jae-ik Kim, senior presidential secretary for economic affairs during the Chun Doo-hwan government, started import liberalization with a mid- to long-term plan. However, opening up Korea's commodity markets was coordinated by the state. Korea's import liberalization measures progressed gradually over 20 years until the market opened and the diversity of origin system was finally abolished in 1999, compared to Taiwan, which completed the opening of the domestic market in a mere 3 years, starting in 1972 (Kim 2003, pp. 150–152).

Continuity of the Developmental State

The contents and methods of Korean developmentalism have changed completely. The focus of earlier industrial policy, which prioritized cultivation of large firms in the assembly sector with an input-driven strategy, shifted to policy that would foster high-tech companies in the components and materials sector with an innovation-driven strategy. Moreover, the Korean developmental system has institutionalized and decentralized policy formulation and implementation methods to enforce professionalism and consistency of policies, forming an inclusive policy network among industrial ministries, government-funded research institutes, large corporations, component companies, and colleges. Despite disorganization of financial control and protectionism, policy instruments based on the national innovation system also initiate innovation activities of companies and attract new policy partners, especially in the components and materials sector and new high-tech industries.

These changes do not mean the abolition or change of developmentalism itself. The state continues to play a role in coordinating the industrial innovation system as a whole. And Korean developmentalism still has a selective industrial policy rather than a universal one. Finally, when compared with the past, the subsidies for economic development have been relatively reduced, but remain very high compared to other countries.

State Coordination at the Macro Level

According to Carney and Witt (2015), one of the basic features of a developmental state is the existence of a government agency to establish and implement economic policies based on long-term national interests and industrial development (Witt 2015, pp. 548–549). In 1994 the Korean government dismantled the EPB, which was the top policymaking body in the traditional Korean developmental state. However, the functions of establishment and implementation of mid- to long-term policies for each industry still remain in the economic ministries of the Ministry of Commerce, Industry and Energy; the Ministry of Science, ICT and Future Planning; and the Small and Medium Business Administration.

The state, not private economic agents, considers Korea's entire industrial structure and plays a role in identifying its weaknesses and solutions and proposing a vision for the future. The government's role has allowed a relatively quick response during industrial upgrades and economic crises due to exogenous shocks. Faced with the 1997 economic crisis, the Korean government could rapidly shift the paradigm of industrial policy from the assembly industry to the components and materials industry because it had already identified problems and found feasible solutions in the Korean industrial structure. According to an economic bureaucrat from the Ministry of Commerce, Industry and Energy who set policy to nurture the components and materials industry following the 1997 crisis:

> The reason we focused on development of components and materials at that time was the trade deficit, particularly with Japan. However, the Japan trade deficit mainly came from the import of components and materials. There

> was widespread consensus within our government that in order to resolve the trade deficit with Japan, we needed to develop our own parts and materials. In addition, Kenichi Omae ignited our sense of nationalism by despising Korean economic development as a dependent economy. (Former director at the Ministry of Commerce, Industry and Energy, personal communication, June 17, 2015)

The Korean government's role in monitoring structural problems and seeking solutions of the national economy has persisted despite several liberal reforms since the 1997 crisis. The reform direction of the Kim Dae-jung government and subsequent governments has been to continue the state's role in nurturing strategic industries to adapt to international competition following the market opening. To this end, the mid- to long-term industrial development plans and industrial policies have continued. In 1999, with the second industrial development plan, the project for next-generation technology development and the regional project for industrial technology development were promoted. In 2000, the five-year plan was established for SME technology improvement. In 2001, the basic plan for components and materials development was established, and the Act on Special Measures for the Promotion of Specialized Enterprises, Etc. for Components and Materials (the Act on SMPSECM) formed the basis for long-term cultivation of the components and materials industry, which had been a critical weakness in the Korean industrial structure. This policy direction was succeeded by the subsequent governments. In 2004, the Roh Moo-hyun government in 2004 established the Next Generation Growth Engine Development Plan, which continued through the Lee Myung-bak and Park Geun-hye governments as a New Growth Engine Development Policy. In 2005, the 2015 Components and Materials Industry Development Strategy strengthened the development plan for the components and materials industry. The Act on SMPSECM, which had been enforced as a law in force only for ten years since 2001, was extended to expire in 2020 by the Lee government.

In addition to presenting a vision of economic policy and leading the formulation of specific plans, the Korean government has expanded its role as more active coordinator beyond only providing funding in the process of policy implementation. As shown in Table 5.1, when long-term large-scale R&D investment of main industries such as electronics was needed, the state directly promoted technology development along with major domestic large corporations, as with development of Code Division

Table 5.1 State-firm joint technology development ventures

Development project name	*Period*	*Money spent (in 100 million KRW)*	*Participating firms*
Next-generation semiconductor and infrastructure technology (16 M–64 M DRAM)	1989–1997	1914	Samsung Electronics, etc.
CDMA mobile communication terminal	1989–1996	996	Korea Electronics and Telecommunications Research Institute, etc.
HD-TV	1990–1994	1900	LG Electronics, etc.
High-speed medium-sized computer (main computer IV)	1994–1998	570	Daewoo Communications, etc.
TFT-LCD-based technology	1994–1999	568	Samsung Electronics, etc.
TDMA mobile communication terminal	1993–1995	130	Electronic Components Research Institute, etc.
DVDR	1996–2000	1200	LG Electronics, etc.
Next-generation battery	1997–2002	550	Rocket Electric, etc.

Source: KEA (1999, p. 237)

Multiple Access (CDMA), the mobile communication technology of the early and mid-1990s (Jho 2007, pp. 633–639). Developing CDMA technology spanned eight years, from 1989 to 1996, with a total investment of 99.6 billion KRW, and was led by the ETRI, with LG Electronics, Samsung Electronics, Hyundai Electronics, and Maxon Electronics participating. Through the successful development of CDMA technology, the second-generation mobile communication system, Korea, which had no mobile communication technology in the early 1990s, became a powerhouse of information technology (ETRI 2012, p. 58).

Having commercialized CDMA technology for the first time in the world, Korea formed a consortium of domestic and foreign companies to promote R&D of MT-2000, a third-generation mobile communication system, and completed its development within two and a half years. The cooperative development system, centered at ETRI, has continued to develop next-generation mobile communication technologies such as LTE-Advanced systems (ETRI 2012, p. 59).

The cooperative technology development system, directly coordinated by the state, has been Korea's basic framework for industrial innovation.

Government-funded research institutes, large-sized corporations, and small- and medium-sized component companies have jointly formed R&D consortia, which include large-scale projects such as the World Premier Materials (WPM) project to small-scale projects.

State Coordination at the Micro Level

In the changed Korean developmental system, the state has continued interventions and coordination at the micro level by adopting a way of establishing a consortium of government-funded research institutes and companies for joint technology development. This is the division of labor: governmental research institutes coordinate the overall research project and take charge of basic R&D, while firms focus on application technology development to move quickly to commercialization. This path of governance is a feature distinct to the Korean national innovation system compared to other developed countries such as the United States, Europe, and Japan, as well as Asian developing countries such as Taiwan. With Taiwan, for example, national research institutes develop key technologies and then spin them off (Breznitz 2007; Amsden and Chu 2003; Hong and Lee 2000; Yoon 2012, p. 21).

Korea's system includes large-scale research projects such as memory semiconductor development in the 1980s and CDMA technology development in the 1990s, as well as small-scale research projects to develop components for finished products (ETRI officials, personal communication, April 18, 2013; ETRI 2012, pp. 52–68). The World Premier Materials (WPM) project, a large-scale national R&D project launched in 2010, is one example. The WPM project aims to become one of the world's four major powers in the materials industry, promoting ten core materials including magnesium, secondary batteries, and silicon carbide (SiC) semiconductors, with more than 200 participating companies and research institutes. Given the time-consuming process of materials development, this project was planned to evolve over three phases: first, core technology development (from 2010 to 2012); second, application technology development (from 2013 to 2015); and third, commercialization (from 2016 to 2018) (Ministry of Trade, Industry and Energy 2016).

For government-sponsored research projects without direct participation by government-funded research institutes, a system has been formed that allows policy implementation agencies and firms to resolve problems together through an interactive feedback process. For a multiyear project, a designated committee provides annual evaluation of progress of the project. The evaluation committee judges whether the developing technology has lost its marketability, and then it recommends that the company raise its technology level to develop or speed up technology development. Companies can also receive technical assistance through government-affiliated institutes. According to the director of the material component policy team of the Korea Institute for Advancement of Technology (KIAT), one of the major policy enforcement agencies under the Ministry of Trade, Industry and Energy:

> For example, if you have a three-year project, your project is evaluated each year. However, it is important that the target of your development project changes as the market situation moves on. The development targets and performance criteria are collaboratively reconstituted by you and our evaluation committees. In the first year, we evaluate your project based on our Request for Proposal (RFP). However, in the second and third years, our evaluation committees readjust the target of the project considering the market situation—for example, saying that "Japan has already made it; we need to raise the target or shorten the development time." Our team does not evaluate the project firms only on financial performance, but also on marketability of the developed technology. (A team leader on the Korea Advanced Institute of Science and Technology team, personal communication, June 4, 2015)

Hence the state's technology development direction is evaluated and adjusted at the micro level. Such ongoing interaction between state and firms at the policy enforcement stage provides the necessary feedback to establish national industrial policies that can be tightly integrated with industrial fields in the micro level. The state can identify which firms have which technologies in which industries in the process of implementing policy programs and use the information in establishing mid- and long-term industrial visions and making specific policy programs.

The state is a core agent to organize the innovation network for technological advancement. In the changed system the state focuses on establishing an innovative ecosystem in main industries, rather than supporting and funding only a few selective corporations. Since the 2000s, the Korean government has enforced policies to encourage large companies and small- and medium-sized components companies to conduct joint R&D through the so-called Consumer-Related Technology Development projects (Head of the Materials and Components Planning Team of the Korea Institute for the Advancement of Technology, personal communication, June 4, 2015). These projects have not only reduced the uncertainty of technology development for components companies, but also have formed cooperative innovation networks between lead firms and components companies.

Medium- or large-sized corporations may not need the state's R&D subsidies, but they still participate in government-supported R&D programs. They are interested in maintaining relations with industrial policy agencies and government-funded research institutes. Once they form a relationship with the national innovation network through participation in a government project, they have access to more information and opportunities for new projects by government, public institutions, other firms, and universities in the network. According to one midsize company:

> Once we have completed a government-funded project, they gave us information about future projects related to our company. National research institutes and organizations have detailed data about private companies. Thus, when the government has a plan to localize a particular technology, it selects available firms, and sends an offer to them, asking if they can "localize the technology." In national technology development projects, we do not offer first what to do, but the government suggests a task and we play a role in implementing it. For example, we are currently working on a HUD development project funded by the government. (A manager at an electronics component company, personal communication, November 12, 2015)

In short, government R&D support has played an important role in stimulating R&D investment by private companies. The state sets the direction of industrial development, using its innovation network. Participating companies gain constant information from the network and pursue long-term interests by reducing uncertainty of technology development.

Strategic and Selective Industrial Policy

Lee et al. (2004) criticized the position that claims the continuity of Korea's developmentalism through the persistence of industrial policy, pointing out that in liberal economies, such as the United States, the government has R&D policies and provides subsidies especially to health, aerospace, military, and other sectors (Lee et al. 2004, pp. 27–28).

However, US R&D policy cannot be compared with Korean R&D policy. In the United States, R&D support goes to national research institutes and universities rather than directly to companies and supports basic research rather than development of technology that can be commercialized. In contrast, most of Korea's R&D support goes directly to companies and focuses on application and development technology rather than basic research. Supports are concentrated to main industries such as ICT and machinery. In Korea, the economic development sector accounted for half of the total 2011 government R&D budget. In comparison, the United States apportions 60% for the health and environment sector, but its economic development budget is only about 15% (Ministry of Science, ICT and Future Planning, and Korea Institute of S&T Evaluation and Planning 2012, 2015). In short, Korea's government R&D projects serve as an instrument for industrial policy.

With the introduction of the Industrial Development Act in 1985, selective industrial policy continued through its Industrial Technology Development Project (1987), Advanced Technology Development Project (1992), New Industry Development Strategy (1999), Components and Materials Development Project (2000), Next-Generation Growth Engine Project (2003), and select others. In addition, the state has invested heavily in mid- to long-term core technology development with high investment risk. In particular, the government's lead investment in semiconductor, telecommunication, and automotive core technologies has greatly enhanced Korean firms' international competitiveness. The Korean government has reduced direct subsidy in accord with WTO rules, but instead, relies on a way of early investing or financing to firms, and then retrieving the investment or loan from them after the technology has been commercialized.

Policy Instruments: Policy Finance, Tax Benefits

Major policy instruments from the past still exist, including government subsidies, policy finance, and tax benefits. Instead of liberalizing the financial sector, the Korean government has strengthened its policy financial institutions and mobilized funds needed for restructuring, technology investment, and industry development (Yoon 2012, p. 166). However, the government no longer depends on currency evaporation to mobilize massive amounts of money for large-scale facility investments. Instead, it uses maximum subsidies, policy finance, and taxation, as much as government finances and domestic savings allow.

While a major policy finance following the 1985 Industrial Development Act (Gongupbaljunbup) had been the Industrial Development Fund (Gongupbaljungigeum), a major policy finance following the 1998 Industrial Development Act (Sanupbaljunbup) has been the Industrial Infrastructure Fund (Sanupgibanjageum). From 1987 to 1997, the Industrial Development Fund spent 1.2 trillion KRW for development of industrial generic technology; from 1998 to 2007, the Industrial Infrastructure Fund invested almost 4 trillion KRW in industrial structure upgrading, balanced regional development, industrial infrastructure construction, and industrial cooperation. In addition, government subsidies for components and materials promotion, a major industrial policy since the 2000s, amounted to 1.46 trillion KRW between 2000 and 2007 (Yoon 2012, pp. 214, 216; 130). Government subsidies for components and materials development still amount to hundreds of billions of KRW annually. As mentioned earlier, the Ministry of Commerce, Industry and Energy's Materials and Components Policy Division spent more than 600 billion KRW on the budget in 2016. Most of the budget, except for operating expenses, was used for technology development and infrastructure building of the materials and components sector.

Taxation is one indirect policy instrument to expand corporate investment. Tax benefits indirectly attract corporate investment. The Korean government operates a wide range of business investment tax credit systems. According to the Ministry of Economy and Finance's *Tax Expenditure Report*, investment tax remuneration, which amounted to 394.7 billion KRW in 1998, increased to more than five times to 1979.5 billion KRW in 2007, while the temporary investment tax credit system accounted for 94% of the total capital investment tax credit, and the remaining tax credit system stayed at 1–2% (Kim et al. 2008b).

In 1982, the Act on Regulation of Tax Reduction and Exemption (Josegammyungyoojebup) was revised to allow the government to apply the investment tax deduction under Article 72 by Presidential Decree when needed to control the economy. This policy allows the state to flexibly adjust the deductible tax ratio from 6% to 10%. The Roh Moo-hyun government implemented more generous measures for encouraging business investment, including expanding the temporary tax deduction to 15% (Yoon 2012, p. 219). At the economic meeting on July 14, 2003, the Roh Moo-hyun government announced that it would increase the temporary investment tax credit rate by up to 15% in order to establish industrial infrastructures for expanding corporate capital expenditure and create new growth engines. On December 30, 2003, the Tax Exemptions Restriction Act was amended to reduce taxes on SMEs, R&D investments, and facility investment (Yoon 2012, pp. 219–220).

The changes in Korean developmentalism provide the backdrop for qualitative changes in interfirm relations. From an input-driven to a technology-oriented development strategy, the transition from cultivating the finished product assembly enterprises to developing the components-materials SME has improved the technology of components and materials SMEs, thus creating an important opportunity to change the quality of relations between Korean companies. In the next section, we will examine how relations between Korean firms have changed and how they work.

Section 2: Interfirm Relations

Chapter 4 explored interfirm relations in the past Korean development model, which were based on arms-length market relations with the under-developed components and materials industry. Relations between lead companies and their subcontractors depended on market competition like in the Anglo-American countries until the 1970s, but from the late 1970s, a vertical integration system began to be formed by lead companies in main industries. It was a unilateral system, with no horizontal interactive cooperation between the lead company and its subcontractors, signaling technical superiority of the lead company and technical inferiority of its subcontractors.

However, if one axis of the industrial innovation system is state-business collaboration in the new version of Korean developmental state, the other axis is interfirm collaboration based on vertically integrated organizations. Relations between Korean firms in terms of market structure remain unchanged with large conglomerates' superior market power and hierarchical subcontracting practices. Since the 2000s, however, major corporations in main industries have been able to grow into global corporations because of qualitative changes in interfirm relationships. At present, major Korean companies' international competitiveness is based on long-term business relations and close collaboration with component companies. Interdependent collaboration between large companies and component companies is due to the technological growth of Korea's component companies.

Continuity: Large Corporation-Centered Market Organization

Interfirm relations in Korea's industrial innovation system still depend on a large corporation-centered hierarchical structure. Although exclusive transactions have reduced compared to the past, high reliance on a few large corporations continues.

The large corporation-led market structure and innovation ecosystem has not changed much. First, many components companies still depend on exclusive transactions with their main contractor (or parent company), even though the degree of exclusiveness has been relatively relaxed since 2000. According to the KIET, in 2012, 45% of subcontractors of Hyundai Motor Group (including Kia Motors) relied on transactions within the vertically integrated organization, while 32% of subcontractors of GM Korea (previously Daewoo Motors) did so (Cho and Kim 2012, p. 79). According to this study's survey on the Korean automobile industry and electronics industry companies conducted in 2011, 53 companies out of 96 that responded to the survey make more than 50% of their transactions with a main contractor. This exclusiveness was also confirmed by the interviews conducted for this study. Most components companies that participated in the interviews conducted for this study had still traded only with one main domestic contractor, and almost 100% of them had engaged more than 50% of their transactions with a main contractor.

Exclusivity in the Korean interfirm relation has strengthened the control and support system of components companies by large corporations at the vertex of the vertical integration organization. Since the early 1980s, large companies such as Hyundai Motors and Samsung Electronics organized associations of their main subcontractors (Sootakgiupchehyubuihwoi) and began to supervise and support their components makers. Hyundai Motors Cooperative Association (Hyundai Motors Hyupdonghwoi) and Samsung Electronics Cooperative Association (Samsung Electronics Hyupsunghwoi) are typical associations of subcontractors. Registered associations of subcontractors totaled 88 in 2001. According to a study by Dyer and Chu (2000), in the first half of the 1990s, the relationship between parent and component companies in the Korean automobile industry was closer to a liberal US-style relationship, rather than based on high reliability, mutual cooperation, and long-term transactions, as in Japan. Interestingly, they found, however, that a parent company's technological support level for their subcontractors was higher in Korea than in either the United States or Japan (Dyer and Chu 2000). Technical support for its subcontracting companies by the parent company is another aspect of Korean interfirm relations based on closed exclusivity.

Since the 2000s, large companies' support for their components companies has become more systematic and inclusive. For example, in 2002, Hyundai Motors established the Automotive Components Industry Promotion Foundation (Jadongchaboopoomsanupjinheungjedan) in order to improve the quality of their components suppliers by operating quality schools, technology schools, and technology seminars with technical guidance programs within their suppliers' factories. In 2011 they also established R&D support teams to teach Hyundai Motors' R&D expertise to their suppliers. Besides, Hyundai has instituted a guest engineer system, new technology exhibitions and seminars, Suppliers' Tech Day, R&D Motor Show, and so on. According to a general manager at Hyundai Motors:

> Through two conferences per year, together we explore new technology trends and development directions. Our Hyundai research institute occasionally organizes seminars and conferences. And we continue to monitor the companies' efforts to ensure that they can follow our target. ... Our quality management teams often go to parts suppliers and help them to improve their products and production. Our teams encourage them to share their best production know-how. (A general manager on the Business Coordination team at Hyundai Motors, personal communication, October 29, 2015)

Hyundai also improves the parts suppliers' quality management and reliability of components through systematic evaluation indices. A general manager of the Supplier Cooperation team at Hyundai Motors said:

> We manage parts suppliers in a pool structure. In our pool we have approximately 420 first-tier suppliers and about 5000 second-tier and third-tier suppliers. Of these, approximately 2500 second-tier suppliers are required to receive the SQ (Supplier Quality) Mark certification while first-tier suppliers should get Five Star quality certification. The reason for operating the Five Star and SQ Mark systems is that the car directly affects human safety, and we need extreme standards of quality control to ensure safety. ... In recent years, Hyundai and Kia ranked in first and third place in the U.S. Quality Inspection Agency's evaluation. Quality control of the first-tier suppliers is stable now. The problem is in the second-tier. However, in order to improve quality management of second-tier suppliers, we have operated

a special fool-proof quality control system for the past three years. This system examines the defect rate thoroughly by attaching an automatic inspection device to each process, and we share the data with parts suppliers to reduce the defect rates. We call this system process automation. With this system we know exactly where the defects occur and solve the problem quickly. (Hyundai Motors Policy Coordination Team Manager, personal communication, October 29, 2015)

Change: Interdependent Collaboration in Business Relations

How have Korean large corporations been able to succeed rather than lag in the competition for innovation in the global market? A few Korean manufacturing corporations have grown as global players, competing in the global cutting-edge product market. This study holds that major Korean companies' competitiveness is based on qualitative changes in Korean interfirm relations, which have evolved from a unilateral power relation based on large corporations' market dominance to collaborative relations between large assembly companies and component companies. This evolution is also based on the qualitative growth of component companies.

This section examines the results of the survey conducted on the first-tier suppliers in the Korean automobile and electronics industries in 2011, and interviews with firm managers and business associations in the same industries conducted from 2010 to 2016. According to these surveys and interviews, the changes in interfirm relations among Korea's main industries share three characteristics. First, long-term trade relations have been established. Second, they have built a product development system based on close collaboration between large corporations and their core component companies, which, third, has strengthened interdependence and mutual trust.

These findings seem to be counterintuitive because the questions of unbalanced growth and unfair practices between large- and small- and medium-sized enterprises have been major issues in Korean society. After the 1997 crisis, the operating profit margin of Korean large corporations increased from 6.53% in 1998 to 7.83% in 2010, while SMEs' profit margin decreased from 6.01% to 5.55% in the same period (Cho 2012, p. 19). Simply considering the operating profit margin, we find a significant difference between large automobile companies and first-tier nonaffiliated suppliers. For example, in 2009, the operating margin of leading automobile companies was 7%, while the operating margin of first-tier nonaffiliated suppliers was only half of that, at 3.7%. In the communication equipment industry, Samsung Electronics, the leading large company in 2009, had an operating margin of 8.7%, while first-tier nonaffiliated suppliers had an operating margin of 5.5% (Chang et al. 2010, pp. 89–91, 110).

We do not deny that the gap of profit rates between lead firms and their suppliers should be reduced. When that gap is addressed, relations between Korean companies will be sustainable in the long run. However, what should be noteworthy is that growth in technology and sales of core component companies in Korea's main industries has increased since the 2000s, despite the profit margin gap. These changes will have important implications. Interdependent collaborative relations between major companies in core industries and primary core component companies seem to facilitate another change. Components companies that have grown through collaborations with large corporations have recently moved beyond transactions with large conglomerates to become global customers. Such change was difficult to realize even ten years ago, when domestic component companies depended only on the domestic market. It could have been impossible if domestic large companies expanding their overseas production had broken relations with domestic component companies in favor of global or local components suppliers.

Long-Term Transactions

The first characteristic of changed relations between Korean firms is that long-term trade relations have been established. As shown in Table 5.2, according to this study's survey in 2011, the average duration of business

Table 5.2 Transaction practice

		Existence of written contract		*Transaction duration*
		Number of companies (each company)	*Ratio (%)*	*Average (years)*
Survey results	Yes	94	96.9	16.9
	No	4	4.1	
Number of respondents (each company)		97		87

relations between lead companies and their suppliers in main industries has reached 16.9 years, revealing a change from past short-term contractual relationships. These figures are in contrast to a survey result in 1976. According to the *Survey Report of Small and Medium Enterprises* by the Ministry of Commerce and Industry and the Industrial Bank of Korea in 1976, only 46.2% of subcontractors had long-term exclusive subcontracts and 53.8% had irregular or opaque temporary subcontracts (Lee 1979, p. 12; KITA 1977, p. 125).

Hyundai Motors' long-term business relation with its first-tier partners has been fully established. According to Hyundai Motors' internal data, Hyundai Motors (including Kia Motors) had an average trading period of 28 years with their first-tier suppliers in 2014, and 78% of partner companies have had relations for more than 20 years. Additionally, 27 partner companies out of approximately 300 (or 9%) have had continued business relations with Hyundai Motors for more than 40 years since Hyundai Motors was founded in 1967 (Hyundai Motor Group 2015, p. 11).

These long-term trading practices show that business between Korean firms is based on relational networks rather than on market contracts (Herrigel 2010). For example, even when Hyundai's suppliers cannot match Hyundai's requirements, they do not stop business relations but try to adjust in order to meet the requirements. Hyundai Motors' Purchasing Management Team Manager said:

> The current method is different from that of the past, but the essence of our basic relationship is that we are still helping our partners. ... We differ from U.S. customers. In the U.S., the customers make a lot of difficult demands. ... For instance, GM demands that the parts should be made according to their blueprints. If the parts do not meet their criteria, they return them to the suppliers and take only what they are satisfied with. By contrast, Toyota continuously says to: "Make it this way, don't make it that way; we think it's better to make it this way," and "How many defects occur?" and "Solve the problems." Although Toyota demands a lot, they often help suppliers by dispatching their own teams to work with the suppliers. We also work this way. (Hyundai Motors Purchasing Team Manager, August 24, 2010)

Hyundai Motors also manage their component companies every year by evaluating quality, technology, and delivery performance. The purpose of the evaluation is not to cast off components suppliers. If the cut line is not reached, the company has one to two years to improve on its own. If the company shows insufficient improvement, the final evaluation will be to eliminate the company, but that has rarely happened. Hyundai Motors' strategy is to hold business relations for the long term (General Manager of the Procurement Planning and Strategy team at Hyundai Motors, personal communication, June 28, 2011). Relations with domestic components suppliers are a source of competitiveness for Hyundai. This idea seems to be shared by Hyundai Motors' suppliers. The section chief of the Advanced Research Institute at DY Auto (Hyundai Motors' first-tier supplier) noted:

> If Hyundai demands cost reduction and we say it is difficult, Hyundai and our team deliberate together to find what we can adjust. We sometimes reject Hyundai's demand if we cannot find a solution. However, Hyundai and our team usually find solutions together and adjust our conditions. In fact, Hyundai does not ruthlessly cut prices. If Hyundai were to do that, parts suppliers could not survive, and if the current suppliers die, that is not good to Hyundai. As far as I know, no firm has ever been kicked out of Hyundai. (Director of the Advanced Research Institute at DY Auto, personal communication, October 19, 2015)

Interfirm Collaboration

The second characteristic of changed relations between Korean firms is that lead companies and their suppliers work closely together from the early stages of product development. According to survey results, 75% of

Table 5.3 Product development cooperation method with customer companies

	Product development cooperation method with customer company (multiple responses)	*Number of firms (each firm)*	*Ratio (%)*
Survey result	Participation from the beginning of product development	72	75
	Participation from prototype stage	48	50
	Product production with customer company blueprint (rental method)	42	44
	Product production through rental method	11	11
	Companies that do not adopt the rental method	54	56
Number of respondents		96	

Note: The rental method refers to a method of producing products by receiving blueprints from customer companies components companies that responded to the survey said they participated in development of new products from the beginning of product development, and 50% responded they participated from the prototype stage. Only 11% of companies relied solely on the "detailed blueprint," which is a drawing designed by the customer. In a survey conducted by the KIET and the Korea Auto Components Industry Promotion Foundation (Jadongchaboopoomsanupjinheugjedan) of automobile component companies, only 31% of respondents used the "detailed blueprint" method to produce ordered components. Clearly, significant changes have occurred since the early 1990s when 70% automobile components companies relied on components produced by "detailed blueprint" (Cho and Kim 2012, p. 79).

Closer collaboration has been developed between major large corporations and components companies, especially in main Korean industries. When independent development is difficult or time-consuming, technology teams from components companies join the OEM or OEM's R&D personnel stay in the components company to develop components together. For example, Hyundai Motors operate a "Guest Engineer System," which dispatches suppliers' engineers to Hyundai and Kia to develop new car models and conducts joint R&D to ensure design quality early on. It shortens the development period of a new car model, minimizes the risk of design failure, and fosters technicians for partner companies. A considerable number of suppliers participate in the program, with an average of 344 partner engineers from 42 partner companies per month, as of 2014 (Hyundai Motor Group 2015, pp. 33–35).

In the electronics industry, which has much looser interfirm relations due to the high percentage of modular components, close collaboration between large and primary component companies is important for rapid innovation. A manager of a parts supplier making camera lenses for Samsung Electronics, LG Electronics, and Hyundai Motors observed:

> Since the product life cycle is very short, three months for cell phones, we cannot make our new parts every three month if we do not have close and collaborative relations with our customers. Sometimes customer teams such as Samsung and LG come here and stay for two or three months through the development of a new product. We work together to develop new products. (Sekonix department head, personal communication, November 12, 2015)

Now, long-term transaction practices and close collaborative relations between Korean firms strengthen the flexibility and rapid innovation of the Korean industrial system. Relying on close communication with OEMs, Korean components makers complement their relatively lower ability to develop new technologies than global components makers, with "customizing capabilities" to compete with global components companies. A manager of a parts firm supplying electric components to Hyundai Motors, Kia Motors, GM, and Ford said:

> Our competitors are global suppliers like Bosch, Continental, and Denso. … To compete, we focus on price and quick response to customers, because we follow them in the technical aspect. … Global suppliers have more power. They give automakers their standard products and demand automakers to change the auto designs in order to match their part products. Thus Hyundai, domestic manufacturers, and even overseas automakers have difficulties in dealing with these global suppliers. By contrast, we accept our customers' requests almost one hundred percent, and try to customize our products to meet their needs. (Director of the Advanced Research Institute at DY Auto, personal communication, October 29, 2015)

Another Korean parts supplier, which makes a semiconductor component, shared a similar story:

> The world's leading companies are so big that they take a long time to make decisions. For example, if a problem arises in global companies, it takes one month at least, sometimes two or three months, to solve the problem. Sometimes based on their power, they decline to accept that the problem is their fault. By contrast, when problems arise in domestic suppliers, they go to the customer company immediately, on that very day when the problem occurs. We go to customers and deliberate the problem together. Normally we say "we will do whatever we can," and we bring a solution to our customers in most cases within two to three days. Our solutions may or may not be correct, but most problems are usually solved in a week. No matter how difficult the problems are, we solve them at least within a month. This aspect is one of our competitive advantages. (A director in the Quality Assurance Division at MK Electronics, personal communication, November 17, 2015)

Interfirm collaboration is also evidenced through active information sharing based on informal and frequent communications. Many Korean components companies get ideas for product development from trading companies. In Table 5.6, 60% of companies surveyed received ideas for product development from trading companies. In fact, large corporations intentionally offer information on new technology trends to their domestic suppliers and encourage them to develop new technologies. Hyundai Motors Purchasing Team Manager said:

> New technologies are developed and released mainly by global companies. When global suppliers like Bosch, Denso, and Valeo develop and bring new technologies to us, first we assess when to apply them in our autos. Once we decide to adopt the new technology, initially we use what the global company made. But later we encourage and foster our domestic suppliers to quickly localize the technology. We encourage our domestic suppliers to upgrade their technology level. (Hyundai Motors Purchasing Team Manager, personal communication, October 29, 2015)

The same comment surfaced during interviews with the components company. A section chief of the advanced research institute in the DY Auto parts supplier firm noted:

> Hyundai provides basic information on a new technology to us, although it is not the core information about the new technology coming from global suppliers like Bosch. Hyundai gives us a basic conception of the new technology and asks us whether we can develop it. In that case, we actively and positively respond to Hyundai. First, we analyze the patents owned by global competitors, and then we develop a new technology by which we can avoid infringing on the global suppliers' patent right. (A section chief at the Advanced Research Institute at DY Auto, personal communication, October 29, 2015)

Collaboration with government-funded and university research institutes, as well as with customer companies, complements Korean component companies' limited R&D capabilities. According to survey results in Table 5.4, about 72% of respondents cooperated with government or university institutes in technology development. Of the 63 companies that specified cooperation partners, 68.3% had experience with government and 60.3% had experience with universities. The technology director of MK Electronics, a semiconductor parts supplier with long-term relations with Samsung Electronics, SK Hynix Semiconductor, and Anam Electronics said:

Table 5.4 External collaboration of parts companies

	Cooperation experience with government or universities	*Number of firms (each firm)*	*Ratio (%)*	*Cooperation experience with government or universities (multiple responses)*	*Number of firms (each firm)*	*Ratio (%)*
Survey result	Yes	70	72.2	Government	43	68.3
	No	27	27.8	University	38	60.3
Number of respondents		97			63	

> Another competitive advantage of our company is that we have built extensive research and development networks with government research institutes and universities. Among the government-funded research institutes in our networks are KIST and Electronic Components Research Institute, while universities include Seoul National University, Seoul City University, KAIST and Sungkyunkwan University. When feedback and requests come from our customer companies, we immediately contact researchers in our government research institute and university networks because we cannot scientifically analyze the problems internally. These researchers sometimes direct us in acquiring government development funds. In the case of this current technology, KIST proposed a development consortium with Seoul National University and KAIST and get national development funds. The consortium and working collaboratively expands and deepens our research networks. Likewise, our customer teams participate in development consortia. Through our customer teams' involvement, we can easily test our developed parts. This integration facilitates technological development. (MK Electronics Technology Director, personal communication, November 17, 2015)

Formal and informal networks of the industrial innovation system have resulted from collaboration between large assembly companies and components companies and collaboration between government-funded research institutes and companies. Through this network, large companies, component companies, governments, and universities share information about technologies, advantages, and reliability of companies or technicians. The information shared in the network enables a consortium for new technology development to be quickly built when needed.

Interfirm Reliability

Trust between companies has also formed with changes in business practices. As we saw in Chap. 4, Korean interfirm relations were characterized by exploitative and unfair relationships in the past Korean political economic model. According to a Ministry of Industry and Commerce survey at that time, subcontractors answered that low unit price, delayed payment, and excessive market competition created difficulties in business with large companies (Son 1978, p. 170). According to a KITA survey in 1977, parent companies unilaterally decided the delivery price in more than 40% of cases, and the payment method was cash settlement in only 25.6% of cases, with payment under 30 days happening in only 22.4% of cases. As a result, SMEs had difficulties in investing in technology development, equipment, and productivity (Lee 1979, pp. 11–13; Choi 1983, p. 159).

In recent years, however, unfair business practices have declined significantly, especially regarding payment. According to a survey conducted by the Small and Medium Business Bureau in 1993, the unilateral transaction cancellation by contractors reached 20.5% in the manufacturing sector and 36.6% especially in the automobile industry. In 2009, however, cases of cancellation of unilateral transactions by contractors decreased to 4.9% in the manufacturing sector with a decrease to 6.3% in the automobile industry. In 1997, cases of delayed payment exceeded 50% of the manufacturing sector and the automobile industry, but in 2009 that figure decreased in the manufacturing to 28.5% on average. In the automobile industry the figure dropped to 11.2%.

These changes in business practices seem to create trust in the Korean business system. Surveys conducted for this study show that the reliability of relations between Korean firms has significantly improved. As shown in question (h) of Table 5.5, about 60% of responding companies said that they have a trust relationship with their customers, while only about 4% of companies said that they are not in a trust relationship with their customers. These results regarding reliability are related to the level satisfaction of information exchange with customers. In Table 5.5, in evaluating the quantity and quality of information exchanges in questions (a) through (d), positive answers ranked higher than negative answers, while evaluating the possibility of information exploitation in questions (e) through (g), the rate of negative answers was much higher than positive answers.

Results of this survey show a great change when compared with the results of Dyer and Chu (2000), mentioned in Chap. 4. That study analyzed the determinants of "trust" between automobile companies and

Table 5.5 Trust of Korean inter-firm relations

Survey questions	*Responding firms (each firm)*	*Positive*		*Neutral*		*Negative*	
		Number of firms (each firm)	*Ratio (%)*	*Number of firms (each firm)*	*Ratio (%)*	*Number of firms (each firm)*	*Ratio (%)*
(a) Our company provides trading partners with new ideas on product improvement and cost reduction.	97	60	61.9	29	29.9	8	8.2
(b) The trading partners provide our company with new ideas on product improvement and cost reduction.	97	35	36.1	37	38.1	25	25.8
(c) The information provided by trading partners is very helpful to our company.	97	49	50.5	30	30.9	18	18.6
(d) We think that the exchange of information between our company and trading partners is transparent with nothing hidden.	97	31	32.0	36	37.1	30	30.9
(e) The trading partners use the information we give to oversee and use us rather than solving problems.	97	6	6.2	36	37.1	45	46.4
(f) The trading partners try to exploit the deal with our company if the opportunity arises.	97	15	15.5	23	23.7	59	60.8
(g) Trading partners often transfer our know-how to our competitors and seek competition and price reductions.	97	20	20.6	29	29.9	48	49.5
(h) We believe that we are in a trust relationship with trading partners.	97	58	59.8	35	36.1	4	4.1

components suppliers in the United States, Japan, and Korean automobile industries based on surveys conducted in 1992–1994. The trust level of Korean automobile industry firms was somewhat lower than even that of the United States as well as of Japan until the early 1990s, and most factors, such as length and intimacy of transaction relations, continuity of transaction relations, participation of capital, and other indicators, indexed significantly lower for Korea than Japan, though similar or somewhat higher than the United States (Dyer and Chu 2000, pp. 271–272).

Growth of Components and Materials Companies

These changes in the relationship between Korean firms are due in part to the strengthening of component companies' technological capabilities. Limited cooperation among Korean firms existed even in the 1990s. According to Dyer and Chu's empirical study, in the first half of the 1990s, the support level from customers felt by Korea auto components makers was higher than in either the United States or Japan. However, technology support from the customer was inevitable at that time because Korean component companies' technology level was too low. Clearly, interfirm collaboration in the new Korean business system is qualitatively different from the earlier business relation between companies that relied on the parent company's unilateral support.

As components and materials companies become more specialized, their R&D infrastructures have greatly improved. Table 5.6 shows that 96.9% of responding companies have their own technology research institute. In addition, the independent R&D capability of components companies has greatly improved, with 74.7% of responding companies stating that they

Table 5.6 Technology development capabilities of parts companies

	Possession of Technology Institute	*Number of firms (each firm)*	*Ratio (%)*	*Idea source (multiple responses)*	*Number of firms (each firm)*	*Ratio (%)*
Survey result	Yes	95	96.9	Trading partner	57	60.0
	No	3	3.1	Internal	71	74.7
				External Research	16	16.8
Number of respondents		98			95	

depend on their internal resources as a source of ideas for developing new technologies. According to a 2012 survey by the KIET and the Automotive Components Industry Promotion Foundation, among Korean automobile components companies, the way of using "detailed blueprint" in product design was adopted by only 31% of respondents. On the other hand, the way of using "approved drawing," in which the automobile company creates only the basic design of the part and the components company carries out the detailed design, was used by 60.4% of companies (Cho and Kim 2012, p. 79). These findings are consistent with the findings noted in Table 5.3. According to Table 5.3, only 11% of companies relied on "detailed blueprint" in the process of product development. Considering that the sample of this study includes relatively large first-tier component companies, most first-tier component companies in Korea's main industries currently have their own capabilities of design development.

Considering only the components makers interviewed for this research, most have an internal technology development infrastructure including personnel and equipment for technology development, allowing them to benchmark new technologies worldwide and quickly develop products that their clients want. A first-tier parts supplier for Hyundai Motors said that they prepare for orders in advance, based on their long-term relations with Hyundai:

> Once a competitor like a global supplier develops a new product in the market, we disassemble the new product, analyze, and benchmark it. We develop a concept in order to surpass that product. Before a request comes from our customers, we research ways to develop the new technology internally. Our firm has a research team that benchmarks and develops the technology and know-how of production. (Director of the Advanced Research Institute at DY Auto, personal communication, October 29, 2015)

The stable quality of Korean components makers is well recognized by domestic and overseas companies. In fact, the technological capability of Korean components makers allows them to deliver components to global companies. In the case of GM, a global automaker with the most active relationship with Korean automobile components makers, 21 of the total 82 companies selected in 2011 as excellent components suppliers for each sector are Korean companies. Technological capabilities of Korean components companies have grown to the level of becoming globally competitive (Cho and Kim 2012, p. 81). Hyundai Motors' general manager of the business coordination team noted:

> In the past, in order to get business orders from global automakers like GM, our suppliers would obtain a new quality certificate that foreign companies request, although our suppliers get Hyundai's best quality certificates like Five Star and SQ Mark. They did not recognize our quality certificates. But now global companies acknowledge Hyundai quality system certificates. There are a lot of domestic parts suppliers that deliver their parts to global GM. Global GM recognizes excellent parts suppliers and gives prizes to them every year. More than ten Korean parts suppliers have received the prize. (Hyundai Motor policy coordination team leader, personal communication, October 29, 2015)

Synergic Effect of Interfirm Collaboration

According to a general theory of technology economics, the higher the ratio of ordinary profit a firm has, the more financial and organizational resources for technology development it has, so it tends to increase R&D investment (KIET 1997a, pp. 69–74). However, empirical studies on business relations show that interfirm collaboration promotes technology development. Lyons et al. (1990) found that assembly companies can receive high-tech components by establishing cooperation with advanced components suppliers, and components companies can enhance the effects of technology developments when they follow assembly companies' development plans. Studies also show that Japan's subcontracting system is a "quasi-integration" type of division of labor that combines market and organizational factors. It is an innovation-promoting trade relationship that maintains technological superiority of assembly companies by promoting cooperation and innovation activities of component companies and engaging component companies at the technology development process of assembly companies through the so-called competition by visible hands. These studies reveal that the competitiveness of technology development in Japanese component companies is further promoted by a long-lasting cooperative relationship, or integrated systemization with assembly companies (Gittelman and Dunning 1992; Aoki 1988; Womack et al. 1990; Smitka 1991; Dyer and Ouchi 1993; KIET 1997a, pp. 78–80).

Indeed, a mid-1990s survey of Korean automobile components companies showed that a company that had a higher profit rate didn't necessarily have a higher level of technology (KIET 1997a, pp. 69–74). The study found that the technology level of Korean automobile components companies was related with the characteristics of subcontracting relation rather than profit rate. First, it was observed that the more exclusive relationship a Korean automobile components company had with its main contractor, the higher level of technology it had. This phenomenon is closely related to the development process of the Korean automobile industry, where the state pursued a development strategy focused on automobile companies to promote production and export of finished cars, and instead, development of components companies has been left to automobile companies' discretion. Second, the higher the degree of collaboration with their main contractors, the higher the technology level of Korean automobile components companies. The stronger human and asset relationship a components company had with its main contractor, the higher level of technology it had, compared to domestic competitors (KIET 1997a, pp. 80–81).

In sum, interfirm collaboration not only contributes to technology development but also plays an important role to reduce uncertainty in R&D investment. Korean components makers can compete with global components makers, despite being incomparable in terms of R&D investment size, because they minimize costs of R&D and shorten development time by eliminating uncertainties in R&D investment through long-term business relationships, close collaboration, and formal and informal communication processes with domestic large companies.

References

Amsden, A. H. (2013). *Securing the home market: A new approach to Korean development.* Research paper 2013-1. United Nations Research Institute for Social Development (UNRISD). Retrieved April 15, 2015, from http://www.unrisd.org/__80256b3c005bccf9.nsf/0/3c3c2e5f091a961dc1257b7c00470256?OpenDocument&panel=seriespapers&Click=.

Amsden, A. H., & Chu, W.-W. (2003). *Beyond late development: Taiwan's upgrading policies.* Cambridge, MA: MIT Press.

Aoki, M. (1988). *Information, incentives and bargaining in the Japanese economy.* Cambridge and New York: Cambridge University Press.

Baik, N.-K., Joo, H., Jo, D.-H., & Jun, J.-W. (1995). *Daegiup·joongsogiupgan hyupryuksiltae mit ganghwabangan.* Seoul: Korean Institute for Industrial Economics & Trade.

Breznitz, D. (2007). *Innovation and the state: Political choice and strategies for growth in Israel, Taiwan, and Ireland.* New Haven and London: Yale University Press.

Chang, S. -I., Lee, K.-S., Park, K.-S., Lee, H.-G., Hong, S.-I., Jung, E.-M., Kim, J.-K., & Kim, K.-Y. (2010). *Jooyo sanupbyul daejoongsogiup sunggwa mit guraegoojo boonsukgwa jungchaekjuk sisajum.* Seoul: Korean Institute for Industrial Economics & Trade.

Cho, C., & Kim, K.-Y. (2012). *Public policy issues arising from the auto parts business relationship shift in next-generation automotive industry*. Seoul: Korean Institute for Industrial Economics & Trade.

Choi, D.-K. (1983). A study on the systematization of medium & small enterprises. *Kyungyungnonchong, 6*, 143–161.

Chung, C.-K. (1987). Jungchaekgwajung. In Jo, Suk-joon et al. (Eds.), *Hangookhaengjungui yuksajuk boonsuk, 1968–1984* (pp. 504–521). Seoul: Seoul National University Press.

Chung, C.-K. (1988). Kyungjejanggwanhwoiuiwa jungchaekgyuljung. *Korean Journal of Public Administration, 26*(2), 370–380.

Dyer, J. H., & Chu, W.-J. (2000). The determinants of trust in supplier-automaker relationships in the U.S., Japan, and Korea. *Journal of International Business Studies, 31*(2), 259–285.

Dyer, J. H., & Ouchi, W. G. (1993). Japanese-style partnerships: Giving companies a competitive edge. *Sloan Management Review, 35*(1), 51–63.

Electronics and Telecommunications Research Institute. (2012). *Hangookjunjatongsinyungoowon 35nyunsa* [35 years' history of ETRI]. Daejeon: Electronics and Telecommunications Research Institute.

Gittelman, M., & Dunning, J. H. (1992). Japanese multinationals in Europe and the United states: Some comparisons and contrasts. In M. W. Klein & P. J. J. Welfans (Eds.), *Multinationals in the new Europe and global trade* (pp. 237–264). Berlin and New York: Springer Verlag.

Ha, Y.-C. (2006). *Late industrialization and the dynamics of the strong state in South Korea: Debureaucratization and hollowing out*. Seoul: Seoul National University Press.

Han, S.-H. (1988). Hangook jejoupui gyeyulhwa goojo hyunhwanggwa gyeyulhwajungchaek: Saengsangongjung mit boopoomgooksanhwawa gwanryunhayu. *Jungchaekdonghyang, 6*(1), 94–112.

Hart-Landsberg, M., & Burkett, P. (2001). Economic crisis and restructuring in South Korea: Beyond the free market-statist debate. *Critical Asian Studies, 33*(3), 403–430.

Herrigel, G. (2010). *Manufacturing possibilities: Creative action and industries recomposition in the United States, Germany, and Japan*. Oxford and New York: Oxford University Press.

Hong, S.-B., & Lee, C.-G. (2000). *Daemanui gwahakgisoolchejewa jungchaek* [The S&T system and policy of Taiwan]. Sejong: Science and Technology Policy Institute.

Hyundai Motor Group. (2015). *2015 Hyundai·kiajodongcha dongbansungjang choojinhyunhwang*. Seoul: Hyundai Motor Group.

Jho, W. (2007). Liberalization as a development strategy: Network governance in the Korean mobile telecom market. *Governance: An International Journal of Policy, Administration, and Institutions, 20*(4), 633–654.

Jung, H.-S. (2003). Kim Chae-ik Soosukgwa Jungbohwa Jungchaek. In D.-W. Nam et al. (Eds.), *80nyundae kyungjegyehyukgwa Kim Chae-ik soosuk* (pp. 117–142). Seoul: Samsung Economic Research Institute.

Kang, K.-S. (2003b). Keumyoongsilmyungjewa anjunghwa sichek. In D.-W. Nam et al. (Eds.), *80nyundae kyungjegyehyukgwa Kim Chae-ik soosuk* (pp. 83–116). Seoul: Samsung Economic Research Institute.

Kang, C.-G., & Chang, S.-I. (1989). *Sanupjojungui yirongwa silje*. Seoul: Korea Institute for Industrial Economics & Trade.

Kim, L.-S. (1993b). National system of industrial innovation: Dynamics of capability building in Korea. In R. R. Nelson (Ed.), *National innovation system: A comparative analysis*. New York: Oxford University Press.

Kim, L.-S. (1997b). *Imitation to innovation: The dynamics of Korea's technological learning*. Boston: Harvard Business School Press. Korean edition: Kim, L.-S. (2000). *Mobangesu hyuksineuro* (Y.-C. Lim & H.-S. Lee, Trans.). Seoul: Sigma Insight.

Kim, K.-H. (2003). Kim Chae-ik soosukgwa kookjehwa. In D.-W. Nam et al. (Eds.), *80nyundae kyungjegyehyukgwa Kim Chae-ik soosuk* (pp. 143–170). Seoul: Samsung Economic Research Institute.

Kim, C.-Y. (2006). *Choibingookesu sunjingook moontukggaji: Hangook kyungjejungchek 30nyunsa*. Seoul: Randomhouse Korea.

Kim, W.-C., Koo, J.-E., & Song, E.-J. (2008b). *Jooyogookui toojagwanryun josejiwon jedo bigyoboonsuk*. Seoul: Korea Institute of Public Finance.

Korea Electronics Association. (1999). *Junjasanup40nyunsa: 1959~1999*. Seoul: Korea Electronics Association.

Korea Institute for Industrial Economics & Trade. (1997a). *Hangook jadongchasansubui dogeupchegyewa hwalsunghwa bangan*. Seoul: Korea Institute for Industrial Economics & Trade.

Korea Institute for Industrial Economics & Trade. (2012). *Boopoom·sojae miraebijun soorip yungoo*. Seoul: The Korea Institute for Advancement of Technology.

Korea International Trade Association. (1977). *Joongsosoochoolsanupui gyeyulhwa yooksungbangan*. Seoul: Korea International Trade Association.

Kwon, O.-Y. (2010). *The Korean economy in transition: An institutional perspective*. Cheltenham and Northampton: Edward Elgar.

Lee, H.-B. (1969). Choigo gwanli. In H.-B. Lee et al. (Eds.), *Hangookhaengjungui yuksajuk boonsuk, 1948~1967* (pp. 393–407). Seoul: Hangookhaengjungmoonjeyungooso.

Lee, S.-Y. (1979). Joongsogiup gyeyulhwabangane gwanhan yungoo. *Kyungjukyungsangjunmoondaehaknonmoonjip*, 2.

Lee, T.-Y. (2001, September). Boopoom·sojaebaljun gibongyehwoik (MCT-2010). *Sanupgyungje*.

Lee, Y.-H., Chung, S.-K., & Lim, Y.-J. (2004). A comparative study of 'industrial rationalization' and 'corporate reform'—The Chun Doohwan and the Kim DaeJung government cases. *21st Century Political Science Review, 14*(1), 25–54.

Lyons, T. F., Krachenberg, A. R., & Henke, J. (1990). Mixed motive marriages: What's next for buyer-supplier relations. *Sloan Management Review, 31*(3), 29–36.

Ministry of Science, ICT and Future Planning & Korea Institute of S&T Evaluation and Planning. (2012). *2011nyundo Kookgayungoogaebalsaup josa·boonsukbogosu* [2011 Analysis Report on Government R&D]. Seoul: Ministry of Science, ICT and Future Planning.

Ministry of Science, ICT and Future Planning & Korea Institute of S&T Evaluation and Planning. (2015). *2014nyundo Kookgayungoogaebalsaup josa·boonsukbogosu* [2014 Analysis Report on Government R&D]. Seoul: Ministry of Science, ICT and Future Planning.

Ministry of Strategy and Finance (2013, September). 2014 Budget. Press Release. Retrieved November 16, 2013, from http://www.moef.go.kr/nw/nes/detail-NesDtaView.do;jsessionid=HJt1QrE19SzVkLcKUo2YIMts.node10?searchBbsId1=MOSFBBS_000000000028&searchNttId1=OLD_4016779&menuNo=4010100.

Ministry of Trade, Industry and Energy. (2015). *2016nyun yesan mit gigeum-woonyong gyehwoik saupsulmyungjaryo sanupjungchaekgwa, sojaeboopoom-sanupjungchaekgwan, siseutemsanupjungchaekgwan.* Ministry of Trade, Industry and Energy. Retrieved August 10, 2016, from http://www.motie.go.kr/motie/ms/mg/budgeting/bbs/bbsView.do?bbs_seq_n=36&bbs_cd_n=24&currentPage=1&search_key_n=&cate_n=&dept_v=&search_val_v=.

Ministry of Trade, Industry and Energy. (2016, April 7). *World Premier Materials (WPM) Saup, 2dangye saup sunggwajunsihwoi gaechoi.* Policy Briefing. Retrieved August 20, 2016, from http://www.korea.kr/policy/pressReleaseView.do?newsId=156121064.

Smitka, M. J. (1991). *Competitive ties: Subcontracting in the Japanese automotive industry.* New York: Columbia University Press.

Son, G.-S. (1978, September). Yoomyungmoosilhan joongsogiupui gyeyul-hwa. *Sedae.*

Weiss, L. (2003). Guiding globalization in East Asia: New roles for old developmental states. In L. Weiss (Ed.), *States in the global economy: Bringing domestic institutions back in* (pp. 245–270). New York: Cambridge University Press.

Witt, M. A. (2015). South Korea: Plutocratic state-led capitalism reconfiguring. In M. A. Witt & C. Redding (Eds.), *The Oxford handbook of Asian business systems* (pp. 216–237). Oxford: Oxford University Press.

Womack, J. P., Jones, D. T., & Roos, D. (1990). *The machine that changed the world: The story of lean production.* New York: Harper Perennial.

Yoon, D.-Y. (2012). *Crisis of export-led development and the politics of industrial policy, 1980–2007: Idea, institution and developmental governance.* Seoul: Yonsei University Dissertation.

CHAPTER 6

Politics of Evolution

The characteristics of the Korean economic development model are not based on the advantages of the free market, and nor on the rationality of bureaucracy in the developmental state. Korea's sustainable development was possible because it shifted from an earlier input-driven growth strategy to an innovation-driven growth strategy based on technological advancement and the knowledge economy. We argue that Korea's state-led capitalist system has been maintained not merely by market forces but by continuous state intervention. However, continuation of this state-led system does not mean that there has been no change. Rather, the system continues because it could change the method and means of realization.

South Korea has shifted from a structure focusing on economies of scale and nurturing a few conglomerates based on an "input-driven" growth strategy to a comprehensive and inclusive innovation system that includes small- and medium-sized components companies. Interfirm relationships between components makers and large assembly companies have shifted from simple exploitation to long-term collaborative systems in main industries, thus reinforcing the state-led comprehensive innovation system. State intervention, which relied on forced mobilization and concentration of capital in the past, was transformed into a structure based on a democratic legal system. In addition, the policymaking process changed from a hierarchical top-down system centered on the president and a handful of chaebols to a more comprehensive partnership that includes

K. M. Kim, *The Korean Developmental State*,
https://doi.org/10.1007/978-981-15-3465-2_6

relevant government departments as well as industrial associations, government-funded research institutes, private experts, and firms.

We define this transition as the evolution of the Korean capitalist model from an authoritarian developmental system to a democratic developmental system. The question is: How did the Korean capitalist model evolve into a more democratic developmental system—a type of state-led capitalism—rather than an Anglo-American free-market system or corporatist coordinated capitalism with equal participation from labor?

Most discussions on the changes in the Korean capitalist system emphasize the external shocks and pressures of the 1997 financial crisis and globalization. Scholars, including Paul Krugman, say that the developmental state in East Asia has been demolished and transformed into neoliberalism due to the 1997 financial crisis, since governed financial practices have been dismantled and the financial markets have been forced to become autonomous (Krugman 1998; Jayasuriya 2000; Pirie 2008). Even developmental state theorists, like Chang and Evans (2005), observed that the developmental state in Korea has completely disintegrated since 1995 when it joined the OECD. According to Chang and Evans (2005), Korea had to adapt to the free trade rules required by international organizations, such as the WTO and OECD, in the mid-1990s, rendering various financial and industrial policies typical of the 1970s no longer useful.

We agree with previous studies that exogenous environmental changes triggered changes in the Korean political economic model. But the pressure of change itself does not explain the direction of change. Since the end of the 1970s, changes in the international political economic environment have continued to apply pressure to dismantle Korea's state-led developmental system, but the Korean developmental system did not simply shift to a market liberal system or a corporatist system. In addition, large Korean companies began to compete in the globalization of production in the 1990s, but they have tended to strengthen their business relations with domestic components companies rather than cut them off, as in the case of large US corporations.

Some studies emphasize change in the domestic political environment due to democratization. These studies argue that democratization in 1987 disrupted the existing authoritarian developmental state and transformed it into a liberal regulatory state or strengthened the possibility of corporatist regime (Moon and Kim 1996; Moon 1994; Kim 2014; Hundt 2005). By focusing on changes in politics and coalitions of domestic political groups, they contributed to an understanding of the political process of change, rather than emphasizing exogenous shock.

However, this perspective ignores the possibility of change to a more democratic developmental state like Japan on the premise of more inclusive participation, by equating the state-led developmental system with the past imperative mobilization system or the exclusive coalition between the state and chaebols. Even approaches focusing on the dynamics of the domestic political economy emphasize exogenous shocks or one-dimensional aspects like the weakening of state autonomy due to the emergence of interest groups. These approaches lack a systematic analysis of the political process of interactions between key actors, such as state bureaucrats, large corporations, and SMEs, which limits the understanding of the direction of change.

This work attempts to understand the uniqueness of the evolution of Korean capitalism. To understand why the Korean development model has shifted from authoritarian developmentalism to a democratic but still state-led developmentalism, this work relies on a discursive institutional approach that focuses on the interactions of major actors and the reinterpretation of actors' interests in their political processes.

We argue that the Korean economic development model maintained a form of state-led capitalism while introducing a more market-oriented and democratic governance system when faced with the pressure of change for the following reasons. First, it argues that the direction of change in the Korean political economy resulted from political processes of main actors that have adapted to environmental changes. Rather than resulting from the master plan of one institutional actor, the direction of evolution has been determined from a process of constantly rebalancing interests of main actors and rearranging their institutional roles in adapting for survival. This perspective differs from existing change theory, especially seen in class coalition theory, which assumes that a class has a fixed policy preference and the direction of change is determined by the balance of power between classes. The transformation of Korean capitalism is not a consequence of change in the balance of power between major political powers, but rather a process of adaptation and compromise in which major actors such as state bureaucrats, large corporations, and SMEs adapt themselves to changing circumstances to secure the survival and legitimacy of their own organizations.

Furthermore, we argue that the evolutionary process of Korean economic development is not a simple dichotomy of change or continuity;

both change and continuity constitute the same evolutionary process. In short, we suggest that continuity of Korea's state-led capitalism model was possible through changes in policy priorities and instruments, and through continuous efforts of adaptation. Main actors, including the state, changed to produce new industrial strategies for a changing situation both at home and abroad.

In this chapter, we examine the unique characteristics of the evolution of the Korean development model to explain why Korea has moved to a democratic developmental system, still a version of the state-led capitalist system, rather than an American free-market system or a European corporatist capitalism. This chapter focuses on key actors and how they redefine their interests and strategies in the process of real political interactions.

Section 1: Pressure of Change

Changes in International Political and Economic Environment

Change in the Korean development model began with the overproduction crisis in the heavy chemical industry in the late 1970s and the liberalization and stabilization measures of the 1980s. Overproduction resulted from a state development strategy based on industrial linkages rather than market consumption. While rooted in an endogenous cause—the policy of developmental states supporting the heavy and chemical industrialization—the problem was triggered by deterioration of the international economy with the 1970s oil shock. Such changes in the international environment open the door to problems as well as to changes. None of this, however, determines the direction of change. States' responses to the oil shock varied widely, depending on their political economic institutional conditions and their different interpretations of the crisis.[1] This section examines the external crises that triggered changes in Korea's developmental state.

The critical crises of note were the second oil shock in the late 1970s and the Asian financial crisis in the late 1990s. Shortly after the second oil crisis in 1979, the Korean economy experienced a −1.9% in growth rate in 1980, the first negative growth since the rapid economic growth in the early 1960s. To stimulate the economy, the Korean government used a

[1] See Katzenstein (1985), Hall (1986), and Scharpf (2000) for different states' responses to oil shocks.

demand expansion policy, which lowered the interest rate, raised policy finance for export, and raised the target amount of currency. As a result, the increase rate of wholesale price rose from 11.6% in 1978 to 18.8% in 1979 (Nam 2003, pp. 47–48). The bigger problem was that with a shrinking global economy, the heavy and chemical industry's capacity utilization rate decreased, which exposed the industry's overproduction problem. This raised a doubt about Korea's existing state-led industrial policy and provided the opportunity to shift to a neoliberal policy change promoted by neoliberals on the EPB.

Crisis itself can point to a very different direction for solution, depending on how it is understood: what the nature of the problem is, who recognizes it, and how it is framed. However, despite the debate about the wrong policy, the crisis in the late 1970s did not cause the retreat of the developmental state itself and the policy of cultivating major export industries. Although there were some debates and conflicts among policymakers on the solution of crisis, the government's support of strategic industries itself was not recognized as a problem.

The 1997 financial crisis is typically referred as a critical cause of the transformation of the Korean developmental state. In 1997, the Asian financial crisis led to a sharp decline in domestic foreign exchange reserves, which brought the Korean economy to a financial crisis. Korea had to receive funding from the IMF for the first time after it left the aid economy in the 1950s. Korea's economic growth rate dropped to −5.7% in 1998, putting the Korean economy in a deeper recession than in 1979. The turning point of 1997 was once again a great moment of neoliberal change in the Korean economic model, introducing neoliberal reform measures at the expense of IMF aid.

Although 1997 has brought about radical changes that could be called the dismantling of the Korean developmental state, the direction of the solution and change was not toward an Anglo-Saxon free-market economy. In overcoming the crisis, Korea improved its past government financing practices and strengthened more independent financial supervision while continuing various industrial policies to foster the export sector. The government strengthened the competitiveness of large conglomerates through a "Big Deal," a business exchange measure between chaebols, and expanded industrial policy partners to small- and medium-sized components and venture companies. State intervention was strengthened to fundamentally transform the existing development strategy supporting the assembly industry based on large enterprises.

Additional pressures from the United States and international organizations to open and liberalize, while not as severe as the pressure caused by the economic crisis, served as exogenous pressure on the direction of Korean capitalism. Since Korea's transition to an export-oriented strategy in the 1960s, the state has secured more export markets by being part of the global economic system and in return has had to open up the domestic market—an unavoidable structural factor of the industrialization strategy for export growth. Korea became an official member of the General Agreement on Tariffs and Trade (GATT) in 1967 and moved to a member of GATT11 in 1979. In 1989, it began to relax restrictions on imports from nontariff barriers. In 1999, it abolished the import diversification system. As a result, the average tariff rate has fallen from 34.4% in 1981 to 9.8% in 1995, while liberalization of quantity regulation has increased from 70.7% to 92.0%, reaching the liberalization level of OECD countries. Joining the WTO in 1995 and the OECD in 1996 further strengthened the pressure on the Korean economy to open up (CCKE 2011a, pp. 84–85; Kim 2001, p. 82; OECD 1994, p. 64).

Since the end of the 1970s, the protectionism of developed countries has strengthened, and Korea has begun to suffer from trade frictions in export markets. The Korean electronics industry, which had grown rapidly since the 1970s, recorded exports of $55 million in 1970, followed by exports of $1.5 billion in 1988, maintaining a rapid annual growth rate of 37% since 1970. However, this increase in exports caused trade friction with developed countries. In particular, due to Korea's 1982 trade surplus with the United States and again in 1986, the United States and the European Community (EC) introduced a new form of import regulation, antidumping investigation. Starting with the 1983 color TV antidumping suit, the United States imposed antidumping duties on Korean-made electronic components such as PCBs and CPTs, which were exported to US factories such as GoldStar factory in Huntsville, and Samsung Electronics' New Jersey factory. The EC started antidumping proceedings against almost all major products including VTRs, color TVs, CDPs, and videotapes, starting with the microwave oven antidumping suit in 1986. Since 1988, the EC has not granted Korea GSP (general preferential tariff) benefits, making Korea's exports to the EC more difficult. Antidumping lawsuits have also taken place in Canada and Australia since the early 1980s (KEA 1999, pp. 171–174).

Protectionism of developed countries had a characteristic of techno-nationalism as well as direct trade barriers (Ostry and Nelson 1995). The strengthening of techno-nationalism has triggered the qualitative change of Korean capitalism. As the Korean economy grew, more developed countries were reluctant to relocate their technologies to pursuers like Korea. Even with copyright contracts, developed countries refrained from the technology transfer contracts. In particular, Japanese companies, on which Korean corporations were heavily reliant, in the 1980s became severely wary of Korean companies. The pressure of techno-nationalism in these developed countries provided Korea with an opportunity to fundamentally revise its input-driven development strategy, which relied on large-scale capital investment and low-cost labor supply on the premise that foreign technology would be introduced, because introduction of foreign technology became difficult (Kim 1993b, p. 367, 1997b/2000, pp. 56–64).

Techno-nationalism of advanced countries is an external factor that most late developing states face during the course of their development. Yet all late developing states subject to similar conditions do not always succeed, like Korea, in transitioning to an innovation-led economy. South American countries, such as Mexico and Brazil, which were developing countries similar to Korea, failed to shift to an innovative, high value-added production system.

Diverging paths in developing countries depended on interpretations of crises and solutions. Korea had not also recognized the problem as a limitation of input-driven strategy until the mid-1990s, despite the fact that domestic and foreign economic conditions such as techno-nationalism and deepening trade deficits with Japan continued to act as pressures for change. As a result, the transition from an input-driven economy to an innovation-led economy had to be postponed until the late 1990s.

External factors cannot explain every aspect of the transition. The transition to a new system is not merely a natural consequence of the market mechanism but requires political interactions and coordination among major actors. Korea's late 1990s shift to an innovation-led strategy centered on components and materials companies resulted from the politics of main institutional actors in the Korean political and economy, and was initiated especially by the state, as in the great turn to export-oriented strategy in the mid-1960s.

Changes in the Domestic Political and Economic Environment

Some studies hold that democratization and changes in the balance of power between state and large corporations are important factors for explaining the changes of the Korean capitalism system.

As economic growth had continued at more than 10% per year for about 20 years since the early 1960s and especially growth benefits were concentrated in large corporations, large conglomerates came to account for a major portion of the Korean economy. In 1984, the top ten conglomerates in Korea accounted for 67.4% of GNP. R&D investment, which was dependent on the state in the past, began to increase in private sector, mainly by chaebols (Hahm et al. 1994; Yoon 2006, p. 84). At the same time, from the late 1970s, signals emerged that the state could not control large conglomerates. Chaebols' real estate speculation mushroomed, and in the early 1980s, mergers and acquisitions of small- and medium-sized enterprises by large corporations unfolded indiscriminately (Amsden 1989, p. 131).

This brought about the change of relation between the state and large corporations. The growth of large conglomerates meant a relative reduction in the state's economic management capacity and power. In the 1960s and 1970s, organized private sector (chaebol) interests were only secondary considerations in the process of establishing and enforcing the Korean government's economic policies. But in the 1980s and 1990s, the Korean state's influence has gradually weakened. In the early 1980s, the Chun Doo-hwan government's weakening of state control over banks and finances in order to gain the support of the capitalist group decisively weakened the influence of the state on chaebols. Meanwhile, the influence of chaebols on the market increased rapidly (Yoon 2006, p. 88).

This change in balance of power between state and large corporations has caused a great change in the existing authoritarian developmental state. The growth of large conglomerates has made them relatively free from the system in which they depended absolutely on the state's capital procurement policies.

Another domestic political element that sparked a transition to Korean capitalism is democratization. The pressures to democratization in "Spring of Seoul" in 1980 and again in 1987 have become major causes for the past authoritarian developmental state to no longer function. The sudden death of President Park Chung-hee in 1979 and the political instability that led to another coup d'état of the new military group reinforced the desire for democratization, serving as an opportunity to reflect on the overweighted support for large corporations in line with the demands of improvement of political and economic equality. As a result, after the early 1980s, regulations on large corporations and support for SMEs were raised as major agendas, and these demands were adopted by the Chun Doo-hwan regime, which needed policy shifts to justify the coup. However, as we shall see later, the SME support policy at this time was different from the small- and medium-sized components and materials support policy established in the late 1990s. Still, the SME policy starting at this time influenced the formation of new industrial policies in the 1990s through the reflective thinking of industrial policymakers.

The 1987 democratization of Korea served as a direct pressure on the change of Korean political economy. Specifically, it led to the transition from imperative discretion, the main policy tool of the existing authoritarian regime, to legal and institutional discretion of state governance. Democratization also increased the pressure to raise wages so that Korea could no longer stay in a low-wage-based input-driven strategy. Along with democratization, labor and capital began to claim that the state should dismantle its existing method. Labor argued that the state should control the power of the chaebol while raising the problems of imbalanced growth, and capital demanded that the state reduce its intervention in the economy (Kim 2014, pp. 247–248).

However, not all of these new pressures resulted in realistic changes. The problem of chaebol-centered imbalanced growth raised by the labor remains. Nor has Korea been able to develop into a European corporatist capitalism with labor participation, due to the lack of labor organizational capacity. The authoritarian attribute of imperative discretion has disappeared, but the state's industrial policy based on legal and institutional discretion has remained in effect.

In addition, frequent change of political power caused by democratic elections has added new pressure on policy sustainability. Some observers suggest that the economic performance of the Park Chung-hee regime was made possible by its 20-year rule. Indeed, frequent government change currently hampers the efficiency of the Korean developmental system, making it difficult to establish and enforce policies in the long term.

The pressures of these changes, whether international or domestic, have been the backdrop for change or provided opportunities that triggered change, but these pressures did not determine the direction of change. Despite changes in foreign and domestic political and economic order caused by globalization and democratization, Korea has developed a new form of developmentalism. The process of substantial change was endogenous, caused by the politics of major actors in the Korean political economy, who have adapted to exogenous and internal changes, reinterpreting their interests and restructuring their strategies based on their capabilities.

Section 2: Politics of Evolution

Korean developmentalism underwent major changes in content and method through the 1980s and 1990s. In terms of content, the transition from input-driven growth strategy to innovation-led growth strategy was achieved. Changes in methods accompanied the transition from authoritative dirigisme, protectionism, and narrow coalition between state and large corporations to more extensive and more horizontal innovation networks that include SMEs, national research institutes, and university research centers in policymaking and enforcement.

Here exogenous pressure did not determine the direction of change. Rather, the direction of change was determined by the political process in which actors were looking for alternatives based on their institutional capabilities in the face of pressure to change.

Despite the pressures of globalization, Korea's economic system has been based on the state's will to sustain developmentalism rather than seek neoliberal alternatives. State intervention in the Korean political economy has been justified by a commitment to an export-led growth strategy and the need to support strategic industries for export. When the state-led heavy and chemical industrialization was in crisis in the late 1970s, a solution adopted by policymakers lay in cultivation of new export-led industries such electronics industry including semiconductors. Even in the aftermath of the 1997 financial crisis, policymakers emphasized the development of the components and materials industry for upgrade of export-led industries. Export-led industrialization has become an ideological base that justifies the active intervention of the state to strengthen the international competitiveness of strategic industries.

The state's efforts to sustain developmentalism were effective because they were based on the capability of the state to do so. More importantly, the capabilities were reinvigorated by exploring new means and methods amid changes in domestic and international circumstances. In the face of the severe economic crises of the late 1970s and the late 1990s, when doubts and debates were proposed on state-led developmentalism, the Korean developmental state justified the continuation of developmentalism by changing its way of governance, rather than abolishing it. As we saw in Chap. 5, the institutionalized governance system of industrial policy has guaranteed and expanded participation of private sector in the process of policymaking and enforcement, apart from authoritarian dirigisme and reliance on financial control.

The institutional capability of the state has influenced which alternative actors would adopt when faced with the pressure of change. Main actors in the Korean political economy have taken advantage of existing institutional capabilities rather than pursue a completely new alternative every time a crisis arises. In 1997, the state tried to overcome the crisis through a developmental alternative rather than neoliberal or corporatist alternatives. In 1997, Korea faced a serious crisis of state-led developmentalism, but the state tried to overcome the crisis through a developmental alternative, rather than a neoliberal or a corporatist alternative, by suggesting an innovation-led development strategy, once again justifying the continuation of developmentalism. The strategy justified developmentalism by extending the partnership of industry policy to small- and medium-sized enterprises, not just large corporations, and emphasizing the necessity of nurturing components and materials sector.

Still, why could Korea not pursue a corporatist alternative despite strengthening the relative power of large conglomerates in relations with the state and the growth of organized labor after democratization? Simply, it was caused by the weak institutional capability for a corporatist alternative. With the establishment of a progressive government in 1997, a corporatist tripartite consultation mechanism to overcome the crisis was attempted. The government, newly launched through the presidential election in December 1997, established the Korea Tripartite Commission (Nosajungwiwonhwoi). The state hoped to resolve the problem through social consultation rather than conflicts in the crisis situation where the sacrifice of all social actors was required. Labor, recognized as an official negotiating partner at the national level, took a positive stance on participating in the Tripartite Commission. Capital traditionally tended not to recognize labor as an official negotiating partner but participated in the Commission to win concessions regarding layoffs in the context of restructuring. In the crisis situation, the corporatist alternative emerged as a viable option, which means that the will of social actors to solve the crisis by a social consensus existed at that time (Lee 2011, pp. 69–70).

But the results were not so positive due to a lack of institutional capability to realize the will of the actors. Importantly, the institutional capacity of labor was absent. After democratization in 1987, the democratic union movement developed, and gained its legal status with the establishment of the progressive government in 1997, thus giving labor a greater voice than before. Nonetheless, labor's organizational ability in Korea has not yet developed at the macro level and micro level.

At the macro level, limitation of organized labor was caused by the low rate of organized labor and the traditional corporate union system, under which the trade unions at the national level could sanction their umbrella unions, even if they failed to abide by the decision of the national trade unions such as the Korean Confederation of Trade Unions (KCTU) or the Federation of Korean Trade Unions (FKTU). The union density stood at 12.2% in 1998, slightly up in the early 2000s, but declined again, with only 10.3% in 2012. In addition, the strength of traditional corporate-specific unions has raised organizational difficulties in resolving differences of interests between the upper and lower unions. Despite the Tripartite Commission's establishment in 1997 and reaching a certain amount of agreement, the noncooperation of individual labor unions finally led to a deadlock in the Commission (Lee 2011, pp. 86–88). The state also lacked the institutional ability to persuade or force a noncooperative negotiating partner. For this reason, the Commission has maintained only a formal framework, but hasn't yet secured legal and normative binding power.

At the micro level, organized labor has not developed any partnership with management within the company, despite the development of the enterprise-specific union. Historically, by being excluded from the developmental system based on the alliance of the state and chaebols, Korean labor has stood not only against the state but against the capital through conflicts and disputes in pursuit of its own interests, lacking its capabilities as a partner on the supply side. Due to the labor-capital conflict, Korean companies have increasingly limited labor's roles in the production system, rather than enhancing employees' skills and productivity through systematic cooperation with organized labor. Instead, they have developed an engineer-centered production system (Jo 2005).

Hence Korea's corporatist experiments have failed due to a lack of institutional capacity. Indeed, if social consensus could have been reached through compromise as a functional alternative to institutional capacity, Korea could have developed a corporatist alternative similar to Ireland since 1987. However, Korean institutional actors have failed to make corporatism a viable option by failing to address the limitations of institutional capacity as well as ideological conflicts (Kim 2010).

Meanwhile, a developmental alternative, which was more successful than a neoliberal or a corporatist alternative, served as an indirect cause of changes in interfirm relations. In traditional Korean interfirm relationships, large companies have used their relations with domestic components suppliers in limited ways. Since the 1980s, Korean companies have developed a vertical integration system similar to Japan's, but in the system roles of components suppliers limited to only partners for production of simple components rather than as partners for technological cooperation. As referenced in Chap. 4, large companies preferred strategies to import or internalize for core components. This strategy was mainly due to the low development of local components suppliers. If a domestic components supplier localized a core component technology, it could reduce costs for large companies while increasing its bargaining power with foreign components suppliers. Nevertheless, until the mid-1990s, large companies were not interested in raising the technological skills of their domestic suppliers because they deemed it not worth their time or cost.

However, since the late 1990s Korean large companies have begun developing strategies to strengthen technological cooperation with local components suppliers, which was a political result of the Korean globalization process. After the 1990s, as major industries such as electronics and automobile expanded their overseas production, Korean large companies had difficulty in establishing production networks in overseas production sites. They then recognized the need for a components procurement system that could secure their bargaining power but still guarantee a technological level. This motivated large companies to use their components suppliers at home. Nevertheless, a strategy to use domestic components suppliers would have been a still highly uncertain option for large Korean companies, if domestic components suppliers had failed to achieve the technological level demanded by large companies.

Korean components and materials companies began to be strengthened in the late 1990s when the state established an innovation-driven industrial policy centered on components and materials companies and started fostering components and materials industries. Prior to the government's incentive policy, Korean small- and medium-sized components suppliers lacked the resources and motivation to invest in technology development on their own. The incentive policy created a virtuous cycle that further promoted technological advancement of components suppliers by strengthening their technical cooperation with successful large business groups. The explosive growth of the components and materials industry since the 2000s was the result of domestic production increase in the Korean globalization process.

This virtuous cycle, established between large companies and components suppliers, is limited to core components suppliers in main industries. Yet this form of interfirm collaboration is a new practice in the Korean political economy, which is an engine to maintain the growth and competitiveness of Korean core industries.

In the following sections, this study traces how Korea has succeeded in transforming from an input-oriented economy to an innovation-driven economy in the face of the late 1990s crisis, focusing on relationships between state and business and between lead firms and their suppliers. Adjusting to changing international political and economic environments, how could Korean policymakers reproduce developmentalism by strengthening its legitimacy rather than abandoning it? Despite increasing belief in neoliberal efficiency, why have Korean firms moved from their traditional arms-length relationship to a selective but closely cooperative one?

Relationship Between State and Business

The economic crises of the late 1970s and the late 1990s and the pressure of globalization and democratization have raised doubts about the state-led developmental principle. Initially, the question "Were the economic policies going in the right direction?" lay at the heart of the matter. For example, criticism was raised that the 1970s heavy and chemical industries led to excessive investment and caused a serious economic crisis with the second oil shock late in the decade. The second question related to more fundamental problems: "Is state-led developmentalism effective as an economic development model?" It was a question of whether the state could make better judgments than the market. For instance, the problem of overinvestment in the late 1970s was pointed out not a mere misjudgment of the state but an inevitable limitation of state intervention itself.

However, such pressures of change did not result in the dismantling of the state-led developmental system; state-led developmentalism was directly related to the organizational understanding of bureaucratic groups, especially economic policymakers. But this was no mere resistance of institutional actors who benefit from the system, as explained by the path dependency of institutionalism. The system cannot continue simply with organizational understanding, given that the effectiveness of state-led developmentalism is constantly being challenged by changes in the international and domestic environments. New justification for the continuity of the system was necessary to promote the survival and stability of the organization. Main institutional actors in Korean developmentalism, especially economic policymakers, have sought new justification for continuing developmentalism by changing the direction and governance of industrial policy to solve the problems raised to state-led developmentalism. The validity of this justification to date suggests an absence or weakness of a new "path-breaking" alternative to the legitimacy of developmentalism, whether neoliberalism or corporatism, in Korea.

In this section, we explore the relations between state and business for reasons for how the state could maintain its state-led developmentalism despite changes in domestic and international political and economic situations. In particular, we focus on policymakers who defined the causes of crises and led the solutions and companies that adjusted to policy change. We will also examine how state-led industrial policies have been redefined and justified amid competition among major economic ministries.

Competition in Bureaucracy and Transformation of Industrial Policy Governance

Transformation in Korean developmentalism arose from internal politics among economic ministries. Competition between the EPB and the Ministry of Commerce and Industry, which started from the heavy and chemical industrialization policy of the mid-1970s, triggered a change in Korean developmentalism, but at the same time made its continuity possible. In Korea, neoliberalists have played an important role in criticizing and adjusting classical developmentalism rather than offering an alternative of their own.

Stabilization Policy

With the doubts about classical state-led developmentalism, bureaucrats on the EPB, who disagreed with heavy chemicals industrialization driven by the Ministry of Commerce and Industry in the mid-1970s, raised their voice with the severe economic crisis in 1979. The EPB led the stabilization measures in 1979 and shifted the way of organizing industrial policies from support by industry to support by function in the mid-1980s.

On April 17, 1979, the EPB announced its economic stabilization measures (4.17 Measures), with the idea that the government-led heavy chemical industry promotion policy would change to a private-led policy based on the market economy principle of self-regulation. The four elements of the stabilization plan included: first, financial liberalization; second, restriction of heavy and chemical industries investment and promotion of light industries; third, restraint of artificial price control; and fourth, import liberalization. The measure was firmly set in the direction of "stability, autonomy, and openness," which means that the fundamental economic policy priority would change from growth to price stability, from government-led economic management to private-led market economy, and from protection to market opening and competition (Kang 2003b, pp. 105–106).

These new economic plans were embodied in the Chun Doo-hwan government in 1982. While the EPB promoted the Fifth Five-Year Economic Development Plan (1982–1986) reflecting a stabilization policy, it initiated the change of the contents and methods of industrial policy. Hosting the Industrial Policy Council in May 1983, the EPB set forth the main points of "the basic tasks and direction of the 1980s industrial policy" as follows: (1) to reorganize the selective support system for strategic industries into functional support systems such as technology and human resource development and energy supply, (2) to reduce various regulations on import restriction and market entry restrictions to expand openness and competition, and (3) to permit government intervention in areas where it is difficult to anticipate autonomous development by the free market by establishing clear support criteria and term.[2] It revised the Fifth Five-Year Economic and Social Development Plan in December 1983, reflecting the new tasks and direction of industrial policy (Kim 2006, pp. 2–3). These measures were evaluated as liberal, compared with the typical 1970s Korean developmentalism, which placed priority on growth rather than macroeconomic stability and on selective rather than universal policy (Yoon 2013).

It is worth noting that this liberalistic "stabilization policy" originated not from an exogenous crisis or pressure itself but from the interpretation of the crises by economic bureaucrats of EPB and economic experts in the Korea Development Institute (KDI). In early 1978, a task force for

[2] The Industrial Policy Council is a deliberation coordination agency established within the EPB. Its chairman is the deputy prime minister, and the committee consists of ten ministers, the senior presidential secretary for economic affairs, and the administrative coordinator at the prime minister's office (Kim 2006, pp. 12–14).

fundamental inspection of the Korean economy was made, which was formed by EPB officials including Kim Je-ik, who later became the Senior Secretary for Economic Policy to President Chun Doo-hwan, and young economic scholars in KDI. And the discussions of the team became the beginning of the "stabilization policy." According to the former Deputy Prime Minister Kang Kyung-sik, who participated in the team at that time, any policies made by the team as well as the process of making the team were not due to external recommendation or pressure.

> In early 1978 the task force team first began to check the economy, and around March it reported to Vice Prime Minister Nam Deok-woo with its early results. We took a year to prepare for the stabilization measures, and we had an opportunity in early 1979 to report to the president. We hadn't known that British prime minister Thatcher was promoting similar reforms until we began to promote the stabilization measures. We followed no foreign precedent in the process of reviewing our measures. There were no suggestions, and no pressure from international organizations such as the IMF, and no recommendations from domestic or foreign economic experts or research institutes such as KDI. (Kang 2003b, pp. 97–99)

In addition, the pressure of liberalization in Korea was not raised by market participants. Market players, including large conglomerates, expressed concern rather than welcome liberalization measures because they worried about the intensification of the market competition caused by opening policy (Kang 2003b, p. 104).

On the other hand, the liberalization of the early 1980s stands out not because it led to the dismantling of Korean developmentalism, but because it failed to. The EPB's liberalization measures brought about change in ways of governing industrial policy, rather allowing Korea's developmentalism to continue. The adaptation of Korean developmentalism was caused both by the resistance of classical developmentalists and by the liberalists' response, reinforcing the reason to explain the evolution of the Korean political economy model by endogenous politics rather than exogenous factors.

Industrial Development Act: Developmentalists' Response

The Industrial Development Act of 1986 was the Ministry of Commerce and Industry's countermeasure against the policy shift led by Kim Jae-ik (Jae-ik Kim), previous senior economic presidential secretary, and the

EPB. The Industrial Development Act, a turning point of Korean industrial policy, marked a change in governance method, not the abandonment of industrial policy. The Ministry of Commerce and Industry established an institutional framework that allows a wide range of private participation in the industrial policy governance system through the Act. The Ministry of Commerce and Industry tried to overcome the criticism of inefficiency of state intervention raised by excessive investment in the heavy and chemical industries in the late 1970s.

The Industrial Development Act's two axes were liberalization (Minganjayoolhwa) and industrial restructuring (Sanuphaprihwa). For liberalization participation by the private sector was institutionalized as part of the process of selecting industries, which needed to be restructured. The Industrial Development Act stipulated two policy coordination bodies, the Industrial Policy Council (Sanupjungchaesimuihwoi) and the Industrial Development Council (Gongupbaljunsimuihwoi), to deliberate and select restructuring sectors. While the Industrial Policy Council was a policy coordination agency within the government including the deputy prime minister and other ministers, the Industrial Development Council was a private-led policy coordination body composed of private industrialists and experts. The Industrial Development Act institutionalized the process of collecting opinions from the private sector into the industrial policy governance system through the official body, the Industrial Development Council.

However, industrial restructuring meant the persistence of selective industrial policies by state intervention. During the implementation of the Industrial Development Act, the Ministry of Commerce and Industry strived to bring the initiative of industrial policy back from the EPB. The first selection of restructuring sectors was designated by the Minister of Commerce and Industry, not voluntarily by companies nor by arbitration of a private review panel (Kim 2006, p. 16). Although the Industrial Development Act has shifted the focus of support from industry to function, the Ministry of Commerce and Industry has continued support by industry through its industrial restructuring policy. In July 1986, the Ministry of Commerce and Industry designated automobile, heavy construction equipment, marine diesel engine, and heavy equipment industries as "industries to supplement competitiveness." The Industrial Development Act, revised six times from March 1989 to November 1995, also reintroduced the legal basis for establishing the Ministry's long-term vision and industrial policies (Kim 2006, p. 17).

The Ministry of Commerce and Industry's will to maintain the industrial policy initiative could be realized by reestablishing the role of the industrial policy. The Ministry justified the industrial policies by emphasizing the need to upgrade main industries and to reinforce industrial competitiveness through technology development. With the implementation of the Industrial Development Law, the Ministry introduced its Industrial Technology Development Program (Gongupgibangisoolgaebalsaup), deemed a breakthrough program to support the development of industrial technology. The government selects urgently needed technologies and encourages company-affiliated research institutes or industrial technology research associations (Sanupgisoolyungoojohap) to develop them. In the program, the government supports up to 80% of the total development cost, and if the development is successful, the government-funded subsidy will be returned as a technology fee within five years. The subsidy provided by the Industrial Technology Development Program was minimal at first—4.6 billion KRW in 1987, 4.8 billion KRW in 1988, and 7.1 billion KRW in 1989, but the amount gradually expanded (KEA 1999, pp. 155–156).

In the liberalization process of the 1980s, competition between industrial ministries led to expansion, rather than reduction, of industrial policies for state-led development. Industrial ministries have justified their roles and expand their influence through new industrial policies. For example, the Ministry of Science and ICT (2017–present) has evolved through the Ministry of Information and Communication (1994–2008) and the Ministry of Science, ICT and Future Planning (2013–2017) from the Ministry of Communication (1948–1994). It has been expanded by competing with the Ministry of Commerce and Industry. In the 1980s, when the Ministry of Communication expanded into the information and communication technology business, the Ministry of Commerce and Industry had to give control of the semiconductor or ICT business on a large-scale project to the Ministry of Science and Technology or the Ministry of Communication. Instead, the Ministry of Commerce and Industry began to focus on the components localization policy (Boopoomkooksanhwajungchek). The Ministry established a plan to achieve a 70% self-sufficiency rate of components and materials through the Five-Year Plan for Components and Materials Development spanning from 1987 to 1991. To do this, it formed an industrial policy consultation committee to build up the machinery and components and materials industry and had the KEA organized a task force to localize electronic components. The plan continued another five years and was expanded to "Measures to foster capital goods industry" in 1995 (KEA 1999, p. 363). A director of the general services division of the Ministry of Science, ICT and Future Planning said:

> The Participatory (No Moo-hyun) Government's Ministry of Information and Communication performed such functions as fostering the IT industry, communication services, managing frequency resources, postal service, and promoting informatization. However, conflicts existed between the Ministry of Information and Communication and the Ministry of Commerce, Industry and Energy regarding the functions of each ministry sector, especially related to the promotion of the device industry. The service industry was wholly in charge of the Ministry of Information and Communication. However, some equipment businesses are closely related to broadcasting or communication services, including device, semiconductor, secondary batteries, and network equipment businesses. With regard to supporting the device industry, there is some overlap between the two ministries. The Ministry of Commerce, Industry and Energy, for example, asked the robot industry to be promoted entirely by itself, although it recognized the robot industry as part of the ICT ecosystem. When the Ministry of Information and Communication was established in the Kim Young-sam government, it began to foster information and communication as a national strategic industry. Since then, the information and communication industry has become more important than traditional industries fostered by the Ministry of Commerce, Industry and Energy. It caused a sense of crisis within the Ministry of Commerce, Industry and Energy. That Ministry worried about reducing or abolishing its roles in the industrial policy. The Ministry of Commerce, Industry and Energy did not want to lose the initiative in fostering the information communication device industry, so conflict arose over competing interests in the information and communication industry. (A director in the general services division of the Ministry of Science, ICT and Future Planning, personal communication, May 12, 2015)

From the mid-1980s until the mid-1990s, the Ministry of Commerce and Industry had tried to establish its new role with industrial infrastructure technology and intermediate goods and capital goods industry policies, to little effect. Its policy priority lay in industrial rationalization, not in technology development or nurturing of intermediate goods industries. Until then, the ministry's major policy partners were still large conglomerates, not small- and medium-sized companies. And because of their rising power, the Ministry of Commerce and Industry appeared to be losing its autonomy after the 1980s. Thus, the Ministry's attempts to establish a new role were unsuccessful. But these attempts enabled industrial policymakers to quickly seek alternatives when a new crisis hit in the late 1990s. And what was impossible before the mid-1990s emerged as a new alternative in the late 1990s crisis, based on a shift in perception of industrial bureaucrats.

Alternative of the Economic Planning Board: Decentralized but Developmental

The economic planner, who led economic policy with the slogan of liberal reform in the 1980s, had no intention of discontinuing industrial policies or denying the need for state intervention. Rather, the alternative industry promotion initiative led by liberalists has inspired the alternative model of Korean industrial policy.

Korea's market-driven economy (Minganjoodokyungje) promoted by the EPB did not mean abandoning its industry promotion policies in the 1980s. Kim Jae-ik, who led the economic stabilization measures at the EPB in the late 1970s, directed market opening, financial reform, and industrial policy conversion as senior secretary to the president for economic policy in the Chun Doo-hwan government. However, the government still set the direction of development and promoted the advancement of strategic industries in the export market. By establishing the Industrial Policy Council led by the EPB under the Industrial Development Act, the EPB institutionalized the role of control tower to lead and coordinate industrial policies. Since late 1980, the economic secretary's office, led by Kim Jae-ik, also established a comprehensive policy to promote and develop electronics industries. Established in March 1981, the policy focused on expanding the share of industrial devices and electronic components in the electronics industry, focusing on three strategic items—semiconductors, computers, and electronic exchangers—away from home appliances. This landmark measure included both support and regulation by the government and continued for almost a decade. At that time, the operation rate of the Korean electronics industry was at over 100%, with productivity at 80% to 90% of that of Japan, indicating that investments in electronics should continue to expand. Thus, this policy included financial measures to induce more than twice as many investments over five years (Jung 2003, pp. 125–128).

It seems to be contradictory that Kim Jae-ik and his followers in the government, who pushed for a stabilization plan based on liberalist ideas and a series of liberal reforms, led the support policy for a strategic industry, electronics. However, "liberalism" of liberal policymakers within the Korean government, especially the EPB bureaucrats including Kim Jae-ik, should be distinguished from Anglo-American liberalism. The liberal idea of Korean officials seems to have been refracted at the process of policymaking and implementation. The economic policymakers also seemed to justify promoting strategic industries by changing policy governance.

More important in this period of change is the change in industrial policy governance than in turn to liberalization. Measures to foster the electronics industry in the 1980s have led to a shift in governance of policymaking and implementation in Korea. Unlike the top-down way led by government bureaucracy, experts within companies, academia and research institutes, government officials, and Blue House secretaries came together to present alternatives in the policymaking process for the electronics industry. Responsibility for directing the work was assigned to Oh Myung and Hong Sung-won in the secretary office to the president for economic policy, but the actual work was carried out by businessmen, researchers, academics, and government officials from the Ministry of Commerce and Industry, the Ministry of Communication, and the Ministry of Science and Technology.

The industrial development measures completely changed implementation process as well as policymaking. The semiconductor, computer, and electronic exchanger sectors required rapid technological innovation, and Korean companies in those sectors were far behind foreign competitors at that time. Therefore, the government organized and coordinated joint research projects between companies to avoid or reduce cost by unnecessary competition in R&D investment and to maximize investment efficiency. This shift was a breakthrough policy in Korea's industrial history (Jung 2003, pp. 122–129).

For example, in 1986, the government designated 4 M DRAM development as a national project in order to prevent duplication of investments in the semiconductor industry and formed a consortium with Samsung Electronics, GoldStar (the present LG), and Hyundai Electronics, led by the ETRI. The consortium spent $110 million over three years (1986–1989), with government spending reaching 57%. The government also pursued national R&D projects to develop 64 M DRAM and 256 M DRAM (Kim 1997/2000, pp. 206–211). These joint R&D projects brought successful results in the 1990s with CDMA and LCD panel technologies.

In short, the Korean bureaucracy's policy shift following heavy and chemical industrialization in the 1970s did not simply mean abolition of state-led industrial policy or transition to liberalism as some studies have suggested (Yoon 2013). Liberal ideas and policies were introduced in the process of bureaucratic competition, but policymakers used them to achieve their initiative to lead and control industrial policies' bureaucratic competition. However, policy shifts resulting from liberal ideas began to change the contents and methods of traditional state-led developmentalism in Korea. The direction and governance of Korean industrial policy have dramatically changed, but these changes have been led by the state in the competition between bureaucratic groups.

Ideational Shift of the State and Transition to Innovation-Driven Economy

While the content of Korean developmental principles has changed greatly from the classical developmentalism, the direction of change has been to a new version of developmentalism rather than neoliberalism or corporatism. Why has Korea evolved to a new form of developmentalism, despite the pressures of globalization and democratization?

In the late 1990s, Korea abandoned its components-oriented strategy centered on assembly conglomerates for an innovation-driven strategy centered on components and materials companies. This shift was based on a question about existing strategies' effectiveness. At the heart of the matter were the ideas that input-oriented growth strategies were no longer valid and that large companies did not have to be the only partners in industrial policy.

As in the late 1970s, the economic crisis of the late 1990s called into question the effectiveness of Korean state-led developmentalism. But even at this time, while industrial policymakers, who were main institutional actors of Korean developmentalism, interpreted the crisis from their own perspective and presented feasible alternatives, other actors, especially employers or laborers, could not present their tangible alternatives, whether neoliberalism or corporatism. Neoliberal reforms were introduced by the IMF, but they were imposed externally, not formed and agreed to internally. The neoliberal discourse surrounding the 1997 crisis was not a favorable alternative for all the key actors in the Korean political economy, the state, business, and labor.

Policymakers, mainly of the Ministry of Commerce, Industry and Energy, assigned themselves a new role by highlighting that the problem of the Korean economy lay in a structural crisis, and not merely a temporary liquidity crisis caused by the exogenous crisis. Their interpretation of crisis was based on a deepening trade deficit in the Korean economy, especially with Japan. In 2001, imports of components and materials from Japan accounted for 28.1% of total imports of components and materials, and the trade deficit of components and materials with Japan was 10.5 billion dollars, which led to continued dependence on Japan for the components and materials industry (KIET 2012, p. 9). A former official of the Ministry of Commerce, Industry and Energy observed:

> In 1997, the Act on Special Measures for Development of Venture Businesses was created. At that time, I was in charge. A huge trade deficit existed because Korea had imported almost all components for export. Until then, however, policymakers thought that if exports would continue to increase, it would eventually lead to a trade surplus. The reasons for the crisis in 1996 and 1997 may be partly due to corporate mismanagement, but the bigger problem was due to such illusions by the government. They saw trade deficits as temporary or transient. (Former head of the Ministry of Commerce, Industry and Energy, personal communication, June 17, 2015)

The trade deficit problem, especially with Japan, had been chronic in the Korean economy since the adoption of the input-driven strategy in the 1970s. Thus, despite the trade deficit worsening in the past, it was not recognized as a problem of input-driven growth strategy itself, but rather a problem that could be solved by increasing exports. However, in the mid-1990s economic bureaucrats' thoughts were different from the past, in that they saw the input-driven strategy itself as causing the trade deficit. The former Vice Minister of Knowledge Economy who was involved in industrial policy at the time recalled:

> In Korea, there had been a limit to input-driven growth since the late 1980s and early 1990s. However, noticing this limit was delayed due to the special boom in the international economy in the late 1980s. In the mid-1990s when the boom disappeared, the balance of payments began to deteriorate in earnest. Then big companies tried to survive the crisis by diversifying their businesses. Facing the limitations of input-driven growth, however, no matter how much manpower and capital were applied, their marginal profits deteriorated. For example, Samsung diversified into petrochemicals, a new business, instead of investing in R&D and innovation when profits deterio-

> rated in electronics, their main business. Like Samsung, big companies followed suit, putting capital into new businesses, which expanded insolvency. That was why we went to the IMF regime. At the Lewisian turning point we should have gone to an innovation-led economy. But neither the government nor private sector had that idea then. In particular, large companies did not have that idea at all. The financial system was designed to lend to large companies when they wanted money. So the debt ratio of Daewoo went up to 1200% in the late 1990s. Samsung was at about 500- to 600%, and the average was over that. As the business became bankrupt, the bank became insolvent with the debt. (Former Vice Minister of Knowledge Economy, personal communication, June 22, 2015)

This ideational shift was already held by industrial policymakers before the external crisis triggered the domestic economic crisis. When the crisis became visible in the fall of 1997, it was possible to quickly switch to an industrial policy based on promoting components and materials companies, because industrial bureaucrats had grasped the structural problems of the Korean economy and had sought solutions. The Act on Special Measures for the Promotion of Venture Businesses, so-called the Special Act on Venture Businesses, generally known as a representative policy of the Kim Dae-jung government, had already been prepared by industrial policymakers who recognized the structural crisis of the Korean economy at the end of the Kim Young-sam government. A former bureaucrat who was in charge of establishing the Special Act on Venture Business said:

> At the end of the YS government, an economic team led by Deputy Prime Minister Kang Kyung-sik was established. At that time, the Minister of Commerce, Industry and Energy was Lim Chang-ryeol, and Deputy Minister was Han Duck-soo. And Kang Kyung-sik is the first person to focus on this illusion phenomenon. Kang Kyung-sik insisted that it would be serious if we leave it as it is, and that something need to change. Then the concept of "venture companies" came up. In the background, the Act on Special Measures for the Promotion of Venture Businesses was established. However, the original title of the law was the Special Act on New Technology Knowledge Intensive SME, not the Act on Special Measures for the Promotion of Venture Businesses. The National Assembly changed the name of the act because the name was too long. The core purpose of the act was not to support small businesses but to restructure and innovate them, which meant to reorganize low-paying and labor-intensive small businesses and to make innovative small businesses the basis of the Korean economy.

(Director of the Capital Goods Industry Bureau at the Ministry of Commerce, Industry and Energy, personal communication, June 17, 2016)

The purpose of the Act that would nurture technology-innovative SMEs was diluted and distorted in the process of policymaking and implementation. This serves as a background for establishing the Act on Special Measures for the Promotion of Specialized Enterprises, etc. for Components and Materials (hereinafter referred to as the Special Act on Components and Materials) a few years later, despite the introduction of the Special Act on Venture Business. When the request for aid from the IMF to overcome the crisis was accepted, a major restructuring of the business and financial sector began as a countermeasure, which resulted in large-scale unemployment. The new government needed policies to create new jobs. As a result, the purpose of the Special Act on Venture Business, which was intended to foster technologically innovative SMEs, started to be distorted to absorbing victims of restructuring by encouraging start-ups. The former bureaucrat who participated in establishing the special law for venture businesses recalled:

> The Special Act on Venture Businesses turned into a kind of law promoting job creation [in the process of overcoming the crisis]. It increased another type of small and midsize enterprises. Originally, the law was introduced to turn existing small and medium businesses into knowledge- and technology-intensive SMEs, but the government began to use it for wrong purposes. They focused on expanding more jobs by increasing the number of venture companies. (Former Ministry of Commerce, Industry and Energy officials, personal communication, June 17, 2015)

But the crisis also served as an opportunity for industrial policymakers. In 1999, Japanese economist Kenichi Ohmae, who visited Korea when various solutions were being sought to overcome the crisis, criticized the structural problems of the Korean economy by comparing it to "a cormorant," the type of bird used by fishermen to catch fish traditionally. This analogy prompted the president to step forward and look for ways to solve the structural problems of the Korean economy. A bureaucrat who was involved in the enactment of the Special Act on Components and Materials said:

> When the Korean economy faced a foreign exchange crisis with the bankruptcy of large companies including Hanbo and Kia in 1997, some raised questions about whether the principle of growth of the assembly-based manufacturing until the 1990s had reached its limit. Of course, in the past there have been concerns that the Korean economy tended to fluctuate with the yen, and at the core of that problem was a serious trade deficit in components and materials. In 1996, the trade deficit stood at more than $20 billion, with the trade deficit in components and materials at $30 billion. Under these circumstances, it has been steadily pointed out that we should promote the components and materials industry to solve the limits of the assembly industry led by large companies. At that time, moreover, the story of the cormorant raised by a renowned Japanese economist Kenichi Ohmae was drawing attention. He compared the Korean economy to a so-called "cormorant" economy, which meant that if Korea exported, the added value of the components and materials sector would go to Japan. That is, the trade imbalance in components and materials sector was the main culprit of the Korean financial crisis. With social interest in this debate rising, it was said that President Kim Dae-jung berated the minister of Commerce, Industry and Energy, asking what solutions the Ministry was preparing to solve the problem. As a result, one of the two major pillars of industrial policy was corporate restructuring, and the other, as a new growth engine, was a policy of promoting the components and materials industry. (Policy Director of the Ministry of Commerce, Industry and Energy, personal communication, May 27, 2015)

The president's request to resolve the components and materials trade imbalance became an opportunity for the industrial policymakers who had complaints that the Special Act on Venture Businesses had been distorted to a job creation policy. They began to drive a policy to nurture technology-innovative companies again, which resulted in the Special Act on Components and Materials of 2000.

Policies on promotion of components and materials industry since the 2000s starting from the Special Act on Components and Materials differ from previous policies on localization of components in three ways. First, while the existing components localization policy was a complementary measure in the large assembly industry strategy, the strategy to nurture high value-added intermediate goods emerged as a new core. It was a paradigm shift in that it changed the main object of industrial policy. Another official involved in the enactment of the Special Act on Components and Materials recalled:

> I think the role of the government lies in presenting a vision. However, more important is that the government show its strong willingness to realize it. The Special Act on Components and Materials is the expression of the will. Once a law is made, the budget is secured by law, and thereby manpower moves in that direction. Furthermore, introducing a special law means to put a special priority to it. A special law shows that the resources of the state are distributed through selection and concentration, and that the policy is not a temporary end, but a part of the long-term vision. (Former director of the industry planning office at the Ministry of Commerce, Industry and Energy, personal communication, April 1, 2015)

The components and materials industry policy established at this time secured the persistence of the policy, while the previous components localization policy had been continuously marginalized due to policies to promote the production and export of the end products, despite the need for intermediate components. Second, the policy shift attempted to truly globalize the components and materials industry (Nuclear Industrial Policy Director of the Ministry of Commerce, Industry and Energy, personal communication, May 26, 2015).

Third, the new policy on components and materials included a qualitative change of the meaning of localization. Until the 1990s, localization meant only localization of production, not of technology. Thus, the trade deficit in the components and materials industry had been deteriorated even though the official localization rate had kept high. In the case of automobiles, the localization rate already reached 90% in the 1980s, but the trade deficit did not decrease until the 1990s, because the localization rate was calculated on the basis of the finished product assembly industry. Even if a domestic components supplier imported and assembled core components and then supplied them to a finished car, the components in terms of the finished car were considered localized. However, after the late 1990s economic crisis and a social debate on the "cormorant economy," attempts were made to newly define localization. In 2001, the Special Act on Components and Materials addressed these problems, emphasizing the importance of technology localization. A policymaker who participated in the Special Act on Components and Materials said:

> At that time, for instance, there were no exact statistics on how much value added would be created in Korea if we exported 10 billion dollars of goods. For example, if Hyundai Motors imports electronic control devices from Japan, it will be caught as imports from Japan, but if Hyundai make a parts

> company, the company imports the device from Japan, and then Hyundai buys the components from the company, and the components are caught as localized goods in the official statistics. So, with the help of the Korea Customs Service, we analyzed millions of imported customs records, hoping to precisely assess the value added to Korea. The import clearance letter provides the final destination of the item. Therefore, it analyzed all imported goods of the five major industries including electronics, cars, shipbuilding, and general machinery. ... The survey played a big role in moving prime minister Park Tae-joon. At that time, if Samsung Electronics exported $10 billion, the profit to Korea would have dropped less than 40%. For Hyundai Motors it seems to have been around 50 to 60%, and for shipbuilding corporations it was about 80%. This was not made public because it was a business secret for those corporations. Anyway, these statistics showed evidence that the economic structure of Korea was a kind of "cormorant economy" at the time. (Nuclear Industrial Policy Director of the Ministry of Commerce, Industry and Energy, personal communication, May 26, 2015)

In other words, the policy to foster components and materials at this time was based on the reflection that innovation through the assembly industry had been stretched to the limit, and the result was a shift in industrial policy to innovation through components and materials industry. Once the components and materials industry became the center of the industry policy, localization policy by the Korean government became to focus on localization of technology, not of simple assembly.

The state, not the private sector, took the initiative for transition. Individual companies were not concerned with the total trade balance. They did not care about whether their domestic suppliers imported components or developed their own. What was important for them was only whether their suppliers could deliver the components they wanted on time. As we see in the interview with the industrial policymaker, large companies maneuvered the localization rate by using foreign components, which were imported by their domestic suppliers, as the government induced localization of components. Large companies were also interested in localizing components, since the cost of components would be reduced only if domestic components suppliers developed their own components with their own technologies. However, individual conglomerates had no reason to share uncertainty in technology development with components suppliers. Until the mid-1990s, the state had not recognized the trade deficit as a serious problem. Since the Korean economy had been growing based on an industrial structure centered on assembled goods, importing intermediate goods had been considered inevitable. The Korean government had been interested only in growing exports. However, after the mid-1990s, economic policymakers shifted their ideas of structural problems in the Korean economy.

In the late 1990s, another reason the Korean government shifted the main objects of its policies from large companies to small- and medium-sized businesses was because of policymakers' idea that only large companies could be partners with their policies with growth of large companies. At the same time, the idea that small-sized and medium-sized businesses should produce more meaningful and effective policy outcomes had grown among industrial bureaucrats.

Policymakers' ideational shift is related to strengthening market autonomy, especially in terms of large conglomerates. The policy turn by the Chun Doo-hwan government in the early 1980s created dual effects: one was the survival of developmentalism and the other was the change of balance of power between the state and large business. That is, the state could persist in its developmental system by permitting the strengthening of private power. Through the policy shift in the early 1980s, the Korean government strengthened market autonomy by expanding private participation in establishing industrial policies and easing barriers to market entry. At the same time, it began the liberalization of financial, capital, and commodity markets. The intent was not disbandment of developmental industrial policies but to increase the efficiency of industrial policies in the changing political and economic environment. However, the policy shift that increased the autonomy of large companies enabled the continuation of industrial policy while weakening the state's control over large companies (OECD 1996, p. 48; Cho 2003, pp. 85–86).

More importantly, from the microscopic perspective, policymakers had felt that the state's role had reduced in the partnership with large companies due to their growth. Policymakers needed new partners to justify the persistence of their developmental policies. Meanwhile, the idea grew that small- and medium-sized businesses should become major partners in policy. An executive director of the Korea Electronics Industry Cooperative Association noted:

> In fact, Korea no longer needs industrial policies for large companies. Conglomerates can develop their business by themselves because they have the manpower, capital, and technology. Therefore, it is time to nurture small and medium-sized businesses. Germany is still one of the world's top export-

> ers because there are many strong medium-sized companies with sales of more than 100 billion won. The Korean government has been also shifting its direction toward strategies for promoting small and medium-sized businesses. (An executive director at the Korea Electronics Industry Cooperative Association, personal communication, July 1, 2011)

A general manager of the KEA noted:

> Now our large companies have self-sustaining capabilities in any sector. So the government mainly focuses on supporting SMEs. For example, patent issues have been a major problem for large companies in the 1980s and early 1990s. But now that our SMEs have grown bigger, claimants of patents began to claim SMEs, too. In the case of small and medium-sized companies, there is no countermeasure if they are unexpectedly involved in a patent lawsuit. (A KEA general manager, personal communication, June 1, 2011)

Indeed, government-initiated research institutes, which formed R&D consortia mainly through partnership with large companies in the 1980s and 1990s, are expanding partnerships with small and medium components suppliers. The ETRI managers and researchers who have been leading large-scale government-funded R&D projects since the 1980s commented:

> In the past, there were many big projects—for example, development of CDMA, TDX, and memory semiconductors and so on. In those projects large companies mainly participated, and jointly developed and commercialized technologies. In recent national projects, however, mainly SMEs and midsize companies participate and collaborate with government-funded research institutes. Many SMEs that have not participated in government-funded research tasks can often receive technology transfer from government-funded research institutes. (ETRI managers, personal communication, April 18, 2013)

Moreover, small- and mid-sized businesses began to be recognized as major players in the Korean economic structure, not just from the point of view of subcontractors who supplement the finished product industry. Until the 1980s, small businesses were more likely to be seen as an incidental part of the industrial production system led by large companies. However, since the 2000s, they have played indispensable roles for securing national competitiveness in its main industries. As overseas investment was actively carried out, especially as outsourcing was strengthened and global production networks developed, the industrial competitiveness of a country is now under international division of labor. As a main agent of these production networks, small and medium components business began to draw attention. They are also seen as necessary for sustainable growth of the Korean economy, as well as contributing to job creation and social integration (Kim 2007, pp. 97–98). The policy for promoting components and materials companies established during this period was completely different from existing policies for small businesses. A policymaker in charge of establishing the Special Act on Components and Materials observed:

> We insisted that when we make the law, we must eliminate the concept of SMEs from the concept of components and materials companies. Therefore, we suggested that the law should cover firms that specialize in components and materials business but should not restrict the size of firms. We started with that idea at the time, but the law included the concept of restricting firm size due to many benefits such as tax exemption. Thereafter, the Special Act on the Promotion of Growth and the Strengthening of Competitiveness of Middle-Standing Enterprises (the Special Act on Middle-Standing Enterprises) was created. In 2009, when I was chief of the department of industrial technology development, Assistant Vice Minister of Knowledge of Economy Ahn Hyun-ho asserted that we should introduce the concept of "middle-standing" enterprises, and then we prepared to introduce the act together. The significance of the Special Act on Middle-Standing Enterprises is to break away from the dichotomy between large and small businesses. In fact, the idea began with the Special Act on Components and Materials, but it was not realized until the Special Act on Middle-Standing Enterprises was enacted in 2014. (Director General for Nuclear Power Industry Policy at the Ministry of Commerce, Industry and Energy, personal communication, May 26, 2015)

The focus of the past SME policy was on protecting them or correcting unfair practices between them and large enterprises. However, the components and materials policy in the 2000s was designed to nurture specialized components and materials companies, not just for protecting SMEs. Industrial bureaucrats held that the components and materials enterprises that occupied the middle part of the Korean industrial structure could not grow and develop only by protecting them. Based on this perspective, a former industrial policymaker pointed out that the recent issues of "win-win cooperation" or "mutual growth" of large corporations and SMEs present a critical problem but that the direction of debate is wrong:

> The cooperative relationship between large and small businesses is formed by the culture of the country, not by the government. In those days, large companies were already big enough not to listen to the government, so the government set a limit to control them. Also, what to do with their components supplier is entirely the policy of the assembler and not the government. However, if there is an unfair part to subcontracting, it can be dealt with by law. If the government had approached the gap between large and small corporations in the material market in an essential way, which means to strengthen competitiveness, the government policy would have been much more effective on the growth of small and medium businesses. Moreover, it would have given more momentum to the policy for the components and materials sector. (Former Vice Minister of Knowledge Economy, personal communication, June 22, 2015)

According to the former policymaker, an integrated economy based on knowledge and cooperation must need the advancement of the intermediate industry, which should be achieved by nurturing small and medium components suppliers rather than forcing large companies to form win-win relations with their suppliers. The industrial policymakers' idea that established the policy to support the components and materials sector in the late 1990s was totally different from the earlier focus on protecting SMEs in the dimension of social justice.

For this reason, the components and materials policy established in the late 1990s could be driven by the fact that it included small and medium companies as main policy partners. Yet the policy that focuses on the technological capability of a company, not its size, has sometimes caused tension with the earlier application of the SME policy. As the policy has focused on supporting small businesses rather than competitiveness of components and materials from the terms of politics, the Ministry of Commerce, Industry and Energy established policies to foster medium-sized businesses by introducing the Special Act on the Promotion of Growth and the Strengthening of Competitiveness of Middle-Standing Enterprises in 2016.

In sum, whenever a problem or a crisis arose, Korean developmentalism could be sustained by economic policymakers, who must create their new tasks and roles in the growth of the national economy for their organizational survival. Yet no matter how much policymakers try to justify their role in the national economy, the Korean developmental system would have been scrapped if it could no longer be socially justified. In Korea, however, there remains a shared perception that the state's intervention in economic growth is necessary and justifiable. A current director of the Ministry of Commerce, Industry and Energy, who was involved in the extension of the Special Act on Components and Materials, said:

> Neither the ruling party nor the opposition party could have questioned it [Special Act on Components and Materials]. One of the tasks I'm in charge of right now is to restructure the old national industrial complexes. Opposition lawmakers are more active in promoting and innovating industrial complexes. Likewise, there was no problem in passing the Act, because promoting the materials and components sector had no opposing interests in either the ruling party or the opposition parties. For R&D budget, both sides also consider that it is necessary for economic growth. They are all [politically] neutral issues. There is a shared consensus that we should go together for national development. (Director General of Regional Economic Development Policy at the Ministry of Trade, Industry and Energy, personal communication, June 10, 2015)

Finally, national consensus remains on export-oriented growth strategy by state intervention. Despite two severe crises in the late 1970s and late 1990s and changes in the international and domestic conditions, the idea that the Korean economy could achieve economic growth only through exports due to the narrow domestic market, and for this matter the state should actively support the export sector for the national economy, has survived. Although many problems have been presented on state-led and export-oriented strategy, no alternative has risen as a feasible option. Meanwhile, whenever Korea has faced a crisis, export-oriented strategy by state intervention has been presented as the only feasible solution to overcome the crisis, which has been a major factor in keeping state-led capitalism in Korea.

Policy Shift and Changing Large Companies's Strategies

State-led industrial policy in Korea continued despite changes in its contents and means because of private actors' demand for state support as well as policymakers' organizational interests and their roles in the Korean economy. Korean conglomerates have grown through active support of the state from the start. Korean developmentalism, focused on cultivating large enterprises with economies of scale, achieved a visible outcome by establishing gigantic conglomerates in the 1970s. However, the larger and more competitive corporations supported by the state became, the more the state had to rely on large companies' performance. Large companies grew through various benefits from the state, but they felt repulsed by the state's dirigisme. However, as we have seen in this section, Korean conglomerates have refused government regulations but not government support by industrial policies. Rather, corporate and business organizations have utilized institutionalized frameworks since the 1980s to take full advantage of the benefits available through government policies, while participating in the policy formulation and enforcement process. Business sector expectations of state support are another reason to maintain Korean developmentalism, and not to transition to Anglo-American free-market system.

Korean large conglomerates have always been keen to seek maximum benefits from state policies, and less state interference. Even under the authoritarian developmentalism associated with political dictatorship in the 1970s, large businesses took full advantage of the space for rent-seeking between the goal and the implementation of state policy. In particular, the greater the state's dependence on the performance of certain large companies in certain strategic industries, the greater the space for their rent-seeking. A major example was Shinjin Motors, which was a beneficiary of the unification policy (Ilwonhwajungchek) in the passenger car sector until the late 1960s. In accordance with the policy, the car maker used its monopoly status to the fullest, but maintained a negative attitude toward localization of components, which was another state policy. The rate of components localization of Shinjin, whose main business was to import Toyota Motor's KD (knockdown) components and assemble them, fell short of expectations of the state, at 21% in 1966 and 23.6% in 1967. According to a plan for components localization of Shinjin when it was first selected as the only plant to produce passenger cars, the rate had to reach 38% in 1966 and 50% in 1967. Shinjin tried to solve the problem politically by persuading or maneuvering policymakers, including ministers, rather than trying to localize components (Korea Automobile Manufacturers Association & Korea Auto Industries Cooperative Association [KAMA & KAICA] 2005, pp. 149, 168).

Even when liberalization measures were implemented in earnest in the new military regime in the early 1980s, large companies' position was ambivalent. They wanted the agricultural sector to be liberalized but wanted trade barriers in the manufacturing market to remain. Most of all, they wanted to privatize banks and liberalize government control over financial markets. At that time the state took some liberalization measures on financial markets by privatizing some banks and allowing large conglomerates to enter the nonbank financial sector, instead of starting a phase of trade liberalization (Amsden 1989, pp. 133–134).

In 1984, when the promotion laws by industry were abolished and the Industrial Development Act was established to shift to a support policy by function such as human capital training and R&D, the business sector generally accepted the change of policy. Despite their concern about reduction of government support by the abolishment of policies by industry, the business sector was interested in the deregulation measures by the policy shift and the legal basis for institutionalizing its formal participation in the policymaking process through the Industrial Development Council. Rather than denying the industrial policy itself, the business sector had more interest in maximizing industrial policy benefits by raising their voice, in the changed industrial policy governance. After interministerial coordination, review opinions were submitted by the Federation of Korean Industries (FKI), the KITA, and the Federation of Korean Industries (SME) cooperatives, but they did not include any opposition to the major direction of policy, and rather, they requested to materialize the new support system and to raise the legal status of the Industrial Developmental Council, which would secure the participation of the private sector. Also, at the meeting with business sector hosted by the Korean Chamber of Commerce and Industry (KCCI), business worried about the government's reduction of support (Kim 2005, pp. 9–10).

Companies also adopted an ambivalent stand over the large-scale research projects led by the government. The government promoted a large-scale joint project between large companies in order to reduce the gross national R&D cost in main strategic industries such as semiconductors. Companies wanted to minimize the risk of uncertainty by reducing the cost of technology development through government support, but they were also interested in minimizing government interference. They were more interested in technology development funds and infrastructure provided by the government rather than in cooperation (Kim 1997/2000).

Companies have participated in policy programs in order to realize their interests and actively use them. For example, in the Enlarged Meeting for Technology Promotion held by the president, Kang Jinkoo, the CEO of Samsung Semiconductor Communication Co.

(Samsungbandochetongsin) and chairman of the KEA, suggested that the government and companies should jointly develop in order to compete with developed countries in the development of more highly integrated semiconductor technology, as did VHSIC or VLSI of Japan. Samsung Electronics Communication Co., GoldStar (current LG) Semiconductor, and Hyundai Electronics formed a semiconductor research union for the development of 4 M DRAM. And a joint R&D system was established with the ETRI under the support of the Ministry of Commerce and Industry, the Ministry of Science and Technology, and Ministry of Postal Service (KEA 1999, p. 154).

In the second half of 1999, when the Kim Dae-jung government examined the plan for fostering the components and materials sector, the business sector officially demanded the enactment of a special law promoting the components and materials sector. In July 2000, the Federation of Korean Industries (FKI) officially proposed to form a "National Competitiveness Strengthening Committee" composed of 30 members including ministers of relevant ministries such as the Ministry of Commerce, Industry and Energy, the heads of related government agencies, and heads of economic associations (*Korea Economic Daily*, July 26, 2000). On March 22, 2001, the government decided to organize a public-private joint committee to pursue the Vision 2011 Project in order to review the economic policy direction for takeoff of the Korean economy. First, selection of items for technology development was made by five economic organizations including FKI, and the Industrial Technology Foundation. The FKI established a support group for the components and materials industry under its jurisdiction and actively cooperated with government policies. In addition, application, evaluation, support, and follow-up of investment and financing programs of the Industry Foundation Fund for specialized components and materials companies were assigned to each industry-specific association including the Machinery Industry Promotion Association, the Korea Association of Mold Industry Cooperative, the Korea Textile Industry Association, and the KAICA. They were entrusted directly by the government and were responsible for the operation of the fund for promoting the components and materials sector. The public-private joint competitiveness conference was also organized and operated under the Roh Moo-hyun government. This inclusive public-private network is currently the institutional basis of Korea's state-led industrial policy (Yoon 2012, pp. 221–222).

As such, Korea's large companies are not interested in creating their own alternative to the state's vision on the national economy and taking the initiative but in participating in state policy and making full use of it. This role of large companies provides a space where Korean developmentalism can still exist.

Interfirm Relationship

As noted in Chap. 4, until the 1970s the typical relationship between Korean companies depended more on an arm's-length market than on a long-term collaboration in the Japanese or German style. In the late 1970s, vertical integration began between large companies and components suppliers. However, the Korean system of vertical integration was based on a division of labor of production process, unlike Japan's vertical integration system based on functional division of labor and cooperative relations between lead companies and components suppliers. The market dominance of large companies and the relatively low development of components suppliers further weakened the status of components suppliers within the vertical integration structure. Nevertheless, through the 1980s and 1990s, the Korean vertical integration system grew, and more importantly, an interdependent and cooperative relationship between lead companies and components suppliers in main industries has been developed, as seen in Chap. 5. How was this change possible?

In Korea, state-led developmentalism has made a critical impact on the formation of interfirm relationships. The input-driven growth strategy centered on large companies in the 1960s and 1970s formed a close interest-sharing system between the state and large conglomerates, excluding SMEs and labor, while the innovation-led growth strategy centered on components and materials companies since the late 1990s has established more inclusive innovation networks based on close cooperation between large conglomerates and their parts suppliers, including SMEs.

Tension Between the State and Large Companies

Despite the Korean government's strong policy of components localization from the beginning of industrialization, Korea's components industry was inferior to the finished goods industry until the policy of nurturing technology-oriented components and materials companies was established in the late 1990s. First, the government's policy was to prioritize the development of the finished goods industry rather than the intermediary goods industry. Second, the earlier government's policy to nurture the components industry played a crucial role in forming a structure that would hinder the natural growth of components companies. Nevertheless, the transition from the finished goods assembling industry to the components and materials industry in the late 1990s was also led by the Korean government, which had not abandoned its will to nurture the components industry even in a tension between the state and large conglomerates.

Before the full-fledged transition to fostering the components and materials industry, why couldn't the development of the Korean components industry be delayed despite the components localization policy? How could Korean components companies manage to survive in unfavorable business and policy conditions until the 1990s, as seen in the Korean automobile industry?

Components Industry Policy Based on Horizontal Integration

From the early 1960s, the Korean government has held a strong policy of components localization based on systemization of components production in the automobile industry. Called the "horizontal integration" (soopyungjuk gyeyulwha) policy, it intended to restrict the finished-car companies' entry into the components industry and foster one specialized components supplier per a core component. This policy aimed to prevent excessive market competition among components suppliers, to realize their economies of scale, and to nurture competitive components suppliers. While the components industry policy based on horizontal integration continued into the mid-1970s, the government did not achieve its goals in components supplier specialization and components localization. The government's policies did not create a virtuous circle structure between the assembly industry and the components. Large conglomerates in the assembly didn't have any preference to localize components. Their interests lay in importing components from advanced foreign companies. Moreover, the government's idealistic components industry policy resulted in the deterioration of the components industry, showing that no matter how worthy the goal of a policy, it cannot function properly if it does not meet the preferences of the policy's partners at the enforcement stage.

In the early 1960s, when the Korean government set up a plan to nurture the automobile industry, its policy for components industries was based on "integration" (gyeyulhwa). According to the 1964 Automobile Industry Promotion Plan, automobile manufacturing factories were integrated into a components manufacturer by core component to meet domestic automobile demand through a single assembly line, marking the start of a horizontal integration. But "horizontal integration" had not been realized until the late 1960s because the policy for finished vehicles was based on "unification" (Ilwonhwa), which was to allow only one assembly line by vehicle. For example, a factory for cars was allowed only to Shinjin. In practical terms, the horizontal integration system was established in 1969 through "Samwonhwa," which was to allow three automobile assembly manufacturers, and through "unification," which was to allow one components manufacturer per item. This policy change was to drive the policy of components localization. With horizontal integration, one components factory had to deliver all the same components to three assembly companies. For cars, the target of localization rate started from 38% in 1969, through 58% in 1970 and 75%, and was to achieve the full localization in 1972. For buses and trucks, it was to achieve the full localization in 1974. This basic plan was in fact focused on nurturing the components industry. It had components manufacturers produce 75% of automobile components except engines and bodies and forced automobile companies to buy the targeted rate of local components in the targeted year (KIET 1997b, p. 58; KAMA & KAICA 2005, pp. 150–151).

However, despite the government's strong horizontal integration policy, the components industry continued to slump, and the localization of components slowed down as well. The problem was in the government's policies. There were some conflicts between the policies for the assembly industry and for the components industry. In the implementation process of the policies, the conflicts were solved by prioritizing the interests of large assembly companies, which held an advantageous market status. As a result, the development direction of the industry gradually moved away from the state's original intent.

The first problem was that the Five-Year Plan for Automobile Industry Promotion in 1962 weakened domestic components companies' voluntary will to develop their own components. The policy prohibited the import of finished automobiles but allowed the import of components and factory facilities. Further, according to Article 7 of the Enforcement Decree of the Act on Protection of the Automobile Industry (Jadongchagongupbohobup) in 1962, the facilities and components imported for the manufacture and assembly of automobiles were exempted from customs duties. The policy caused intense oppositions from domestic components companies. They thought that even if they developed their own products, it would be difficult to compete with imported products (KAMA & KAICA 2005, pp. 141, 146).

The second problem was that the development direction of the entire automobile industry was subjected to the will of the monopolistic market rulers created by the policy, large conglomerates. The physical power and institutional capabilities of the government were always not so effective at encouraging them to do something. Even if the tariff exemption on imported components hindered components companies' will to develop their own components, the problem could be solved if the assembler had a strong will to localize components. However, according to the integration plan, Shinjin Motors, which was selected as the only automobile assembly plant at that time, enjoyed the status of market leader, but was not active in localization of components. The localization rate of Shinjin Motors, which was manufacturing assembled automobiles with imported KD components from Toyota, was only 21% in 1966 and 23.6% in 1967. According to the localization plan established by Shinjin Motors when it was first selected as the only assembly plant for automobiles, the localization rate had to reach 38% in 1966 and 50% in 1967. Nevertheless, Shinjin was not interested in raising the rate, only trying to solve this problem through political deals with government ministers and politicians (KAMA & KAICA 2005, pp. 149, 168). Wŏn-ch'ŏl O, former policymaker, who led industrial policy in the Ministry of Commerce and Industry during the Park government, said:

> Even Shinjin Motors did not want to lose money by using expensive Korean components because the prices of imported goods from Japan were cheaper. It was too much to demand patriotism from private companies that are only seeking self-interest. Finally, Korean corporations continued to import foreign components and thus it was impossible to expect to localize various main components including car engines. (O 1996, p. 94)

In other words, the domestic components industry could never grow if it depended on the interests of large companies. Ironically, it was the government that created such understanding of large companies. The government created exclusive market power of large companies through the unification policy of automobile companies in the 1960s. The policy was based on an input-driven growth strategy to nurture competitive enterprises through economy of scale, rather than favoring certain companies selected by the government.

However, as the Korean government did not achieve its goal of localizing components, it changed its policy from "unification" to "Samwonhwa" in the automobile industry. Even if it slightly undermined its policy priority of "economic realization of scale," it intended to strengthen the government's relative power by strengthening the competitive system among conglomerates. However, monopoly market dominance continued until the development of Hyundai's domestic car model Pony, in the 1970s, even after Asia and Hyundai were selected as car manufacturing companies in 1968. In addition, government policy has helped to maintain the monopoly status of Shinjin in the market. To boost the performance of localization rate quickly, the government regulated the production amount of each automobile company depending on its localization rate in the 1969 Automobile Industry Development Plan. In the case of buses and trucks, however, the government applied for the rule strictly, whereas with passenger cars, only two-thirds of production amount was allocated according to localization performance, and the remaining one-third reflected the production performance of the previous year. As a result, Shinjin could get the greatest amount of production, enjoying its status of market leader. As the localization rates of the three automobile companies were almost similar, the allocated amounts depending on the localization rate were almost the same. But Shinjin was the overwhelming leader in production performance. For this reason, Shinjin had little incentive to actively increase its localization rate (KAMA & KAICA 2005, p. 152).

The third issue was related to the most fundamental problem of automobile industry policies until the early 1970s. The Korean government established a policy to promote the automobile industry through importing and assembling knockdown components of foreign models in the early 1960s. The knockdown production was considered inevitable due to the lack of technology and demand at the time, but it resulted in suspension of production due to frequent model changes and increases in production costs and decreases of quality due to small-quantity production. This sequence led to a decrease in demand generation, reduction of production, lack of investment funds due to financial difficulty, and a decrease in localization.

Under such a vicious circle, neither assembly companies nor components suppliers could have any incentive to localize components. For small components suppliers with low technology levels, quality problems occurred for a considerable period of time even if they developed components, and their lower wages did not give them higher price competitiveness than imports, because they could not realize the economy of scale due to small demand. In addition, since the assembly companies could easily import KD components, they were not attracted to localization of components that cost time and money (KAMA & KAICA 2005, pp. 196, 267). According to the memoirs of the former chairman of Hyundai Motor Co., in the case of finished vehicles, it was much easier and even profitable to produce automobiles by assembling KD components than to localize components. According to the chairman, "in the short term, it was much easier and profitable for us to import core components and assemble and buy cars. In fact, if we or Shinjin depended on assembly-production, we could raise profits without any big investment" (Chung 2000, p. 178).

Yet in the mid-1970s, the Korean automobile industry shifted away from relying on KD components assembly for foreign models toward a domestic model strategy, the most important takeoff in the Korean automobile industry. This transition was made by the state's strong intentional industrial policy, without input from the assemblers. However, this policy shift worked because of a simultaneous change in the understanding of the assemblers with regard to the state's policy instruments.

Finally, despite the state's strong willingness to foster the components industry, the growth of components suppliers was delayed, and localization could not be achieved by the mid-1970s because the policy for the components industry, based on horizontal integration, was in conflict with assemblers' interests. An integration system presupposes close cooperation between the components supplier and the parent company, but under the horizontal integration, it was difficult to form close relationships between suppliers and their lead firm because lead firms were reluctant to share their supports to suppliers with other competitors (KAMA & KAICA 2005, pp. 177, 187).

The industrial structure that the Korean government wanted to build through its policy of horizontal integration appears to have been a German style of industrial structure, which features a horizontal network between professional components suppliers and automotive makers. But this model requires components suppliers with high technological capabilities. In the early 1960s, however, the Korean automotive components industry was confined to the manual production level. Furthermore, the technological gap between car makers supported by the state and components suppliers became more intense through the 1960s. Under these circumstances, cooperation between finished-car makers and components suppliers could be achieved only through unilateral support from the finished-car maker.

However, under the horizontal integration, a car maker didn't have any incentive to support and nurture a specific components supplier. In the case of Dongyang Machinery Co. (Dongyanggigye), which specialized in producing gears at that time, the government expected the company to grow a more specialized company through cooperation with Shinjin, but Shinjin was not interested in it. Instead, Shinjin established Korea Spicer, a joint company with Spicer Co., headquartered in the United States, which defeated the plan of the government to build a specialized gear-components factory (KAMA & KAICA 2005, p. 152). Hyundai, too, wanted to manufacture core components in-house rather than use external components suppliers in the process of developing its own model. Hyundai presented to the government the proposals to develop internally the transmission and rear axle for Hyundai's Pony several times. However, the government did not permit in-house production of the core components by Hyundai. Finally, Hyundai had to hand over the production of the components to Dong Yang Warner and Korea Spicer (KAMA & KAICA 2005, pp. 268–269). Despite Hyundai's failure to internalize core components, it is clear that assemblers did not want to develop core components with domestic components suppliers.

In sum, the Korean components industry was delayed until the mid-1970s, despite the policy authorities' commitment to foster the components industry. Although the Korean government pushed for policies to foster the components industry through integration, it failed to achieve the expected performance in the components industry by prioritizing the policy for assembly based on KD production and by preventing the growth of the domestic components industry. The Korean components industry policy from the 1960s to the early 1970s failed because no market actor could find its own interests within the framework of the policy. Still, the Long-Term Automobile Industry Promotion Plan of the mid-1970s showed unexpected success with the government's intention and market actors' interests combined.

Domestic Car Model Development and Adoption of Vertical Integration Policy

In the mid-1970s, the state-led process of developing Korea's domestic car model provides some important implications. First, the gradual upgrade in Korea's industrial development process was state-led, not market-led. Second, the policy works only when it matches corporate interests. Third, the experience of policy success or failure can have a significant impact on future policy formation. Development of domestic car models in Korea was led by strong policy. On the other hand, initially car makers did not participate in the policy actively. However, as a car maker began to pursue its interest by using the policy, other car makers also moved to follow the policy. The policy began to work effectively. Furthermore, the policy's success has strengthened cooperation between the state and assemblers, which in turn led to policy changes in the components industry.

Following the development of unique domestic models, the Korean government moved its components industry policy from horizontal integration to vertical. The development process of unique domestic models strengthened large companies' willingness to secure a stable procurement system of components. Yet in the early days of the project, the government maintained components industry policies based on horizontal integration. The government believed that the policy would be necessary for the development of the components industry. And the development process of the automobile industry after the early 1960s strengthened the belief that nurturing components suppliers should not be left to large companies. However, trust between the state and large assemblers established in the unique domestic model development project enabled a drastic policy shift for the components industry in the late 1970s, which was a decisive occasion for shaping the typical relationship between Korean companies.

In the mid-1970s, the Korean government abandoned its previous policy centered on the assembly of KD components for development of the unique domestic model. Despite initial concerns, this strategy succeeded due to the strong will of policymakers coupled with the interests of large assemblers, resulting in a dramatic increase in localization of components as well as the development of the domestic model, Pony.

The Korean government's Long-Term Automobile Industry Promotion Plan was established after the president announced its heavy chemicals industrialization policy at his New Year's press conference on January 12, 1973. The core of the Long-Term Automobile Industry Promotion Plan was to promote development of a unique domestic model of small passenger car and nurture the components industry for increased localization rates. According to this long-term plan announced in May of 1974, the automobile sector should produce a small passenger car with a production price of about $2000 and with more than 95% of localization rate by 1975 and achieve the production of 500,000 cars and export of 75,000 cars by 1981. A specialized production system by car size was also implemented. The plan required that Kia, Hyundai Motor Co., and GM Korea specialize in producing 1000 cc models, 1300 cc models, and 1400 cc models, respectively.

In the components sector, the plan separated the policies for car makers and for components companies. Car makers were required to construct factories for engines and bodies among core car components. For the remaining components, the phased horizontal integration policy was maintained based on the principle of one factory for one component. To support the plan, car tariffs increased sharply from 150% to 250%. For the components sector, the plan included the expansion of tariff exemptions for raw materials needed for localization, the import reduction, and the abolishment of tariff exemption of KD components (KAMA & KAICA 2005, pp. 201–202).

The policy shift was caused by policymakers' ideational change. As localization of components was not achieved as intended, despite repeated industrial policy changes, policymakers recognized that the problem was the automobile industry's strategy itself, which relied on the assembly of KD components (KAMA & KAICA 2005, pp. 196, 267). Despite the introduction of the "Samwonhwa" policy in the automobile industry in 1968, which licensed three automakers, the localization rate remained limited. As seen in Table 6.1, the localization rates of Shinjin's Corona and Crown were only 38.2% and 27.4% each, Hyundai's Cortina 31.3%, and Asia's Fiat 124 21.1%. The government determined that the problem was caused by the three car makers' dependence on the assembly of KD components.

Table 6.1 Trends of parts localization of cars in the late 1960s (Unit: %)

		1967	*1968*	*1969*
Shinjin	Corona	23.6	27.6	38.2
	Crown	–	21.6	27.4
Hyundai	Cortina	–	22.5	31.3
Asia	Fiat 124	–	–	21.1
Shinjin	Diesel buses	64.7	66.8	77.5
	6-ton cargos	–	24.7	34.0
Kia	Three-wheeled trucks	26.0	35.0	41.0

Sources: Korea Development Bank (1971) and KAMA and KAICA (2005, p. 186)

However, despite the government's policy turnaround, the unique domestic car model could not have been developed without an economic and technological base unless automakers responded to the policy. Then, how did automakers become more responsive to government policy, despite initial objections?

As the honorary chairman of Hyundai Motor Group, Chung Se-young, recalled, automotive manufacturers had no incentive to voluntarily develop their own models. When the official documents were sent asking the four automakers—GM Korea,[3] Kia, Asia, and Hyundai—to present their plan to construct a factory for producing a unique car model, they strongly resisted the project. Especially GM Korea had no reason to accept the drastic policy change, as it held the position of market leader in the existing system. By one account, GM Korea CEO Kim Chang-won got angry at a meeting with the Commerce-Industry Minister Lee Nak-sun after receiving an official letter on the development of a unique model from the government, saying "People who have no idea of cars make the policy of automobile industry." Chief executives of the other automakers who received the official letter also said that policymakers were unaware of the actual situation in the market and that the plan was recklessly created by "an armchair theory" (KAMA & KAICA 2005, p. 200).

However, this initial backlash from automakers began to change as Hyundai turned to actively participate in the plan. Hyundai's strategy shift was caused by the failure of the joint venture with Ford to build an engine casting plant. What held the two companies apart was the issue of export market restrictions and business areas. The main purpose of Hyundai's joint venture with Ford was to export its compact cars through Ford's worldwide sales network. Ford, however, refused to let Hyundai use its sales network to enter foreign markets, which Ford had already entered. In the business areas, Ford insisted that the joint venture would exclusively produce certain components under its strategy to push for a multinational exchange system of components, while Hyundai aimed to build a comprehensive automotive plant. For this reason, at a time when Hyundai was not making progress in negotiations with Ford, Shinjin succeeded in working with GM and Kia to build a comprehensive automotive plant, in the works since the 1960s. In the midst of internal problems and external pressure of competition, Hyundai eventually set the company's basic

[3] Shinjin invested $24 million each with GM on June 7, 1972, and established GM Korea with a 50:50 share.

strategic direction toward the development of a unique model (KAMA & KAICA 2005, pp. 192–193, 208–209).

However, the change in Hyundai top management's strategy met strong opposition from the company's internal staff because Hyundai did not have enough capital and technology to develop its own car model.

> I thought that producing cars only for a small Korean domestic market was not profitable and that we should develop an original national car model for export. If we co-produce cars by joint venture with multinational car makers, we could not develop an original car model because they insisted that we should assemble and sell their car models. Moreover, we could not export the cars that we produced because they were already selling the cars of the same model in the world market. Therefore, we had to create our own models in order to export our products ourselves. … However, my idea of developing our original model faced a wall from the start. As soon as I came up with the idea of an original car model, the whole management including executives opposed the plan. "It is not possible to develop an original model. How are we able to design our own model when we can barely copy the drawing for assembly of the Cortina, even though we're assembling it?" It was an honest remark from the chief technical officer at the time. He told me that not only did we lack the ability to catch up with the technology, but it was too risky to develop our original model because of the huge investment of time and money. Yoon, the managing director, even told me, "Are you trying to collapse the company?" (Chung 2000, pp. 178–180)

Yet despite the absolute lack of objective conditions and strong internal opposition, Hyundai executives' thinking began to move with the government's Long-Term Automobile Industry Promotion Plan. An individual company Hyundai could pursue a long-term strategy despite uncertainties due to incentives and benefits provided by the state policy. Hyundai was the only company out of the four automakers to build its own model development plan based on the government's long-term automobile promotion plan and gained the government's full support. Development of a unique domestic model and construction of a factory for it required a massive amount of money. According to Hyundai Motor Company, the first phase (1973–1975) required a total of $71.12 million. Of that amount, $52.21 million, accounting for most of these funds, was to be financed by international loans, while the remaining $19.14 million was to be financed internally through capital increase and retained earnings. However, the government's final approval for international loans amounted to $61.15 million, far exceeding the planned amount (KIET 2014, pp. 46–47).

Hyundai Motors' unique model development project finally produced the Pony 1 in November 1975, thanks to the government's full support. With the launch of the Pony, the Korean automobile industry had reorganized its landscape around Hyundai. Hyundai's share of production in the Korean passenger car industry rose to 55.5% in 1976 when the Pony began to be produced in full swing and 62.4% in 1977. Hyundai's domestic market share remained firm afterward. GM Korea (Shinjin), which had enjoyed a monopoly position from the mid-1960s to the early 1970s, accounted for 9.7% of Korea's auto production in 1977, the smallest of the three major car makers (KIET 1997b, pp. 51–52).

Hyundai's change in strategy and its success are all the more meaningful in that it changed not only individual companies but also the strategies of other automotive makers. As Hyundai dramatically increased the localization rate through development of its own domestic models, other automotive manufacturers began to work to increase the rate (KIET 1997b, p. 53). Hyundai Pony had achieved 85% localization rate with its launch in 1975 and exceeded nearly 90% in 1976. Pony's success and the development of domestic components suppliers during its development became a stimulus for other car makers. Unlike Hyundai, Kia and GM Korea originally planned production of the KD model, not development of the original domestic model. With the KD model, the localization rate would have been limited, as it was already confirmed in the previous period. Kia Brisa had a localization rate of 26% in 1974, the first year of production, with a localization rate at 63% in 1975, but Brisa II reached 90% localization rate in 1977, as seen in Table 6.2. GM Korea (changed to "Saehan Automobile" in 1976) launched Gemini in 1977 as a national car model with an initial localization rate of 70%. Since 1979, it increased its localization rate to more than 80%.

Pony's success best illustrates how the Korean economy worked at that time. Hyundai Motors was a latecomer among the Korean automakers, with only 1.7 billion KRW of capital, and lacked a technical base and experience in mass production. It could be impossible for the company to develop its original domestic model that required investment of more than 40 billion won without the full supports by the state policy. The state could also successfully pursue such a long-term and risky policy despite the absence of sufficient industrial and technological infrastructure because a company like Hyundai actively responded to policies.

Table 6.2 Trends of parts localization of cars in the late 1970s

	Car models	*1975*	*1976*	*1977*	*1978*	*1979*	*1980*	*1981*	*1982*	*1983*	*1984*
Kia	Brisa	63	78	89	89	89	92	92			
	Brisa II	86	86	90	90	89	90	91			
	Fiat 132				62	62	62	62			
	Peugeot				20	20	20	20			
Hyundai	Pony	85	90	90	91	92	93	93		97	98
	Stellar	60	61	61	61	62	62	62		97	97
	Granada					21	21	21	28	28	
GMK	Chevrolet	72									
(Saehan)	Gemini			70	75	82	85	86	86	86	86
	Rekord	58	58	60	62	62	62	64	65	65	75

Sources: Korean Institute for Industrial Economics & Trade (1997, p. 53)

The history of the Korean automobile industry until the early 1970s showed that the existence of policies itself could never ensure the intended results. The actors targeted by a policy find ways to use or bypass the policy to their advantage. In a state-led economic system, policy plays an important role, but is likely to accompany rent-seeking and political corruption. Until the early 1970s, the development process of the Korean automobile industry showed that success of policies could not be explained by the balance of power between the state and the company or by the policy means of the state. When the policy met the interests of market actors, the outcome showed unexpected results.

Success of Domestic Model and Conversion to Vertical Integration System

The successful development of Korean domestic models in the mid-1970s upgraded the Korean automobile industry and further strengthened the cooperation between the state and large companies, leaving the state dependent on them and bringing a transformation of components industry policy. The government changed its components industry policy from horizontal integration to vertical integration (soojikjuk gyeyulhwa) in the late 1970s. The latter is to organize the components supply chain by automaker vertically, while the former is to arrange components companies by item, where components companies supply the same components to all automakers in the domestic market.

The relationship between Korean firms formed by the vertical integration policy at this time allowed an opportunity to determine typical power relations between Korean firms. From the government's perspective, the vertical integration policy made large assembly companies directly foster and manage their components suppliers. For large assembly companies, the vertical integration system allowed their suppliers to be placed in their own closed hierarchy. Yet unintended consequences played an important role in shaping and transforming the characteristics of Korean business relationships. Vertical integration increased components suppliers' dependence on their lead companies and further intensified the dependence of the components industry itself on the understanding of large assembly companies.

In 1978, the Korean government introduced the vertical integration system, which allowed a closed supply chain between a specific parent company and components suppliers. This policy shift was based on the limits of horizontal integration policy to strengthen cooperation between assembly companies and components suppliers. Vertical integration encouraged assembly companies to support components suppliers, while horizontal integration ensured economies of scale for components suppliers. The vertical integration system was implemented in earnest in 1979 following the first amendment of the Small Business Enterprise Promotion Act (Joongsogiupgyeyulhwachokjinbup) of December 1978. After 1979, the government pursued a joint project plan for the designated integration businesses. The joint project plan sets a joint business plan of a components supplier and an assembly company for the manufacture of the designated integration item, thereby allowing and encouraging the assembly company to directly foster a specific components supplier. The government also expanded the scope of integration components, imposed obligations on assembly companies, and strengthened penalties on them (KIET 1997a, p. 65).

The government's policy shift to vertical integration was related to the transformation of the mindset of automobile assembly companies. Under the government's localization policy, the assembly companies had reluctantly used domestic components and had not cared about nurturing components suppliers. However, when development and mass production of domestic models began and production of finished vehicles increased in earnest in the mid-1970s, assembly companies felt the need to nurture components suppliers themselves, but incentives in the horizontal integration system for assembly companies to nurture components suppliers were limited. The government's vertical integration policy then allowed assemblers to take responsibility for specific components suppliers and to enjoy the benefits they generated there (KIET 1997a, pp. 65–66).

However, under the government-led vertical integration system, collaboration between parent company and subcontractors remained only formal rather than substantial. Then, in the 1980s, the government took steps to transform its policy into a privately centered one. To that end, in 1982 the government encouraged mutual cooperation between a lead company and suppliers' businesses by reinforcing the operation of the integration promotion committee (gyeyulhwachoojinhyupuihwoi) and in 1983 revised the Act on Integration Promotion of Small- and Medium-Sized Companies (Joongsogiupgyeyulhwachokjinbup), delegating a part of the leadership of promoting integration to the privately centered committee to promote integration of small- and medium-sized companies (Joonsogiupgyeyulhwachokjinhyupuihwoi). Further, the government supported and induced the building and operation of suppliers' associations (soogeupgiupchehyubuihwoi) by lead company to establish a voluntary integration. Thus, in 1984 and 1985, the Daewoo Cooperation Association, the Dong-A Cooperation Association (predecessor of SSangyong Cooperation Association), the Hyundai Cooperation Association, and the Asia Cooperation Council were formed. The Kia Cooperation Association had operated on its own since 1977. Since 1985, a number of suppliers' associations have been organized even under the umbrella of first-tier components suppliers (KIET 1997a, pp. 66–67).

The organization and activities of the suppliers' associations show the characteristics of a closed vertical integration structure centered on lead companies, which have become a typical feature of the relationship between Korean firms. Suppliers' associations in Korea have been organized, managed, and supplied by lead companies, rather than organized and operated voluntarily by suppliers. For example, to be a member of the Hyundai Cooperative, components companies must obtain a recommendation from Hyundai Motors. Its requirements include that the company should supply core components necessary for production of Hyundai Motors, with a transaction period with Hyundai at over two years and a ratio of delivery to Hyundai at over 40%. Expenses of the Hyundai Cooperative have been almost 100% subsidized by Hyundai Motors (KIET 1997a, pp. 67–69).

The positive effect of the vertical integration system is the support of the lead company to its suppliers. The lead company's support has focused especially on skill and quality education, and technology exchange for suppliers. This is why the growth of the Korean intermediate goods industry had been delayed until the late 1990s when a new industrial policy centered on components and materials was established.

However, the relationship between Korean companies depended on unilateral support from the lead company, rather than bilateral cooperation, for a long time. Under the vertical integration system, fostering components companies with independent technology capabilities was limited, because the dependence of nurturing components companies on lead companies was intensified. This is why the growth of the Korean components industry had been delayed until the late 1990s when a new industrial policy was established. As observed, the closed hierarchy of the traditional Korean business relations and thereby the underdevelopment of the Korean components until the late 1990s was ironically an unintended result of the state policy. The vertical integration policy adopted to increase the components localization rate and build a collaborative system between lead companies and their suppliers extended the relatively late growth of components companies in Korea.

However, the policy idea of fostering technology-specialized components companies continued to survive. In the late 1990s, the industrial policy focused on components and materials was based on the idea. Furthermore, the policy began to transform Korean business relations, by changing large assembly companies' understanding on their interests and strategies. Next, we focus on how the understanding of interfirm relationships could change at the microscopic level.

Establishing a Cooperative Innovation System

As seen in Chap. 5, Korea's large assembly companies turned to cooperative innovation systems with domestic components suppliers, moving from hierarchical and unilateral relations. This turn resulted from many problems large companies faced in using foreign components. Korean conglomerates began fostering Korean components suppliers as an alternative to avoid market forces of foreign companies, especially Japanese components suppliers. The policy shift to nurturing components and materials companies in the late 1990s enabled large assemblers' turn of strategies to work.

For large Korean assemblers, components localization is always one of the best options, because the absolute beneficiaries of components localization are them, rather than Korean components companies. As we know, until the 1990s, Korea's leading industries depended on foreign countries for most of their core components. At that time, the strategy of foreign components companies exporting their items to Korean assemblers was as follows. At first, they sell their products to Korean manufacturers at an unreasonably high price because they have the stronger bargaining power in the transactions with Korean manufactures. Then, if a Korean components company succeeds in localizing the components that they export to Korean assemblers, they lower the prices of their products to defoliate the Korean supplier with their price competitiveness. Their strategies actually jeopardized the survival of many Korean components suppliers and discouraged Korean suppliers' will to develop their own technology and components. However, this situation is very favorable to Korean assemblers in the short term because they can reduce their delivery cost, whether they use foreign components or localized Korean components. Chung Se-yung, honorary chairman of Hyundai Motors, reflected this understanding of large Korean companies:

> If we make the machine by ourselves, we can repair it when it breaks down. And if we ourselves produce a car component that we buy in foreign countries, we can secure competitiveness in car prices. In fact, there are many instances where the prices were lowered by 30–50% after imported components were localized. If a component is localized, its production cost is revealed. So we can in effect kill two birds with one stone by preventing foreign companies from setting exorbitant prices. (Chung 2000, p. 278)

Foreign companies' strategies influenced Korean assemblers' strategies. Despite the benefits of components localization, they were reluctant to foster domestic suppliers to localize components because the time and cost of supporting localization was useless due to foreign components' lower pricing. The case of an electronic components supplier that produces a bonding wire, which is a semiconductor part, demonstrates this. A director who has been in charge of R&D at a semiconductor equipment company for a long time said:

> Bonding wire is priced only by processing costs except for the price of gold, which is the material. In the past, however, Japanese companies that exported bonding wire asked us to pay high gold prices for the processing cost, even though the actual cost of processing was less than 10% of the price of gold. So even if a Japanese company cuts 50% of its processing costs, we still had room to cut our processing costs. First, if we produce the goods

> domestically, we can reduce the transportation cost, and if we develop the product with our own technology, we don't need to pay the technology royalty to the outside. Thus, although the Japanese company cut the price by 50% at that time, we were able to drop the price of the product by 40–45%, which was a competitive price. Korean customers began to buy our products because our products showed no difference in quality and our products were cheaper than Japanese products. Technology ranged from simple to difficult. (A director of quality assurance division at a semiconductor equipment company, personal communication, November 17, 2015)

Furthermore, Korean assemblers' interest in fostering domestic components suppliers had been increasing in the process of expanding their overseas production in the 1990s, after having difficulty in procuring components on foreign soils. Korean OEMs, latecomers, needed to build more competitive production networks on foreign soils than other advanced multinational companies from Germany, Japan, and the United States. Then, the relationship with domestic components suppliers was an alternative for their successful business in foreign soils.

Since the early 1990s, Korean electronics companies such as Samsung and LG have increased their overseas production rapidly, since the domestic production price was no longer competitive due to sharp wage increases in Korea and increasing overseas production of Japanese competitors in Southeast Asian countries. While Korean companies had been dependent on domestic production until that time, Japanese companies had already built the global production network in Southeast Asia by combining their high technology and low wages for the US market. In the case of the automobile industry, overseas production began in earnest in the late 1990s.[4]

Early overseas expansion of Korean assemblers was attempted independently by individual companies, while Japanese competitors had expanded their overseas production jointly with their domestic suppliers. Japanese assemblers wanted to take full advantage of capacities and close collaboration practices with their advanced home suppliers on foreign soils. However, Korean assemblers could not adopt the same strategy as their Japanese competitors when they began to expand their production overseas. The technological capabilities of Korean components companies had neither advanced as much as those of Japanese suppliers nor was the relationship between Korean assemblers and their domestic suppliers

[4] In the automobile industry, some overseas production took place in the 1980s, but overseas production began in the late 1990s.

as close as the Japanese business relationship. Because of that, Korean assembly companies faced difficulties in components procurement systems overseas.

They had three options for components procurement in overseas locations. One was to use advanced global components suppliers like Bosch; the second was to use locals; and the third, to bring partners from home, as did Japan. However, the first and second were not good options for most Korean companies such as Hyundai and Samsung. Global components companies such as Bosch had much greater bargaining power than Korean assembly companies, so they were unable to obtain components at competitive prices. They already had transactions with other large multinationals like Ford, Volkswagen, and so on, which had greater bargaining power due to their lager production capacity than Korean companies. Therefore, it was difficult for relatively small-sized Korean assemblers to procure from advanced global suppliers at competitive prices. On the other hand, when using components from local companies, quality was still unstable. Particularly in China, which was relatively underdeveloped, local components suppliers had quality problems (Kwon and Kim 2018).

After experiencing the difficulties of components procurement in the overseas production, Korean large companies turned to fostering domestic components suppliers and entering overseas with them, as Japanese companies did. According to a manager at Hyundai Motors, Hyundai expanded its business globally with domestic components suppliers in the 2000s because they thought that they could not compete with larger-sized and advanced multinational assemblers if they used the first or second option to procure components.

> We grounded in Alabama, USA, in April 2002. We took many domestic components suppliers since our competitiveness was derived from them. We tried to take domestic suppliers, which produced items we thought were important, which is core to our competitiveness. In fact, it was the right strategy for our partners [to go together with us]. It was hard to penetrate the market once they go out [alone]. For example, if they go abroad with us, they can secure profitable turnover since our Alabama plant would have a capacity of 300,000 units. In this respect, our partners could have a stable customer on foreign soil, and we were able to use our domestic partners for core components. Perhaps our way was successful. (A general manager on the Procurement Planning and Strategy team at Hyundai Motors, personal communication, August 24, 2010)

Further, Korean assembly companies realized that their competitiveness could come from their own relationship with domestic components suppliers by experiencing the benefits of close collaboration with domestic components suppliers in the globalization process. The aforementioned Hyundai purchasing team manager focused on "competitiveness," meaning not only technological and price competitiveness that OEMs and components suppliers each would bring, but more importantly, the innovative capability that could come from the relationship and collaborative synergy between the two. Then, the exclusive and hierarchical relationship between the Korean companies, which had been considered a weakness in the Korean business system, began to be an alternative system for innovative activities, where knowledge and information accumulated from assemblers and suppliers could be quickly collected, rearranged, and applied in informal and routine interactions based on long-term, exclusive transaction practices.

> In order to have competitiveness in quality and price, we must distinguish ourselves from advanced automobile companies, which grounded their plants on foreign soil. We thought that we should not use the same suppliers to differentiate ourselves from the first-movers, so it would be advantageous to utilize the companies that we had worked with in Korea, since they already knew our production processes and rules. The process of developing and producing a car differs from company to company. For example, if we need 100 suppliers, we already know 90 of them and we don't know 10 of them, and we can concentrate on bringing those 10 suppliers to our process. However, if only ten companies of 100 are known to us, and 90 are not familiar to us, it is hard to manage them intensively. (A general manager on the Procurement Planning and Strategy team at Hyundai Motors, personal communication, August 24, 2010)

New knowledge itself is important for innovative activities, but equally important is accumulating and organizing knowledge and ideas to materialize innovation. Korean assemblers including Hyundai Motors were able to minimize the cost by reestablishing relations with domestic components suppliers in the process of growing as a global top player. In these transformed relationships Korean assemblers could induce faster innovation by sharing the burden of technology development with their home suppliers.

However, the change of firm strategy is always risky because it accompanies uncertainty. The late 1990s policy to nurture components and materials contributed to the turn of Korean large companies' strategies, as the state paid for the risks that they could face.

Understanding the Part Suppliers

As seen in Chap. 4, the hierarchical and exclusive relationship between Korean firms was caused by the relative underdevelopment of the Korean components sector, which was related to the lack of R&D in components companies. Given the absence of policy supports and demand guarantee, it was risky for small components companies to invest in R&D autonomously. As seen in Chap. 3, the Korean components industry has led the growth of the whole national economy since the 2000s, based on close collaborations with domestic large assemblers in R&D activities. How could an interdependent collaborative relationship be formed between key components suppliers and the assembled large companies? Why have Korean components suppliers kept an exclusive and hierarchical relationship with large domestic assemblers, rather than finding new partners abroad?

The gap between major assembly companies and components suppliers has grown since the 1970s due to input-driven policies centered on assembly companies. Hence it was not easy for Korean components suppliers to pioneer their own overseas markets. Instead, relationship with large domestic assembly firms gave the advantage of stability in transactions and trickle-down effects due to the growth of large assemblers, despite unreasonable and unfair practices. These advantages led small- and medium-sized components suppliers to maintain business relationships with domestic large companies. Further, as the transaction relationship continues, components suppliers have also perceived the close relationship with domestic assemblers as their competitive edge. This shift in awareness has played an important role in evolving the relationship between Korean companies in main industries from hostile distrust to interdependent cooperation.

For Korean components suppliers, domestic OEMs have been relatively stable customers, only if they meet the technology, quality, and price that their customers demand. For small components suppliers, securing stable customers is an important incentive. A general manager of a first-tier supplier of Hyundai Motors said:

> Manufacturers should maintain sustainability of sales. If sales are not sustained, the company will decline. If the cost goes on, but the profit reduces

and the debt increases, the company enters into a vicious circle. So sales should increase or at least be maintained. To do so, companies must secure at least one reliable customer. (A planning team manager at an engine components supplier of Hyundai Motors, personal communication, November 10, 2015)

Korean components suppliers wanted to secure stable customers to ensure minimum demand. Instead, they had to bear large assemblers' unfair business practices such as cutting unit prices or delaying payment. Korean components suppliers failed to develop business associations based on horizontal solidarity among them like German components companies, which made it difficult for them to protest or discuss collectively. The most feasible option for Korean components companies has been to become stable and cooperative partners of domestic assemblers, rather than resisting against them or seeking an "exit" strategy.

While large domestic assemblers were growing, components suppliers also grew, thus diminishing components suppliers' interests in expanding their business with foreign OEMs. By improving competitiveness through cooperative relations with domestic conglomerates, they have achieved substantial benefits including sales growth. As large Korean assemblers such as Samsung Electronics and Hyundai Motors have increased their total sales explosively with overseas production, their components suppliers have had no time to expand their business with foreign assemblers.

Over the past decade, the portion of transactions with Hyundai Motors (including Kia Motors) has continued to increase. To date, 92–93% of our sale Over the past decade, the portion of transactions with Hyundai Motors (including Kia Motors) has continued to increase. To date, 92–93% of our sales are from Hyundai and Kia. Our company's sales growth rate in the past 10 years is an average of 15%. ... When I moved to this company from Daewoo, there was a lot of work. As the company grew rapidly, we had to add new lines in the plant, build a new plant, and develop new components every day. (A planning team manager at an engine components supplier of Hyundai Motors, personal communication, November 10, 2015)

In fact, the growth of large Korean assemblers led directly to the growth of partner companies. According to Hyundai Motors' report, the average sales of their first-tier companies increased from 73.3 billion KRW in 2001 to 258.9 billion KRW in 2014. The number of first-tier suppliers with over 100 billion KRW of sales increased from 62 with 21% share to 148 with 56% share. Quantitative growth of components suppliers has been remarkable since the 2000s, as their lead companies expanded production overseas and many components suppliers entered the market together. The number of first-tier and second-tier suppliers that deliver components to Hyundai-Kia Motors in overseas production sites increased from 34 companies in 1997 to 608 companies in 2015 (Hyundai Motor Group 2015, pp. 12–17). In the early 2000s, Korean components suppliers, not large in scale and lacking overseas experience, were able to reduce the risk of overseas investment and establish a foundation for growth as a global supplier through joint globalization with domestic OEMs.

> When Hyundai and Kia Motors go abroad, they build their plants adjacently. For example, if Hyundai built a factory in Alabama, Kia built its factory in Georgia. Then, the components suppliers who have entered the United States together with them took their places in the middle between Alabama and Georgia to supply their components to both sides, so the profitable quantity of supply could be secured. Since 200,000 units are supplied to one factory, 400,000 units will basically be secured. In addition, the suppliers could get an opportunity to grow even more by providing additional supplies to local automobile companies. (A general manager on the business coordination team of Hyundai Motors, personal communication, October 29, 2015)

Another reason why Korean components suppliers have maintained close business relationships with domestic OEMs is that the relationship itself has played an important role in the process where Korean components companies have grown as new agents of the Korean innovation system. Decentralization of the Korean innovation system has not gone entirely to global outsourcing as in the United States, nor has it gone to a consultation model based on a local or industry level as in Europe. The Korean innovation system has maintained the vertical integration centered on large conglomerates, but under the system, components companies have developed as new agents of innovation. Limited decentralization of the Korean innovation system is related to the roles of domestic OEMs in the growth of Korean components suppliers. Indeed, the relationship between Korean OEMs and their domestic components suppliers itself is an important part of the current Korean innovation system.

Positive feedback gained through formal and informal communications between Korean companies has been the basis of closer collaborations for advanced technology development. Based on knowledge as well as evaluation accumulated from experiences of collaborations, Korean companies can organize new R&D teams by reducing the cost of looking for new partners. This is a virtuous cycle of the current Korean innovation system. Korea has thus developed a way to make use of the benefits of collaborative innovation within a somewhat closed pool between large assembly firms and components suppliers.

> The work process we are currently doing with Samsung SDI is the same as the work process we did with Anam Semiconductor and Samsung Electronics. As we make prototypes, Samsung SDI gives feedback and then we both repeat the process several times. In our current WPM project, the material that we are developing is a business that costs at least 10 billion dollars to invest in technology. However, since there are reliable customers, and they and we develop the technology together, we have not reached our targets yet, but we are almost there. (A director at the quality assurance division of a semiconductor equipment manufacturer, personal communication, November 11, 2015)

However, a recent trend to open innovation has put new pressure on Korean companies. Both large Korean assemblers and components suppliers have incentives to overcome the limits of a relatively closed structure of transaction. The understanding of Korean assemblers, which had preferred a closed relationship with their suppliers, has recently changed to a more open business relationship to secure more innovative sources and more competitive prices. Components suppliers also want to expand their new customers because they are now equipped with technical skills and abilities. Establishing a new innovation system, which permits more creative ideas, while keeping the benefits of a stable and close partnership, thus remains a challenge for Korean companies.

References

Amsden, A. H. (1989). *Asia's next giant: South Korea and late industrialization.* New York: Oxford University Press.

CCKE (The Compilation Committee for the Korean Economy for 60 Years). (2011). *The Korean economy: Six decades of growth and development: Summary.* Seoul: Korea Development Institute.

Chang, H.-J., & Evans, P. (2005). The role of institutions in economic change. In S. Paula & G. Dymski (Eds.), *Reimagining growth: Towards a renewal of development theory* (pp. 99–140). London and New York: Zed Books.

Cho, Y. J. (2003). The political economy of financial liberalization in South Korea. In C. H. Lee (Ed.), *Financial liberalization and the economic crisis in Asia* (pp. 82–103). New York: Routledege.
Chung, S.-Y. (2000). *Miraeneun mandeuneu gusida*. Seoul: Haerimchoolpan.
Hahm, S. D., Plein, L. C., & Florida, R. (1994). The politics of international technology transfer: Lessons from the Korean experience. *Policy Studies Journal, 22*(2), 311–321.
Hall, P. (1986). *Governing the economy: The politics of state intervention in Britain and France*. New York: Oxford University Press.
Hundt, D. (2005). A legitimate paradox: Neo-liberal reform and the return of the state in Korea. *Journal of Development Studies, 41*(2), 242–260.
Hyundai Motor Group. (2015). *2015 Hyundai·kiajodongcha dongbansungjang choojinhyunhwang*. Seoul: Hyundai Motor Group.
Jayasuriya, K. M. (2000). Authoritarian liberalism, governance and the emergence of the regulatory state in post-crisis East Asia. In R. Robison, M. Beeson, K. Jayasuriya, & H. Kim (Eds.), *Politics and markets in the wake of the Asian crisis, Asian capitalisms* (pp. 315–330). London and New York: Routledge.
Jo, H.-J. (2005). *Hangookjuk saengsanbangsikeun ganeunghanga?* [A study on the possibility of "hyundaism": Korean production system and employment relations]. Paju: Hanulacademy.
Jung, H.-S. (2003). Kim Chae-ik Soosukgwa Jungbohwa Jungchaek. In D.-W. Nam et al. (Eds.), *80nyundae kyungjegyehyukgwa Kim Chae-ik soosuk* (pp. 117–142). Seoul: Samsung Economic Research Institute.
Katzenstein, P. J. (1985). *Small states in world markets: Industrial policy in Europe*. Ithaca, NY: Cornell University Press.
Kim, L.-S. (1997b). *Imitation to innovation: The dynamics of Korea's technological learning*. Boston: Harvard Business School Press. Korean edition: Kim, L.-S. (2000). *Mobangesu hyuksineuro* (Y.-C. Lim & H.-S. Lee, Trans.). Seoul: Sigma Insight.
Kim, K.-S. (2001). *Woorinaraui sanup·mooyukjungchek jungegwajung*. Seoul: Institute for Global Economics.
Kim, Y.-B. (2005). The industrial policy processes of Korea in 1980s: The case of the industry development law. *The Journal of International, 8*(1), 237–255.
Kim, C.-Y. (2006). *Choibingookesu sunjingook moontukggaji: Hangook kyungjejungchek 30nyunsa*. Seoul: Randomhouse Korea.
Kim, J.-I. (2007). Joongsogiupui Yukhal Jaejungrip. In Korea Development Institute (Ed.), *Woori Kyungjeui Sunjinhwareul Wihan Jungboo Yukhalui Jaejungrip* (pp. 97–157). Seoul: Korea Development Institute.
Kim, K.-M. (2010). Changes in Korean labor market regimes. *Seoul Journal of Korean Studies, 23*(2), 247–269.

Kim, E. M. (2014). The South Korean developmental alliance between business, labor and government. In I.-C. Yi & T. Mkandawire (Eds.), *Learning from the South Korean developmental success: Effective developmental cooperation and synergistic institutions and policies* (pp. 235–258). New York: Palgrave Macmillan.

Korea Automobile Manufacturers Association, & Korea Automobile Industries Cooperative Association. (2005). *Hangookjadongchasanup 50nyunsa*. Seoul: Korea Automobile Manufacturers Association and Korea Automobile Industries Cooperative Association.

Korea Development Bank. (1971). *Hangookui sanup*. Seoul: Korea Development Bank.

Korea Electronics Association. (1999). *Junjasanup40nyunsa: 1959~1999*. Seoul: Korea Electronics Association.

Korea Institute for Industrial Economics & Trade. (1997). *Hangook jadongchasansubui dogeupchegyewa hwalsunghwa bangan*. Seoul: Korea Institute for Industrial Economics & Trade.

Korea Institute for Industrial Economics & Trade. (2012). *Boopoom·sojae miraebijun soorip yungoo*. Seoul: The Korea Institute for Advancement of Technology.

Korea Institute for Industrial Economics & Trade. (2014). *Kyungjebaljunkgyunghummodulehwasaup*. Sejong: Ministry of Economy and Finance and Korea Institute for Industrial Economics & Trade.

Krugman, P. (1998). *What happened to Asia?* Retrieved October 28, 2015, from http://web.mit.edu/krugman/www/DISINTER.html.

Kwon, H.-K., & Kim, K. M. (2018). Varieties of globalisation and national economy: Korea's experience from a comparative perspective. *Journal of International Relations and Development* (Online available). https://link.springer.com/article/10.1057/s41268-018-0162-0.

Lee, J.-W. (2011). *Study on politics of social pacts in South Korea: Presidential commission on industrial relations reform and Korea tripartite commission*. Seoul: Seoul National University Master's Thesis.

Moon, C.-I. (1994). Changing state-business relations in South Korea since 1980. In A. MacIntyre (Ed.), *Business and government in industrializing Asia* (pp. 142–166). Ithaca, NY: Cornell University Press.

Moon, C.-I., & Kim, Y.-C. (1996). A cycle of paradox. In A. Leftwich (Ed.), *Democracy and development: Theory and practice* (pp. 139–167). Cambridge: Polity Press.

Nam, D.-W. (2003). Chongron: "Kim Chae-ik"gwaui Inyun. In D.-W. Nam et al. (Eds.), *80nyundae kyungjegyehyukgwa Kim Chae-ik soosuk* (pp. 25–57). Seoul: Samsung Economic Research Institute.

O, W.-C. (1996). *Hangookhyung kyungjegunsul: Engineering approach 4*. Seoul: Kia Economic Research Institute.

OECD. (1994). *OECD Economic surveys: Korea*. Paris: OECD.
OECD. (1996). *Economic surveys: Korea*. OECD.
Ostry, S., & Nelson, R. R. (1995). *Techno-nationalism and techno-globalism: Conflict and cooperation*. Washington, DC: The Brookings Institution.
Pirie, I. (2008). *The Korean developmental state: From dirigisme to neo-liberalism*. London: Routledge.
Scharpf, F. W. (2000). Economic changes, vulnerabilities, and institutional capabilities. In F. W. Scharpf & V. A. Schmidt (Eds.), *Welfare and work in the open economy: From vulnerability to competitiveness* (pp. 21–129). Oxford and New York: Oxford University Press.
Yoon, J.-H. (2006). *Hangookgisooljungchaekron: Hangook hisoolneungryuk baljun 40nyunsa*. Seoul: Gyeongmunsa.
Yoon, D.-Y. (2012). *Crisis of export-led development and the politics of industrial policy, 1980–2007: Idea, institution and developmental governance*. Seoul: Yonsei University Dissertation.
Yoon, H.-K. (2013). The change of the economic role of Korean government and the change of the market institution: A discursive institutionalist approach. *Journal of Korean Politics, 22*(1), 163–187.

CHAPTER 7

Conclusion

To identify the reasons for the Korean economy's rapid and continuous growth over the past 50 years, we have analyzed the unique characteristics of the Korean development model, how it has changed during that time, and the causes and mechanisms of change in dynamic, comparative-historical, and endogenous terms.

The neoliberalism theory of market economy and the classical state-led developmentalism theory, which have attempted to explain the cause of Korea's economic growth, cannot dynamically identify the evolution of the Korean economic development model through their respective lenses. This work has dynamically explained the characteristics of the Korean economic development model in terms of change, thus surpassing the static explanations of existing studies.

Our analysis revealed that the typical characteristics of the Korean economic development model include strategies of continuous state-led developmentalism. Up until the 1970s, the state deeply intervened in the economy based on the state's powerful dirigisme. The state hand-selected industries and companies, relying on its authority to set policy through financial control, by means of bank nationalization, distribution of policy funds, and the business license system. The policy decision process was a closed and narrow structure, involving a small number of key bureaucrats, with the president at the center, and private corporations serving only as sub-partners in the export promotion policy.

K. M. Kim, *The Korean Developmental State*,
https://doi.org/10.1007/978-981-15-3465-2_7

However, in the 2000s, following the 1997 crisis, the direct means of policymaking that relied on financial control or imperative discretionary authority was no longer an option. With each government, the state continues to advance industries by presenting a new vision of industrial policies and creating programs, such as the Kim Dae-jung government's venture business promotion or promotion of components and materials, the Roh Moo-hyun government's next-generation growth engine policy, the Lee Myung-bak government's new growth engine policy, and the Park Geun-hye government's creative economic policy.

However, Korea's state-led developmentalism has changed in content, means, and methods. Unlike the 1970s when the government developed large corporations through massive capital input, since 1997, the government has focused on industry policies to develop technology-intensive and higher value-added industries and create a system of innovation that fosters synergies of cooperation between small, medium-sized, and large corporations. The means of policy has changed, now providing incentives that focus on R&D support rather than massive capital inputs. Policy governance has also changed, increasing broader participation while the state serves as a coordinator, forming a consortium of private corporations with government-funded research institutes. The state also has formed an ecosystem of industrial innovation through joint private and public R&D projects.

We can best understand these changes in the Korean economic development model from a comparative perspective, identifying the type of Korean capitalism after 1997 in terms of various types of capitalism, rather than through the lens of state developmentalism or state-led capitalism with Korean developmental characteristics. We distinguished Korean capitalism after 1997 from the Anglo-Saxon free-market model or the privately led European corporatism model in that the state does not rely on the market to advance major industries and promote new industries; it intervenes in and controls systems of industry innovation. Korea has changed to a system of democratic developmentalism, which relies on a more comprehensive and democratic governance system than in the past.

Then why did Korea not keep its system of developmentalism of the 1970s? Why not turn to an Anglo-American model of market liberalism or European-type corporatism model?

To understand the unique evolution of Korean capitalism, we have followed the discursive institutionalism approach that examines not only the external impact of change but also the major actors and political processes.

We argue that the Korean economic development model maintained the form of state-led capitalism while adopting a more market-oriented and democratic governance system in the face of pressures to change. Major actors in the Korean political economy had adapted themselves to the environmental changes. Hence, the Korean economic development model did not emerge from a master plan but resulted from actors continuously rebalancing their institutional roles for survival. This viewpoint is distinguished from the theory that actors with a fixed understanding and policy determine the change in direction in order to win power. With Korean developmentalism, major actors such as state bureaucrats, large corporations, and small- and medium-sized corporations compromise with each other in changed situations in order to secure the survival and legitimacy of their own organizations.

We further argue that the evolution of Korean economic development affirms that the Korean model could be maintained through change, and that change was possible through maintenance.

References

Acemoglu, D. (2005). Politics and economics in weak and strong states. *Journal of Monetary Economics, 52*(7), 1199–1226.

Akyüz, Y., Chang, H.-J., & Kozul-Wright, R. (1998). New perspectives on East Asian development. *The Journal of Development Studies, 34*(6), 4–36.

Albert, M. (1993). *Capitalism against capitalism*. London: Whurr.

Amable, B. (2003). *The diversity of modern capitalism*. Oxford and New York: Oxford University Press.

Amsden, A. H. (1989). *Asia's next giant: South Korea and late industrialization*. New York: Oxford University Press.

Amsden, A. H. (2013). *Securing the home market: A new approach to Korean development*. Research paper 2013-1. United Nations Research Institute for Social Development (UNRISD). Retrieved April 15, 2015, from http://www.unrisd.org/__80256b3c005bccf9.nsf/0/3c3c2e5f091a961dc1257b7c00470256?OpenDocument&panel=seriespapers&Click=.

Amsden, A. H., & Chu, W.-W. (2003). *Beyond late development: Taiwan's upgrading policies*. Cambridge, MA: MIT Press.

An, C.-Y., & Kim, J.-H. (1995). Daewoijihyang mooyukjungchaekgwa sanupbaljun. In D.-S. Cha & K.-S. Kim (Eds.), *Hangookgyungje bansegi: 21Segi yeoksajuk pyunggawha 21segi vision* (pp. 321–369). Seoul: KDI..

Anchordoguy, M. (1989). *Computers Inc.: Japan's challenge to IBM*. Cambridge, MA: Harvard University Press.

Aoki, M. (1988). *Information, incentives and bargaining in the Japanese economy*. Cambridge and New York: Cambridge University Press.

Aoki, M., Kim, H.-K., & Okuno-Fujiwara, M. (1997). *The role of government in East Asian economic development: Comparative institutional analysis*. Oxford: Clarendon Press.

K. M. Kim, *The Korean Developmental State*,
https://doi.org/10.1007/978-981-15-3465-2

Baik, W.-K. (2003). Haengjunggarosuui Kim Chae-ik. In D.-W. Nam et al. (Eds.), *80nyundae kyungjegyehyukgwa Kim Chae-ik soosuk* (pp. 171–202). Seoul: Samsung Economic Research Institute.

Baik, N.-K., Joo, H., Jo, D.-H., & Jun, J.-W. (1995). *Daegiup-joongsogiupgan hyupryuksiltae mit ganghwabangan*. Seoul: Korean Institute for Industrial Economics & Trade.

Balassa, B. (1978). The 'new protectionism' and the international economy. *The Journal of World Trade Law, 12*(5), 408–436.

Berger, S. (2013). *Making in American: From innovation to market*. Cambridge, MA: MIT Press.

Bhagwati, J. N. (1978). *Foreign trade regimes and economic development: Anatomy and consequences of exchange control regimes*. Cambridge: Ballinger Co. National Bureau of Economic Research.

Bhagwati, J. N., & Srinivasan, T. N. (1979). Trade policy and development. In R. Dornbushch & J. A. Frenkel (Eds.), *International economic policy: Theory and evidence* (pp. 1–35). Baltimore: Johns Hopkins University Press.

Blank, S. (1978). Britain: The politics of foreign economic policy, the domestic problem of pluralistic stagnation. In P. J. Katzenstein (Ed.), *Between power and plenty: Foreign economic policies of advanced industrial states* (pp. 89–137). Madison: University of Wisconsin Press.

Blyth, M. (2002). *Great transformation: Economic ideas and institutional change in the twentieth century*. New York: Cambridge University Press.

Bobo, B. F., & Sintim-Aboagye, H. (2012). *Neo-liberalism, interventionism and the developmental state: Implementing new partnership for Africa's development*. Trenton: Africa World Press.

Boyer, R. (1997). French statism at the crossroads. In C. Crouch & W. Streeck (Eds.), *Political economy of modern capitalism: Mapping convergence and diversity* (pp. 71–101). London: SAGE Publications Ltd.

Breznitz, D. (2007). *Innovation and the state: Political choice and strategies for growth in Israel, Taiwan, and Ireland*. New Haven and London: Yale University Press.

Byun, S.-K., Kim, H.-J., & Kim, T.-Y. (2002). Analysis for 1990's national growth factors led by export-driven strategy; Focused on mobile communications industry. *International Telecommunications Policy Review, 9*(2), 115–141.

Carney, R. W., & Wit, M. A. (2015). The role of the state in Asian business systems. In M. A. Witt & C. Redding (Eds.), *The Oxford handbook of Asian business systems* (pp. 538–560). Oxford: Oxford University Press.

CCKE (The Compilation Committee for the Korean Economy for 60 Years). (2011a). *The Korean economy: Six decades of growth and development: Summary*. Seoul: Korea Development Institute.

CCKE (The Compilation Committee for the Korean Economy for 60 Years). (2011b). *The Korean economy: Six decades of growth and development: Economy*. Seoul: Korea Development Institute.

CCKE (The Compilation Committee for the Korean Economy for 60 Years). (2011c). *The Korean economy: Six decades of growth and development: Industry*. Seoul: Korea Development Institute.

CCKM (The Compilation Committee for the Korean Miracle). (2013). *The Korean miracle I*. Paju: Nanam.

Chang, H.-J., & Evans, P. (2005). The role of institutions in economic change. In S. Paula & G. Dymski (Eds.), *Reimagining growth: Towards a renewal of development theory* (pp. 99–140). London and New York: Zed Books.

Chang, S. -I., Lee, K.-S., Park, K.-S., Lee, H.-G., Hong, S.-I., Jung, E.-M., Kim, J.-K., & Kim, K.-Y. (2010). *Jooyo sanupbyul daejoongsogiup sunggwa mit guraegoojo boonsukgwa jungchaekjuk sisajum*. Seoul: Korean Institute for Industrial Economics & Trade.

Cherry, J. (2005). 'Big deal' or big disappointment? The continuing evolution of the South Korean developmental state. *The Pacific Review, 18*(3), 327–354.

Cho, Y. J. (2003). The political economy of financial liberalization in South Korea. In C. H. Lee (Ed.), *Financial liberalization and the economic crisis in Asia* (pp. 82–103). New York: Routledege.

Cho, Y.-J (1995). Kwangbok ihoo woorinaraui geumyoongjungchaeke daehan pyungga mit apeuroui jungchaekgwaje. In Korea Institute for Public Finance (Ed.), *Kwangbok hoo 50nyunganui jose mit keumyoongjungchekui baljungwa jungcheckbanghyang* (pp. 11–89). Seoul: Korea Institute for Public Finance.

Cho, C., & Kim, K.-Y. (2012). *Public policy issues arising from the auto parts business relationship shift in next-generation automotive industry*. Seoul: Korean Institute for Industrial Economics & Trade.

Cho, T.-H., Kim, J.-H., & Schreyer, P. (2012). *Woorinara 2000nyundai joongban ihoo sangsansungjoodohyung kyungjero ihang*. BOK issue paper series, no. 2012-2, 1–12.

Choi, D.-K. (1983). A study on the systematization of medium & small enterprises. *Kyungyungnonchong, 6*, 143–161.

Choi, B.-S. (1991a). *Economic policymaking in Korea: Institutional analysis of economic policy changes in the 1970s and 1980s*. Seoul: Chomyung Press.

Choi, J.-W. (1991b). 1980nyundae jooyosanupjungchaek gyuljunggwa gyungjaengjungchek yukhalgwa hangye. *KDI Journal of Economic Policy, 13*(2), 97–127.

Choi, J.-B. (1995). *Haebang ihoo hangookui geumyoongjungchaek*. Busan: Kyungsung University Press.

Choi, D.-S. (2014). *Giupe daehan jungboo R&D toojajiwonui jungchaekhyogwa boonsukyungoo*. Research report 2014-030. Korea Institute of S&T Evaluation and Planning. Retrieved May 24, 2015, from https://www.kistep.re.kr/c3/sub2_5.jsp?brdType=R&bbIdx=7736.

Chu, Y.-W. (2009). Eclipse or reconfigured? South Korea's developmental state and challenges of the global knowledge economy. *Economy and Society, 38*(2), 278–303.

Chung, C.-K. (1987). Jungchaekgwajung. In Jo, Suk-joon et al. (Eds.), *Hangookhaengjungui yuksajuk boonsuk, 1968–1984* (pp. 504–521). Seoul: Seoul National University Press.

Chung, C.-K. (1988). Kyungjejanggwanhwoiuiwa jungchaekgyuljung. *Korean Journal of Public Administration, 26*(2), 370–380.

Chung, S.-Y. (2000). *Miraeneun mandeuneun gusida*. Seoul: Haerimchoolpan.

Cohen, S. (1977). *Modern capitalist planning*. Berkeley: University of California Press.

Cohen, É. (1992). *Le colbertisme 'High Tech': économie des telecom et du grand projet* [High-Tech colbertism: The economics of telecoms and the grand project]. Paris: Hachette.

Cole, D. C., & Lyman, P. N. (1971). *Korean development: The interplay of politics and economics*. Cambridge, MA: Harvard University Press.

Cox, A. (1986). *State, finance and industry*. Prentice Hall: Harvester Wheatsheaf.

Crouch, C. (1993). *Industrial relations and European state traditions*. Oxford: Oxford University Press.

Davidheiser, E. B. (1992). Strong states, weak states: The role of the state in revolution. *Comparative Politics, 24*(4), 463–475.

Delsen, L. (2002). *Exit polder model? Socioeconomic changes in the Netherlands*. Westport: Praeger.

Dyer, J. H., & Chu, W.-J. (2000). The determinants of trust in supplier-automaker relationships in the U.S., Japan, and Korea. *Journal of International Business Studies, 31*(2), 259–285.

Dyer, J. H., & Ouchi, W. G. (1993). Japanese-style partnerships: Giving companies a competitive edge. *Sloan Management Review, 35*(1), 51–63.

Dyson, K. (1980). *The state tradition in Western Europe*. Oxford: Martin Robertson.

Ebbinghaus, B. (1999). Does a European social model exist and can it survive? In G. Huemer, M. Mesch, & F. Traxler (Eds.), *The role of employer associations and labour unions in the EMU: Institutional requirements for European economic policies*. Aldershot: Ashgate.

Economic Planning Board. (1994). *Kyungjebaeksu*. Seoul: Economic Planning Board.

Electronics and Telecommunications Research Institute. (2012). *Hangookjunjatongsinyungoowon 35nyunsa* [35 years' history of ETRI]. Daejeon: Electronics and Telecommunications Research Institute.

Estrin, S., & Holmes, P. (1983). *French planning in theory and practice*. London: Allen & Unwin.

Evans, P. B. (1985). Transnational linkage and the economic role of the state. In P. Evans, D. Rueschemeyer, & T. Skocpol (Eds.), *Bringing the state back in* (pp. 44–77). Cambridge and New York: Cambridge University Press.

Evans, P. B. (1995). *Embedded autonomy: States and industrial transformation*. Princeton: Princeton University Press.

Evans, P. B. (2008). *In search of the 21st century developmental state.* Centre for global political economy working paper 4. Brighton: University of Sussex.

Evans, P. B. (2010). Constructing the 21st century developmental state: Potentials and pitfalls. In O. Edigheji (Ed.), *Constructing a democratic developmental state in South Africa* (pp. 37–58). Cape Town: HSRC Press.

Evans, P. B., & Heller, P. (2015). Human development, state transformation, and the politics of the development state. In S. Leibfried et al. (Eds.), *The Oxford handbook of transformations of the state* (pp. 691–713). Oxford: Oxford University Press.

Evans, P. B., & Rauch, J. (1999). Bureaucracy and growth: A cross-national analysis of the effects of 'Weberian' states structures on economic growth. *American Sociological Review, 64*(5), 748–765.

Fioretos, O. (2011). *Creative reconstructions: Multilateralism and European varieties of capitalism after 1950.* Ithaca: Cornell University Press.

Frank, C. R. (1975). *Foreign trade regimes and economic development: South Korea.* New York: National Bureau of Economic Research.

Fredrick, W. F. (1985). The problem of actor designation in political analysis. *Comparative Politics, 17*(2), 127–152.

Gittelman, M., & Dunning, J. H. (1992). Japanese multinationals in Europe and the United states: Some comparisons and contrasts. In M. W. Klein & P. J. J. Welfans (Eds.), *Multinationals in the new Europe and global trade* (pp. 237–264). Berlin and New York: Springer Verlag.

Gorter, C. (2000). The Dutch miracle? In G. Esping-Andersen & M. Regini (Eds.), *Why deregulate labour markets?* (pp. 181–210). Oxford and New York: Oxford University Press.

Ha, Y.-C. (2006). *Late industrialization and the dynamics of the strong state in South Korea: Debureaucratization and hollowing out.* Seoul: Seoul National University Press.

Haggard, S. (1990). *Pathways from the periphery: The politics of growth in the newly industrializing countries.* Ithaca, NY: Cornell University Press.

Hahm, S. D., Plein, L. C., & Florida, R. (1994). The politics of international technology transfer: Lessons from the Korean experience. *Policy Studies Journal, 22*(2), 311–321.

Hall, P. (1986). *Governing the economy: The politics of state intervention in Britain and France.* New York: Oxford University Press.

Hall, P. (Ed.). (1989). *The political power of economic ideas.* Princeton: Princeton University Press.

Hall, R. B. (2003). The discursive demolition of the Asian development model. *International Studies Quarterly, 47*(1), 71–99.

Hall, P. (Ed.). (2015). The changing role of the state in liberal market economies. In S. Leibfried, E. Huber, M. Lange, J. D. Levy, F. Nullmeier, & J. D. Stephens (Eds.), *The Oxford handbook of transformation of the state* (pp. 426-444). Oxford: Oxford University Press.

Hall, P., & Soskice, D. (2001). *Varieties of capitalism: The institutional foundations of comparative advantage*. Oxford: Oxford University Press.
Hamilton, G., Zeile, W., & Kim, W. J. (1990). The network structures of East Asian economies. In S. Clegg & G. Redding (Eds.), *Capitalism in contrasting cultures* (pp. 105–130). Berlin and New York: de Gruyter.
Han, S.-H. (1988). Hangook jejoupui gyeyulhwa goojo hyunhwanggwa gyeyulhwajungchaek: Saengsangongjung mit boopoomgooksanhwawa gwanryunhayu. *Jungchaekdonghyang, 6*(1), 94–112.
Hansen, B. (1968). *Fiscal policy in seven countries, 1955–1965*. Paris: OECD.
Hart-Landsberg, M., & Burkett, P. (2001). Economic crisis and restructuring in South Korea: Beyond the free market-statist debate. *Critical Asian Studies, 33*(3), 403–430.
Hasan, P. (1976). *Korea: Problems and issues in a rapidly growing economy*. Baltimore: World Bank.
Hemerijck, A., & Manow, P. (2001). The experience of negotiated reforms in the Dutch and German welfare states. In B. Ebbinghaus & P. Manow (Eds.), *Comparing welfare capitalism* (pp. 217–238). London: Routledge.
Hemmert, M. (2007). The Korean innovation system: From industrial catch-up to technological leadership? In J. Mahlich & W. Pascha (Eds.), *Innovation and technology in Korea: Challenges of a newly advanced economy* (pp. 11–32). Heidelberg: Physica-Verlag.
Herrigel, G. (2010). *Manufacturing possibilities: Creative action and industries recomposition in the United States, Germany, and Japan*. Oxford and New York: Oxford University Press.
Hillebrand, W. (1996). *Shaping competitive advantages: Conceptual framework and the Korean approach*. London: Routledge.
Hong, W. (1975). *Trade and development in Korea*. Honolulu: University of Hawaii Press.
Hong, S.-B., & Lee, C.-G. (2000). *Daemanui gwahakgisoolchejewa jungchaek* [The S&T system and policy of Taiwan]. Sejong: Science and Technology Policy Institute.
Hundt, D. (2005). A legitimate paradox: Neo-liberal reform and the return of the state in Korea. *Journal of Development Studies, 41*(2), 242–260.
Hundt, D. (2009). *Korea's development alliance: State, capital and the politics of rapid development*. London: Routledge.
Hyundai Motor Group. (2015). *2015 Hyundai·kiajadongcha dongbansungjang choojinhyunhwang*. Seoul: Hyundai Motor Group.
IMD. (2013). *IMD world competitiveness yearbook 2013*. Lausanne: IMD International.
Institute for International Trade. (2010). *Jooyo mooyukdonghyangjipyo* [Main trade indicators]. Seoul: Korea International Trade Association.
Institute for International Trade. (2015). *Jooyo mooyukdonghyangjipyo* [Main trade indicators]. Seoul: Korea International Trade Association.

Jayasuriya, K. M. (2000). Authoritarian liberalism, governance and the emergence of the regulatory state in post-crisis East Asia. In R. Robison, M. Beeson, K. Jayasuriya, & H. Kim (Eds.), *Politics and markets in the wake of the Asian crisis, Asian capitalisms* (pp. 315–330). London and New York: Routledge.

Jho, W. (2007). Liberalization as a development strategy: Network governance in the Korean mobile telecom market. *Governance: An International Journal of Policy, Administration, and Institutions, 20*(4), 633–654.

Ji, J.-H. (2009). The shift in the state form and mode of power exercise in South Korea: From the authoritarian developmental state to neoliberal state power. *Korean Political Science Review, 43*(4), 175–203.

Ji, J.-H. (2011). *Hangook sinjayoojoouiui giwongwa hyungsung*. Seoul: Chaegsesang.

Jo, H.-J. (2005). *Hangookjuk saengsanbangsikeun ganeunghanga?* [A study on the possibility of "hyundaism": Korean production system and employment relations]. Paju: Hanulacademy.

Jo, D.-H. (2012). *Jejo joongsogiupui gyungyungsunggwa mit gyungjaengryk siltae boonsuk*. Seoul: Korean Institute for Industrial Economics & Trade.

Jo, T.-H, Kim, J.-H., & Schreyer, P. (2012). *Woorinara 2000nyundae joongban ihoo saengsansungjoodohyung kyungjero ihaeng*. BOK issue paper series no. 2012-2. Bank of Korea. Retrieved July 3, 2014, from https://www.bok.or.kr/portal/bbs/P0002353/view.do?nttId=181021&menuNo=200433.

Johnson, C. (1982). *MITI and the Japanese miracle: The growth of industrial policy, 1925–1975*. Stanford: Stanford University Press.

Johnson, C. (1985). Political institutions and economic performance: The government-business relationship in Japan, South Korea, and Taiwan. In R. A. Scalapino, S. Sato, & J. Wanandi (Eds.), *Asian economic development: Present and future* (pp. 63–89). Berkeley: University of California Press.

Jones, L. P., & Sakong, I. (1980). *Government, business, and entrepreneurship in economic development: The Korean case*. Cambridge, MA.: Harvard University Press.

Jung, H.-S. (2003). Kim Chae-ik Soosukgwa Jungbohwa Jungchaek. In D.-W. Nam et al. (Eds.), *80nyundae kyungjegyehyukgwa Kim Chae-ik soosuk* (pp. 117–142). Seoul: Samsung Economic Research Institute.

Kang, E. C. S. (2000a). Segyehwa reform of the South Korean developmental state. In S. Kim (Ed.), *Korea's globalization* (pp. 76–101). New York: Cambridge University Press.

Kang, K.-H. (2000b). *Kyungjegebal 5gyenyun gyehwoik mokpyo mit jiphengui pyungga*. Seoul: Seoul National University Press.

Kang, E. C. S. (2003a). The developmental state and democratic consolidation in South Korea. In S. Kim (Ed.), *Korea's democratization* (pp. 220–244). New York: Cambridge University Press.

Kang, K.-S. (2003b). Keumyoongsilmyungjewa anjunghwa sichek. In D.-W. Nam et al. (Eds.), *80nyundae kyungjegyehyukgwa Kim Chae-ik soosuk* (pp. 83–116). Seoul: Samsung Economic Research Institute.

Kang, C. W. (2002). Bad loans to good friends: Money politics and the developmental state in South Korea. *International Organization, 56*(1), 177–207.

Kang, C.-G., & Chang, S.-I. (1989). *Sanupjojungui yirongwa silje*. Seoul: Korea Institute for Industrial Economics & Trade.

Katzenstein, P. J. (1978). *Between power and plenty: Foreign economic policies of advanced industrial states.* Madison: University of Wisconsin Press.

Katzenstein, P. J. (1985). *Small states in world markets: Industrial policy in Europe.* Ithaca, NY: Cornell University Press.

Kim, J.-W. (1986). Sanupbaljungwa jungchaekgeumyoong. *KDI Journal of Economic Policy, 8*(1), 43–76.

Kim, C.-Y. (1990). *Hangook kyungjejungchek 30nyunsa: Kim Chungyum hwoigorok.* Seoul: JoongAng Ilbo.

Kim, J.-K. (1993a). Jungchaekgeumyoongui jaewonjosunggwa gaesunbangan. In D.-H. Song & H.-P. Moon (Eds.), *Kookgayesangwa jungchaekmokpyo: 1993nyundo* (pp. 113–176). Seoul: KDI.

Kim, L.-S. (1993b). National system of industrial innovation: Dynamics of capability building in Korea. In R. R. Nelson (Ed.), *National innovation system: A comparative analysis.* New York: Oxford University Press.

Kim, K.-S. (1994a). Trade and industrialization policies in Korea: An overview. In G. K. Helleiner (Ed.), *Trade policy and industrialization in turbulent times* (pp. 317–363). London and New York: Routledge.

Kim, S.-J. (Ed.). (1994b). *Park Chung-hee side: Geugusun wooriege moousiutneunga.* Seoul: Chosun Ilbo Co.

Kim, E. M. (1997a). *Big business and strong state: Collusion and conflict in South Korean developments, 1960–1990.* Albany: State University of New York Press.

Kim, L.-S. (1997b). *Imitation to innovation: The dynamics of Korea's technological learning.* Boston: Harvard Business School Press. Korean edition: Kim, L.-S. (2000). *Mobangesu hyuksineuro* (Y.-C. Lim & H.-S. Lee, Trans.). Seoul: Sigma Insight.

Kim, E. M. (1999a). Crisis of the developmental state in South Korea. *Asian Perspective, 23*(2), 33–55.

Kim, H.-K. (Ed.). (1999b). *Youngyokui hangookgyungje: Bisa kyungjegihwoikwon 33nyun.* Seoul: Maeil Business Newspaper Co.

Kim, Y.-T. (1999c). Neoliberalism and the decline of the developmental state. *Journal of Contemporary Asia, 29*(4), 441–461.

Kim, K.-S. (2001). *Woorinaraui sanup·mooyukjungchek jungegwajung.* Seoul: Institute for Global Economics.

Kim, K.-H. (2003). Kim Chae-ik soosukgwa kookjehwa. In D.-W. Nam et al. (Eds.), *80nyundae kyungjegyehyukgwa Kim Chae-ik soosuk* (pp. 143–170). Seoul: Samsung Economic Research Institute.

Kim, Y.-B. (2005). The industrial policy processes of Korea in 1980s: The case of the industry development law. *The Journal of International, 8*(1), 237–255.

Kim, J.-I. (2007). Joongsogiupui yukhal jaejungrip. In Korea Development Institute (Ed.), *Woori kyungjeui sunjinhwareul wihan jungboo yukhalui jaejungrip* (pp. 97–157). Seoul: Korea Development Institute.

Kim, C.-Y. (2006). *Choibingookesu sunjingook moontukggaji: Hangook kyungjejungchaek 30nyunsa*. Seoul: Randomhouse Korea.

Kim, K.-M. (2010). Changes in Korean labor market regimes. *Seoul Journal of Korean Studies, 23*(2), 247–269.

Kim, S.-Y. (2012a). Transitioning from fast-follower to innovator: The institutional foundations of the Korean telecommunications sector. *Review of International Political Economy, 19*(1), 140–168.

Kim, Y.-T. (2012b). *Hangookui chaebolgwa baljungookga: Hangookui chebol2* [Chaebol and the developmental state in Korea: High growth, dictatorship and the making of a dominant class]. Paju: Nanam.

Kim, E. M. (2014). The South Korean developmental alliance between business, labor and government. In I.-C. Yi & T. Mkandawire (Eds.), *Learning from the South Korean developmental success: Effective developmental cooperation and synergistic institutions and policies* (pp. 235–258). New York: Palgrave Macmillan.

Kim, W.-K., & Bae, M.-K. (2004). *Hyuksinjoodohyung kyungjewa chongyososaengsansung*. e-KIET Sanupkyungjejungbo, 214.

Kim, J.-H., & Cho, K.-H. (1991). *Gaebanghwawa hadogeupchejeui gaepyun*. Seoul: KDI.

Kim, W.-K., & Kim, I.-C. (2008). Hangook sanupjungchekui gwaguwa hyunje geurigo Mire. *e-KIET Sanupkyungjejungbo, 379*, 1–6.

Kim, K.-M., & Kwon, H.-K. (2017). The state's role in globalization: Korea's experience from a comparative perspective. *Politics & Society, 45*(4), 505–531.

Kim, C.-K., & Lee, C.-H. (1980). *Ancillary firm development in the Korean automotive industry*. Seoul: Korea International Economics Institute.

Kim, S.-H., Han, C.-H., & Jang, J.-H. (2008a). State-society relations in South Korea after democratization: Is the strong state defunct? *Pacific Focus, 23*(2), 252–270.

Kim, W.-C., Koo, J.-E., & Song, E.-J. (2008b). *Jooyogookui toojagwanryun josejiwon jedo bigyoboonsuk*. Seoul: Korea Institute of Public Finance.

Kimiya, T. (2008). *Park Jung-hee jungbooui suntaek* [The park government's choice]. Seoul: Humanitas.

Kirk, D. (2000). *The unravelling of the Korean miracle in the IMF era*. New York: St Martin's Press.

Kjær, P., & Padersen, O. K. (2001). Translating liberalization: Neoliberalism in the Danish negotiated economy. In J. L. Campbell & O. K. Pedersen (Eds.), *The rise of neoliberalism and institutional analysis* (pp. 219–248). Princeton: Princeton University Press..

Kong, T.-Y. (2000). *The politics of economic reform in South Korea: A fragile miracle*. London and New York: Routledge.

Koo, B.-Y. (1981). *Role of foreign direct investment in recent Korean economic growth*. Working paper no. 8104. Seoul: KDI.

Koo, M.-K. (2010). Embracing free trade agreements, Korean style: From developmental mercantilism to developmental liberalism. *The Korean Journal of Policy Studies, 25*(3), 101–123.

Korea Association of Machinery Industry. (2015). *Sojae·boopoomsanup donghyang-gwa Issue* [Korea Materials & Components Industry Trend and Issue], 15-1. Sejong: Ministry of Trade, Industry & Energy.

Korea Automobile Industries Cooperative Association. (1996). *Jadongchagonguppyunram*. Seoul: Korea Automobile Industries Cooperative Association.

Korea Automobile Manufacturers Association, & Korea Automobile Industries Cooperative Association. (2005). *Hangookjadongchasanup 50nyunsa*. Seoul: Korea Automobile Manufacturers Association and Korea Automobile Industries Cooperative Association.

Korea Development Bank. (1971). *Hangookui sanup*. Seoul: Korea Development Bank.

Korea Development Institute. (1980). *Hangookui jadongchagongup*. Seoul: Korea Development Institute.

Korea Development Institute. (1981). *Jadongchagongupui baljunbanghyanggwa jungchaek*. Seoul: Korea Development Institute.

Korea Electronics Association. (1999). *Junjasanup40nyunsa: 1959~1999*. Seoul: Korea Electronics Association.

Korea Federation of SMEs. (1979). *1979 SMEs poll report*. Seoul: Korea Federation of SMEs.

Korea Institute for Industrial Economics & Trade. (1987). *Korea·the United States·Japan·Brazil Jadongchaboopoomgongupboonupchegyeui bigyoboonsuk – dogeupguraesiltaereul joongsimeuro*. Seoul: Korea Institute for Industrial Economics & Trade.

Korea Institute for Industrial Economics & Trade. (1994). *21segireul hyanghan Hangook jadongchasanupui baljunbanghyang*. Seoul: Korea Institute for Industrial Economics & Trade.

Korea Institute for Industrial Economics & Trade. (1997a). *Hangook jadong-chasansubui dogeupchegyewa hwalsunghwa bangan*. Seoul: Korea Institute for Industrial Economics & Trade.

Korea Institute for Industrial Economics & Trade. (1997b). *Hangook jadong-chasanubui baljunyuksawa sungjangjamjaeryuk*. Seoul: Korea Institute for Industrial Economics & Trade.

Korea Institute for Industrial Economics & Trade. (2012). *Boopoom·sojae miraebi-jun soorip yungoo*. Seoul: The Korea Institute for Advancement of Technology.

Korea Institute for Industrial Economics & Trade. (2014). *Kyungjebaljunkgyunghummodelhwasaup*. Sejong: Ministry of Economy and Finance and Korea Institute for Industrial Economics & Trade.

Korea Institute for Public Finance. (1993). *Kwangbok ihoo woorinaraui geumyoongjungchaeke daehan pyungga mit apeuroui jungchaekgwaje*. Seoul: Korea Institute for Public Finance.

Korea International Trade Association. (1977). *Joongsosoochoolsanupui gyeyulhwa yooksungbangan*. Seoul: Korea International Trade Association.

Kronish, R., & Mericle, K. S. (Eds.). (1984). *The political economy of the Latin American motor vehicle industry*. Cambridge, MA: MIT Press.

Krueger, A. O. (1978). *Foreign trade regimes and economic development: Liberalization attempts and consequences*. Cambridge: National Bureau of Economic Research.

Krueger, A. O. (1980). Trade policy as an input to development. *American Economic Review, 70*(2), 288–292.

Krugman, P. (1994). The myth of Asia's miracle. *Foreign Affairs, 73*(6), 62–78.

Krugman, P. (1998). *What happened to Asia?* Retrieved October 28, 2015, from http://web.mit.edu/krugman/www/DISINTER.html.

Kwon, O.-Y. (2010). *The Korean economy in transition: An institutional perspective*. Cheltenham and Northampton: Edward Elgar.

Kwon, H.-K. (2012). Politics of globalization and national economy: The German experience compared with the U.S. *Politics & Society, 40*(4), 581–607.

Kwon, H.-K. (2013). Politics of institutional change: Evolution of the Irish social concertation model. *Comparative European Politics, 11*(4), 481–510.

Kwon, H.-K. (2014). *Politics of social pacts in the era of globalization: Evolution of the Irish social concertation model*. Seoul: Humanitas.

Kwon, H.-K., & Kim, K. M. (2018). Varieties of globalisation and national economy: Korea's experience from a comparative perspective. *Journal of International Relations and Development* (Online available). https://link.springer.com/article/10.1057/s41268-018-0162-0.

Lee, H.-B. (1969). Choigo gwanli. In H.-B. Lee et al. (Eds.), *Hangookhaengjungui yuksajuk boonsuk, 1948~1967* (pp. 393–407). Seoul: Hangookhaengjungmoonjeyungooso.

Lee, S.-Y. (1979). Joongsogiup gyeyulhwabangane gwanhan yungoo. *Kyeongjukyeonggsangjunmoondaehaknonmoonjip*, 2.

Lee, K.-J. (1986). Gongupgibanui goochookgwa gookjegyungjaengryuk jego (1967~70). *Hangookgyungjejungchaek40nynsa*. Seoul: The Federation of Korean Industries.

Lee, W.-Y. (1989). *Direct foreign investment and technology transfer*. Industrial policies of Korea and the Republic of China. Korea Development Institute, Conference Series 89-01.

Lee, T.-Y. (2001, September). Boopoom·sojaebaljun gibongyehwoik (MCT-2010). *Sanupgyungje*.

Lee, H.-G. (2004). *Hangookchaebolsa*. Seoul: Daemyungchoolpansa.

Lee, Y.-H. (2005). *Chaebolui jaemoogoojowa jageumjodal: Hangookui chaebol2*. Paju: Nanam.

Lee, D.-J. (2009). Woorinara Sahwoihabuijoouiui Hyungsikgwa Siljil ganui Gwoiri [Social Corporatism in Korea: The Evolution of KTC]. *Kyungjewa Sahwoi* [Economy and Society], 83, 143–168.

Lee, J.-W. (2011). *Study on politics of social pacts in South Korea: Presidential commission on industrial relations reform and Korea tripartite commission*. Seoul: Seoul National University Master's Thesis.

Lee, S.-J., & Han, T.-J. (2006). The demise of 'Korea, Inc.': Paradigm shift in Korea's developmental state. *Journal of Contemporary Asia, 36*(3), 305–324.

Lee, Y. H., Lim, Y.-J., & Chung, S.-K. (2002). The rise of the regulatory state and government-business relations in South Korea. *Korean Political Science Review, 36*(3), 199–222.

Lee, Y.-H., Chung, S.-K., & Lim, Y.-J. (2004). A comparative study of 'industrial rationalization' and 'corporate reform'—The Chun Doohwan and the Kim DaeJung government cases. *21st Century Political Science Review, 14*(1), 25–54.

Leruez, J. (1975). *Economic planning and politics in Britain*. London: Martin Robertson.

Levy, J. D. (2015). The transformations of the statist model. In S. Leibfried, E. Huber, M. Lange, J. D. Levy, F. Nullmeier, & J. D. Stephens (Eds.), *The Oxford handbook of transformation of the state* (pp. 393–409). Oxford: Oxford University Press.

Levy, J. D., & Samuels, R. J. (1991). Institutions and innovation: Research collaboration as technology strategy in Japan. In L. K. Mytelka (Ed.), *Strategic partnerships: State, firms, and international competition* (pp. 120–148). London: Pinter.

Lew, S.-C., & Wang, H.-S. (2007). Did the financial crisis transform the developmental state—Focused on the public fund in Korea. *Korean Journal of Sociology, 41*(5), 64–97.

Lim, H.-C., & Jang, J.-H. (2006). Between neo-liberalism and democracy: The transformation of the developmental state in South Korea. *Development and Society, 35*(1), 1–28.

Lim, H.-R., & Lee, H.-N. (2009). Political economy of financial supervisory reform in Korea. *Journal of Korean Politics, 18*(1), 119–146.

Little, I., Scitovsky, T., & Scott, M. (1970). *Industry and trade in some developing countries: A comparative study*. London: Oxford University Press.

Lyons, T. F., Krachenberg, A. R., & Henke, J. (1990). Mixed motive marriages: What's next for buyer-supplier relations. *Sloan Management Review, 31*(3), 29–36.

Mahoney, J., & Thelen, K. (2010). *Explaining institutional change: Ambiguity, agency, and power*. Cambridge: Cambridge University Press.

Martin, C. J. (2006). Corporatism in the post-industrial age: Employers and social policy in the little land of Denmark. In J. L. Campbell, J. A. Hall, & O. K. Pedersen (Eds.), *National identity and the varieties of capitalism* (pp. 271–294). Montreal: McGill-Queen's University Press.

Mason, E. S., Kim, M.-J., Perkins, D. H., Kim, K.-S., & Cole, D. C. (1980). *The economic and social modernization of the Republic of Korea*. Cambridge, MA and London: Council on East Asian Studies, Harvard University Press.

Mathews, J. (1998). Fashioning a new Korean model out of the crisis: The rebuilding of institutional capabilities. *Cambridge Journal of Economics, 22*(6), 747–759.

Ministry of Commerce and Industry. (1982). *Joongsogiupjinheungjanggigyehwoik soojungbowan yungoobogosu 1982–1991*. Seoul: Small & Medium Business Corporation.

Ministry of Economy and Finance. (n.d.). *Jungbojejung Gyulsanbogosu* [Report on government's fiscal settlement]. Ministry of Economy and Finance.

Ministry of Education and Science Technology and Korea Institute of S&T Evaluation and Planning. (2013). *2012Kwahakgisooltonggyebaeksu* [2012 white paper on science and technology statistics]. Seoul: Ministry of Education and Science Technology and Korea Institute of S&T Evaluation and Planning.

Ministry of Finance. (1986, January). *Jaejunggeumyoongtonggye*. Seoul: Ministry of Finance.

Ministry of Finance and Korea Development Bank. (1993). *Hangookwoijadoip 30nyunsa*. Seoul: Ministry of Finance and Korea Development Bank.

Ministry of Science, ICT and Future Planning & Korea Institute of S&T Evaluation and Planning. (2012). *2011nyundo Kookgayungoogaebalsaup josa·boonsukbogosu* [2011 Analysis Report on Government R&D]. Seoul: Ministry of Science, ICT and Future Planning.

Ministry of Science, ICT and Future Planning & Korea Institute of S&T Evaluation and Planning. (2013). *2012nyundo Kookgayungoogaebalsaup josa·boonsukbogosu* [2012 Analysis Report on Government R&D]. Seoul: Ministry of Science, ICT and Future Planning.

Ministry of Science, ICT and Future Planning & Korea Institute of S&T Evaluation and Planning. (2015). *2014nyundo Kookgayungoogaebalsaup josa·boonsukbogosu* [2014 Analysis Report on Government R&D]. Seoul: Ministry of Science, ICT and Future Planning.

Ministry of Science, ICT and Future Planning & Korea Institute of S&T Evaluation and Planning. (n.d.). *Survey of research and development in Korea*. Seoul: Ministry of Science, ICT and Future Planning.

Ministry of Strategy and Finance (2013, September). 2014 Budget. Press Release. Retrieved November 16, 2013, from http://www.moef.go.kr/nw/nes/detailNesDtaView.do;jsessionid=HJt1QrE19SzVkLcKUo2YIMts.node10?searchBbsId1=MOSFBBS_000000000028&searchNttId1=OLD_4016779&menuNo=4010100.

Ministry of Trade, Industry and Energy. (2015). *2016nyun yesan mit gigeumwoonyong gyehwoik saupsulmyungjaryo sanupjungchaekgwa, sojaeboopoomsanupjungchaekgwan, siseutemsanupjungchaekgwan*. Ministry of Trade, Industry and Energy. Retrieved August 10, 2016, from http://www.motie.

go.kr/motie/ms/mg/budgeting/bbs/bbsView.do?bbs_seq_n=36&bbs_cd_n=24&currentPage=1&search_key_n=&cate_n=&dept_v=&search_val_v=.
Ministry of Trade, Industry and Energy. (2016, April 7). *World Premier Materials (WPM) Saup, 2dangye saup sunggwajunsihwoi gaechoi*. Policy Briefing. Retrieved August 20, 2016, from http://www.korea.kr/policy/pressReleaseView.do?newsId=156121064.
Minns, J. (2001). Of miracles and models: The rise of and decline of the developmental state in South Korea. *Third World Quarterly, 22*(6), 1025–1043.
Mitsubishi Research Institute. (1987). *The relationship between Japanese auto and auto parts makers*. Washington, DC: Japan Automobile Manufactures Association.
Moon, C.-I. (1994). Changing state-business relations in South Korea since 1980. In A. MacIntyre (Ed.), *Business and government in industrializing Asia* (pp. 142–166). Ithaca, NY: Cornell University Press.
Moon, C.-I., & Kim, Y.-C. (1996). A cycle of paradox. In A. Leftwich (Ed.), *Democracy and development: Theory and practice* (pp. 139–167). Cambridge: Polity Press.
Nam, D.-W. (2003). Chongron: "Kim Chae-ik" gwaui Inyun. In D.-W. Nam et al. (Eds.), *80nyundae kyungjegyehyukgwa Kim Chae-ik soosuk* (pp. 25–57). Seoul: Samsung Economic Research Institute.
Nam, D.-W. (2009). *Kyungjegaebalui gilmokesu: Jiam Nam Duck-woo hwoigorok*. Seoul: Samsung Economic Research Institute.
National Science and Technology Commission. (2012). *2012 White paper of science technology statistics*. Seoul: National Science & Technology Commission and Korea Institute of S&T Evaluation and Planning.
National Science and Technology Commission. (2013). *2012 Kwahakgisoolyungam* [2012 almanac of science and technology]. Seoul: National Science & Technology Commission and Korea Institute of S&T Evaluation and Planning.
No, I.-H. (1986). Daenaewoihwangyungui geupbyungwa kyunghyuppaetunui godohwa (Chongsul). In The Federation of Korean Industries (Ed.), *Hangookgyongjejungchaek40nyunsa* (pp. 560–570). Seoul: The Federation of Korean Industries.
Noland, M., & Pack, H. (2003). *Industrial policy in an era of globalization: Lessons from Asia*. Washington, DC: International Economic Institute.
O, W.-C. (1992, September 17). Sanupjunlyakgoondansa. *The Korea Economic Daily*.
O, W.-C. (1996). *Hangookhyung kyungjegunsul: Engineering approach 4*. Seoul: Kia Economic Research Institute.
O, W.-C. (2006). *Parkchung-heeneun udduke kyungjeganggook mandeulutna: Boolgoolui dojun hanganguí gijuk*. Seoul: Dongsumoonhwasa.
OECD. (1994). *OECD Economic surveys: Korea*. Paris: OECD.
OECD. (1996). *Economic surveys: Korea*. OECD.

OECD. (2012). *Main science and technology indicators, 2012(1)*. Retrieved October 11, 2013, from https://www.oecd-ilibrary.org/science-and-technology/main-science-and-technology-indicators_2304277x.

OECD. (2013). *Main science and technology indicators, 2013(1)*. Retrieved October 11, 2013, from https://www.oecd-ilibrary.org/science-and-technology/main-science-and-technology-indicators_2304277x.

Ostry, S., & Nelson, R. R. (1995). *Techno-nationalism and techno-globalism: Conflict and cooperation*. Washington, DC: The Brookings Institution.

Pack, H., & Saggi, K. (2006). *Is there case of industrial policy? A critical survey*. Washington, DC: World Bank Publication.

Pai, M.-K., & Kim, W.-K. (2004). Chongyososangsansungui Yoin Boonsukgwa Sisajum. *e-KIET Sanupgyungjejungbo, 218*, 1–12.

Park, S.-Y. (2012). Exploring Korea's emerging 'post-developmental' state: Research trends and agendas since the 1990s. *Journal of Contemporary Politics, 5*(1), 63–90.

Park, S.-Y. (2015). Analysis on the cohabitation of developmentalism and neoliberalism in Korea: Changes in the Korean developmental state since the 1990s and varieties of developmental-neoliberal mixes. *Journal of Asia-Pacific Studies, 22*(4), 5–40.

Patrick, H. (1994). Comparisons, contrasts and implications. In H. T. Patrick & Y. C. Park (Eds.), *The financial development of Japan, Korea, and Taiwan: Growth, repression, and liberalization* (pp. 325–372). New York: Oxford University Press.

Pedersen, O. K. (2006). Corporatism and beyond: The negotiated economy. In J. L. Campbell, J. A. Hall, & O. K. Pedersen (Eds.), *National identity and the varieties of capitalism* (pp. 245–270). Montreal: McGill-Queen's University Press.

Pemberton, H. (2004). *Policy learning and British governance in the 1960s*. Basingstoke: Palgrave Macmillan.

Pirie, I. (2005). The new Korean state. *New Political Economy, 10*(1), 25–42.

Pirie, I. (2008). *The Korean developmental state: From dirigisme to neo-liberalism*. London: Routledge.

Pisano, G. P., & Shih, W. C. (2012). *Producing prosperity: Why America needs a manufacturing renaissance*. Boston: Harvard Business Review Press.

Prasad, M. (2006). *The politics of free markets: The rise of neoliberal economic policies in Britain, France, Germany and the United States*. Chicago: University of Chicago Press.

Pyo, H. K., Chun, H., & Rhee, K. H. (2008). Total factor productivity by 72 industries in Korea and international comparison (1970–2005), *BOK working papers*, 324.

Sakong, I. (1993). *Korea in the world economy*. Washington, DC: Institute for International Economics.

Samuels, R. J. (1987). *The business of the Japanese state: Energy markets in comparative and historical perspective.* Ithaca, NY and London: Cornell University Press.

Samuels, B. C. (1990). *Managing risk in developing countries: National demands and multinational response.* Princeton: Princeton University Press.

Scharpf, F. W. (2000). Economic changes, vulnerabilities, and institutional capabilities. In F. W. Scharpf & V. A. Schmidt (Eds.), *Welfare and work in the open economy: From vulnerability to competitiveness* (pp. 21–129). Oxford and New York: Oxford University Press.

Schmidt, V. A. (1996). *From state to market? The transformation of French business and government.* New York: Cambridge University Press.

Schmidt, V. A. (2002). *The futures of European capitalism.* Oxford and New York: Oxford University Press.

Schmidt, V. A. (2008). Discursive institutionalism: The explanatory power of ideas and discourse. *Annual Review of Political Science, 11*, 303–326.

Schmitter, P. C. (1979). Still the century of corporatism? In P. C. Schmitter & G. Lehmbruch (Eds.), *Trends toward corporatist intermediation.* London: Sage.

Shapiro, H. (1994). *Engines of growth: The state and transnational auto companies in Brazil.* Cambridge and New York: Cambridge University Press.

Shim, S.-Y. (2005). Kwagu sungjangjunryakui kyungrouijonsunggwa hyukshinjoodo dongbansungjangui gwajee daehan yungoo [A study on the path-dependency of old growth model and the tasks of innovation-driven accompanied growth model]. *Hangookjungchekhakhwoibo* [Korean Policy Studies Review], *14*(4), 223–248.

Shin, J.-S., & Chang, H.-J. (2003). *Joosikhwoisa hangookui goojojojung: Moousi moonjeinga* (Restructuring Korea Inc.). Paju: Changbi Publishers.

Shonfield, A. (1965). *Modern capitalism: The changing balance of public and private power.* London and New York: Oxford University Press.

Sim, S. Y. (2005). A study on the path-dependency of old growth model and the tasks of innovation-driven accompanied growth model. *The Korea Association for Policy Studies, 14*(4), 223–249.

Skocpol, T. (1985). Bringing the state back In: Strategies of analysis in current research. In P. Evans, D. Rueschemeyer, & T. Skocpol (Eds.), *Bringing the state back in* (pp. 3–43). Cambridge and New York: Cambridge University Press.

Smitka, M. J. (1991). *Competitive ties: Subcontracting in the Japanese automotive industry.* New York: Columbia University Press.

Solow, R. M. (1957). Technical change and the aggregate production function. *Review of Economics and Statistics, 39*(3), 312–320.

Son, G.-S. (1978, September). Yoomyungmoosilhan joongsogiupui gyeyulhwa. *Sedae.*

Stiglitz, J. E., Lin, J. Y., & Monga, C. (2013). Introduction: The rejuvenation of industrial policy. In J. E. Stiglitz & J. Y. Lin (Eds.), *The industrial policy revolu-*

tion I: The role of government beyond ideology (pp. 1–18). London: Palgrave Macmillan.
Streeck, W., & Thelen, K. (2005). *Beyond continuity: Institutional change in advanced political economies.* Oxford and New York: Oxford University Press.
Stubbs, R. (2009). What ever happened to the East Asian developmental states? The unfolding debate. *The Pacific Review, 22*(1), 1–22.
Stubbs, R. (2011). The East Asian developmental state and the great recession: Evolving contesting coalitions. *Contemporary Politics, 17*(2), 151–166.
The Bank of Korea. (1984). *National income account.* Retrieved October 21, 2013, from http://ecos.bok.or.kr/flex/ClassSearch.jsp?langGubun=K&topCode=102Y002.
The Bank of Korea. (n.d.-a). *Kyungjetonggyeyunbo* [Economic statistics yearbook]. Seoul: The Bank of Korea.
The Bank of Korea. (n.d.-b). *Kiupgyungyoungboonsuk* [Financial statement analysis]. Seoul: The Bank of Korea
The Compilation Committee for Korean Electronics Industry for 50 Years (Ed.). (2009). *The miraculous time: 1959–2009 Korean electronics industry for 50 years.* Seoul: Electronic Times.
The Federation of Korean Industries. (1977, October 21). *Junkyungryunhwoibo.* Seoul: The Federation of Korean Industries.
Thelen, K. (2004). *How institutions evolve: The political economy of skills in Germany, Britain, the United States, and Japan.* Cambridge and New York: Cambridge University Press.
Thurbon, E. (2016). *Developmental mindset: The revival of financial activism in South Korea.* Ithaca, NY: Cornell University Press.
Thurbon, E., & Weiss, L. (2006). Investing in openness: The evolution of FDI strategy in South Korea and Taiwan. *New Political Economy, 11*(1), 1–22.
UNCTAD. (1999). *World investment report.* New York: United Nations.
UNCTAD. (2000). *World investment report.* New York: United Nations.
Visser, J., & Hemerijck, A. (1997). *A Dutch miracle: Job growth, welfare reform, and corporatism in the Netherlands.* Amsterdam: Amsterdam University Press.
Wade, R. (1990). *Governing the Market: Economic Theory and the Role of Government in East Asian Industrialization.* Princeton: Princeton University Press.
Weiss, L. (2003). Guiding globalization in East Asia: New roles for old developmental states. In L. Weiss (Ed.), *States in the global economy: Bringing domestic institutions back in* (pp. 245–270). New York: Cambridge University Press.
Whitley, R. (1992). *Business systems in East Asia: Firms, markets and societies.* London and New Bury Park: Sage Publications.
Williams, M. (2014). Introduction & rethinking the developmental state in the twenty-first century. In M. Williams (Ed.), *The end of the developmental state?* (pp. xiii–xxiii, 1–29). London: Routledge.

Witt, M. A. (2015). South Korea: Plutocratic state-led capitalism reconfiguring. In M. A. Witt & C. Redding (Eds.), *The Oxford handbook of Asian business systems* (pp. 216–237). Oxford: Oxford University Press.

Womack, J. P., Jones, D. T., & Roos, D. (1990). *The machine that changed the world: The story of lean production*. New York: Harper Perennial.

Wong, J. (2004). The adaptive developmental state in East Asia. *Journal of East Asian Studies, 4*, 345–362.

Woo, J.-E. (1991). *Race to the swift: State and finance in Korean industrialization*. New York: Columbia University Press.

World Bank. (1993). *The East Asian miracle: Economic growth and public policy*. New York: Oxford University Press.

World Bank. (2012). *Worldwide governance indicator*. Retrieved November 4, 2013, from http://info.worldbank.org/governance/wgi.

Yang, J.-J. (2007). Hankook Sahwoihyubyak Silhumui Choodongryukkwa Hankwe [Social Concertation in South Korea: Could it be Steppingstone to a Coordinated Market Economy?]. *Sahwoikwahakyunkoo, 15*(1), 38–68.

Yoo, J.-H. (1997). Konguphwa Sokdoe Daehan Segyesijang Kyoomoui Younghyang. *KDI Jungchekyungoo* [KDI Journal of Economic Policy], 19(2), 73–157.

Yoo, J.-H. (2004). *Gwanchisesang: Sijanggyungjemani sal girida*. Seoul: Chaegsesang.

Yoon, J.-H. (2006). *Hangookgisooljungchaekron: Hangook gisoolneungryuk baljun 40nyunsa*. Seoul: Gyeongmunsa.

Yoon, S.-W. (2009). Woihwanwigi ihoo Hangookui baljunjoouijuk sinjayoojoouihwa [Internalizing neoliberal globalization in Korea—A case for 'developmental neoliberalization']. *Economy and Society, 83*, 40–68.

Yoon, D.-Y. (2012). *Crisis of export-led development and the politics of industrial policy, 1980–2007: Idea, institution and developmental governance*. Seoul: Yonsei University Dissertation.

Yoon, H.-K. (2013). The change of the economic role of Korean government and the change of the market institution: A discursive institutionalist approach. *Journal of Korean Politics, 22*(1), 163–187.

Yoon, C.-B., & Hong, J.-K. (1989). *Hangookgwa ilbonui junjasanup hadogeupgoojo bigyoboonsuk – gajunsanupeul joongsimeuro*. Seoul: Korean Institute for Industrial Economics & Trade.

Zeile, W. (1989). *Industrial policy and organizational efficiency: The Korean chaebol examined*. Program in East Asian business and development research working paper no. 30. Institute of Governmental Affairs, University of California, Davis.

Zysman, J. (1983). *Governments, markets and growth: Financial systems and the politics of industrial change*. Ithaca, NY: Cornell University Press.

Index[1]

[1] Note: Page numbers followed by 'n' refer to notes.

K. M. Kim, *The Korean Developmental State*,
https://doi.org/10.1007/978-981-15-3465-2

The manufacturer's authorised representative in the EU is Springer Nature Customer Service Centre GmbH, Europaplatz 3, 69115 Heidelberg, Germany. If you have any concerns regarding our products, please contact ProductSafety@springernature.com

Printed and bound by CPI Group (UK) Ltd, Croydon, CR0 4YY

27/09/2026

02223600-0001